revised and expanded

bed and breakfast
Ireland

a trusted guide
to over 400
of Ireland's best
bed and breakfasts

elsie dillard and susan causin

W9-BER-321

CHRONICLE BOOKS
SAN FRANCISCO

Appletree Press

First published in the United States in 1999 by Chronicle Books

ISBN 0-8118-2275-3

Library of Congress Cataloging-in-Publication Data available

Distributed in Canada by
Raincoast Books
8680 Cambie Street
Vancouver, B.C. V6P 6M9

www.raincoast.com

10 9 8 7 6 5 4 3 2 1

Chronicle Books
85 Second Street
San Francisco
California 94105

www.chroniclebooks.com

for the latest information on-line
readers should visit
www.irelandseye.com/breakfast.htm

CONTENTS

OUR FAVOURITE BED AND BREAKFASTS

INTRODUCTION

The exceptional warmth and hospitality of the Irish would be reason enough to visit Ireland, but combined with the scenic and contrasting countryside, Ireland is a perfect choice for a holiday.

Our research has covered the four seasons and we highly recommend a visit to Ireland in the off-season, when it is easy to get around and there is still plenty to interest the visitor. It was a pleasure to visit the much improved roads, note the upswing in the economy, and best of all, to be in Ireland at a time when there are prospects for peace.

Each property listed in this guide has been personally visited by us, and there are no charges for inclusion. Our criteria for entry are based upon the warmth of the welcome and cleanliness of the property, with many other factors being taken into consideration. We have covered every county, and included areas not considered as tourist regions to accommodate business travellers, visiting friends and family gatherings.

Restrictions on pets have been noted. Most establishments are completely non-smoking and many have restrictions on where smoking is allowed. Children are welcome unless stated otherwise. Sometimes the location or style of a house makes it unsuitable for children; however, houses which provide facilities for children are noted. Parking is always available unless mentioned otherwise. We have included details on the number of ground floor rooms, which is helpful for pensioners or visitors with disabilities. Unlicensed premises often allow guests to bring their own wine.

At the time of publication, prices were correct, but these could vary due to the season, special holiday dates, etc. When booking, it is advisable to verify specifics, such as child reductions, single supplements, special break prices, opening times, meals and dietary requirements. Obtaining driving directions is also recommended.

Most entries include the owner's name, but it is possible that a change in ownership may have occurred, which could lead to significant changes in the standard of accommodation.

At the time of publication, and to the best of our knowledge, the facts in this book were correct. However, changes do occur for which we cannot be responsible. We would like to thank Bord

Fáilte and the Northern Ireland Tourist Board for their help in making this book possible.

We would welcome any comments you have on your personal experiences about properties in this book. We would be delighted to receive your recommendations for consideration as future inclusions. Please send your comments and recommendations to Elsie Dillard and Susan Causin, 48 Nursery Road, Great Cornard, Sudbury, Suffolk, England CO10 3NJ or in North America to PO Box 54107, Redondo, WA 98054.

Note:

All prices are per person. A "single supplement" refers to the practice of charging a single visitor who stays in a double room the single room rate plus an additional charge.

The prices listed for accommodation in the Republic of Ireland are given in Irish punts. The prices listed for accommodation in Northern Ireland are given in pounds sterling (British pounds). As prices and exchange rates fluctuate, check the rates when you book your room as well as the method of payment. Some establishments might not accept credit cards.

Dublin and the East

COUNTY DUBLIN

From above Killakee, on the northern slopes of the Dublin Mountains, there is a wonderful view of both city and county. You can see to the northeast of the majestic sweep of Dublin Bay, the beautiful peninsula of Howth Head, and to the south of the bay, South Killiney Head. The city stretches across the plain, divided by the River Liffey, and the large green patch in the northwest is Phoenix Park, one of Europe's finest city parks, covering some 116 hectares.

The county north of Howth has long sandy beaches and fishing villages, which in spite of their proximity to the city, still retain their character and charm, as well as a wealth of archaeological sites. The castle at Howth dates from 1464, but has been altered over the centuries. The gardens, which are open to the public, are famous for their rhododendrons and eighteenth-century formal garden. Malahide Castle belonged to the Talbot family from 1185 to 1976, when the property was sold to the Dublin County Council. It now houses a large part of the National Portrait Collection.

To the south of the Liffey, Blackrock and Dalkey retain their village identity, and the popular Victorian holiday resort of Dún Laoghaire is one of the main sea-gateways to Ireland.

The city of Dublin is beautifully situated and the people have a friendliness and wit that captivates most visitors. Relatively speaking, it is a small and compact city. The city centre, stretching between Parnell Square and St Stephen's Green north to south, and Dublin Bay and Phoenix Park east to west, can be covered easily by foot. Most points of interest in the city lie between these boundaries. Like most European capitals, there is so much to see in the city that it would take weeks to do it full justice, taking in not only the principal sights of churches, museums and galleries, but taking the time to browse and absorb the atmosphere, the people, shops, theatres and pubs as well. Amongst the sights on the top of the list to visit are the National Museum, the National Gallery and the Municipal Gallery, as well as St Patrick's Cathedral dating from 1190; Christchurch Cathedral, restored in the nineteenth century; St Michan's, where intact bodies still lie in vaults; the fine eighteenth-century church of Saint Anne's; and St

Werburgh's Church – which are amongst the most noteworthy churches to visit.

Dublin Castle, with its beautifully decorated State Apartments, was used by the British for state functions, and since 1938 has been the scene of the inauguration of the Presidents of Ireland. The General Post Office in O'Connell Street is where the Free Republic was proclaimed in 1916. The Custom House is one of the most impressive buildings in Dublin. Parliament House, now the Bank of Ireland, was built in 1785 by James Gandon, Dublin's most famous architect.

The Book of Kells is kept in the Library at Trinity College, which is a restful spot away from the bustle of the city.

BALLSBRIDGE

Northumberland Lodge
68 Northumberland Road, Ballsbridge, Co. Dublin
Tel: 01 660 5270 Fax: 01 668 8679

Northumberland is a gracious, comfortable Victorian residence. Many original features remain, such as the leaded light windows in the front door, ceiling coving and fireplaces. The house is furnished in keeping with its character, has pine floors in the entryway, lounge and dining room and is in excellent decorative order. There are several water colours of local scenes on display by a local artist. Bridget and Tony Brady are excellent hosts, who work as a team to provide visitors with a high standard of accommodation in an informal, welcoming atmosphere. The bedrooms are well-appointed and are of a good size. Plenty of information for visitors can be found in the spacious lounge, which has satellite TV and video. Breakfasts include a buffet choice of cereals and juice, followed by a full cooked breakfast. Bridget Brady is happy to make recommendations of local establishments for evening meals. The well-tended gardens are available to guests. Visa, Mastercard, Access accepted.

OWNER Bridget & Tony Brady OPEN All year ROOMS 2 double, 2 twin, 4 family; all en suite TERMS B&B IR£25–40; reduction for children; single supplement (seasonal)

DALKEY

Moytura House

Saval Park Road, Dalkey, Co. Dublin
Tel: 01 285 2371 Fax: 01 235 0633 E-mail: giacomet@indigo.ie

Designed by the architect John Loftus Robinson and built in
1881, Moytura House is a lovely home. It is set in pleasant gardens
in a quiet residential area and has some sea views. Mr Giacometti,
an architect, has his studio in the house, and Corinne has done a
splendid job creating elegant and restful accommodation for bed
& breakfast guests. The house has a relaxed, informal atmosphere,
and is fresh and bright and beautifully furnished. Breakfast is
served in the dining room, and guests have use of a small, elegant
sitting room. Moytura Lodge is within easy walking distance of the
centre of the village of Dalkey, James Joyce's Tower and the DART
railway, which has a frequent service into central Dublin. No pets
and no smoking. American Express accepted.

OWNER Corinne Giacometti OPEN April 1 – October 31 ROOMS 3
double; all en suite TERMS B&B IR£35; single supplement IR£10

DRUMCONDRA

Parknasilla

15 Iona Drive, Drumcondra, Co. Dublin
Tel: 01 830 5724

A friendly welcome awaits visitors at this Edwardian detached
house located in a quiet residential street. Mrs Ryan is a friendly,
chatty person, who likes to make sure her guests have everything
they need. The location is excellent for both the centre and the
airport, with many buses travelling in each direction. The
accommodation is simple, but a good value, and there is a TV
lounge and a breakfast room.

OWNER Mrs Teresa Ryan OPEN All year ROOMS 1 double, 1 twin, 1
family, 1 single; 2 en suite TERMS B&B IR£18–20; reduction for
children; single supplement from IR£2

Joyville

24 St Alphonsus Road, Drumcondra, Dublin 9, Co. Dublin
Tel: 01 830 3221

Roma Gibbons is a delightful, kindly lady who extends a warm welcome to her immaculate red brick Victorian house, situated opposite St Alphonsus Convent and Church 2 km from the city centre. There is a good local bus service; guests would be well advised to take local transport to avoid the parking and traffic problems. The bedrooms are average in size with orthopedic beds. There are no en suite rooms, but there are two shower rooms and two WCs exclusively for guests' use. The family lounge has a marble fireplace, which guests are welcome to share. Roma Gibbons enjoys meeting people and would be happy to recommend pubs and restaurants for evening meals. Joyville is a good value accommodation and is a popular B&B. Visitors to Dublin should reserve in advance.

OWNER Roma & John Gibbons OPEN All year ROOMS 1 double, 3 twin TERMS B&B IR£16; reduction for children; single supplement (seasonal)

DUBLIN 2

Merrion Square Manor

31 Merrion Square, Dublin 2, Co. Dublin
Tel: 01 662 8551 Fax: 01 662 8556

This lovely restored Georgian town house occupies a corner position on Merrion Square. The house has been beautifully furnished and decorated in keeping with its style and it has a welcoming atmosphere and friendly service. Both drawing and dining rooms are elegant, and excellent buffet-style breakfasts are served. The mostly spacious bedrooms are very comfortable and elegantly furnished and all have hairdryers, trouser presses, telephones, TVs and tea and coffee making facilities. Merrion Square is just a short walk from Grafton Street, the National Gallery and Trinity College. No pets. No smoking in the breakfast room. All major credit cards accepted except Diners Club.

OWNER Anne Neary OPEN Closed at Christmas ROOMS 13 double, 4 twin, 3 single; all en suite TERMS B&B IR£35; reduction for children; single supplement IR£10

Number 31

31 Leeson Close, Dublin 2, Co. Dublin
Tel: 01 676 5011 Fax: 01 676 2929 E-mail: number31@iol.ie

Number 31 is an unusual place to find in the heart of Georgian Dublin off busy Leeson Street. Built by the famous Dublin architect Sam Stephenson as his home, it is an oasis of peace and quiet, hidden behind a high creeper-covered wall. The house has many interesting features; the low entrance opens up into a spacious drawing room with a sunken sitting area, featuring a bar, fireplace, high ceilings and tall windows. There are terraces, patios and different levels, and the comfortable en suite bedrooms all have hairdryers, telephones, TVs and tea and coffee making facilities. From the back of the house a winding path leads through gardens to the back door of Fitzwilliam Place – a total contrast of architecture and style, it's a beautiful, classical building with ornate ceilings and enormous rooms. Brian and Mary Bennett acquired this elegant Georgian town house during the last two years, furnishing and decorating it in keeping with the period. Deliberately, Fitzwilliam Place has no public rooms – guests that stay here cross the garden to make use of Number 31's drawing room, and for breakfast, which is quite a feast and is served in either the upstairs dining room or in the enclosed conservatory. Off-street, secure parking is available. It is not suitable for children under 10. Smoking is only allowed in the living room. No pets. American Express, Mastercard, Visa accepted.

OWNER Brian & Mary Bennett OPEN Closed at Christmas ROOMS 3 triple; 14 twin or double; 1 family; all en suite TERMS B&B IR£37–47; single supplement IR£13

The Fitzwilliam Park Hotel

5 Fitzwilliam Square, Dublin 2, Co. Dublin
Tel: 01 662 8280 Fax: 01 662 8281

The Fitzwilliam Park Hotel occupies one of the largest houses on one of Dublin's most elegant Georgian squares, and was built in

1816 on land leased from Richard, fifth Viscount of Fitzwilliam. Most latterly the house was an insurance office and was converted and opened for accommodation in 1997. It has been beautifully furnished and decorated to complement the architecture, and most of the bedrooms are spacious, all having hairdryers, trouser presses, TVs and tea and coffee making facilities. There is a lift installed, light snacks are available from 24-hour room service, and friendly staff are on hand to help with any questions. Breakfast is served in the wonderful drawing room/breakfast room on the first floor, a large, beautifully proportioned room overlooking the square, which retains its original garden layout (it is where the first ladies' singles tennis championship took place in 1877). There is a conference room on the ground floor. No pets. All major credit cards accepted.

OWNER Mary Madden   OPEN All year   ROOMS 11 doubles (5 superior), 1 twin, 1 family, 1 single, 1 triple; all en suite   TERMS B&B IR£42.50; reduction for children by arrangement; single supplement IR£22.50   MEALS Light snacks from room service 24 hours

Trinity Lodge
12 South Frederick Street, Dublin 2, Co. Dublin
Tel: 01 679 5044 / 679 5182 / 679 5184   Fax: 01 679 5223

Trinity Lodge is probably one of the most centrally located guest houses in Dublin, almost next door to Trinity College and surrounded by shops, restaurants, cafés and pubs. A Georgian town house, it has been interestingly renovated and decorated in strong, bright colours, the walls hung with prints of the artist Knuttel (who lives close by). An original of his work depicting the sinking of the *Titanic* hangs over the staircase. The house is elegantly furnished and beautifully equipped, each en suite bedroom having a hairdryer, trouser press, telephone, TV, air conditioning and tea and coffee making facilities. The three suites can sleep up to six people and include a bedroom, sitting room, bathroom and small kitchen. No pets. All major credit cards accepted.

OWNER Pete Murphy   OPEN All year   ROOMS 2 double, 3 twin, 2 single, 3 suites; all en suite   TERMS B&B IR£45; single supplement IR£10–30

DUBLIN 3

Greenmount
124 Howth Road, Dublin 3, Co. Dublin
Tel: 01 833 9522

This Victorian house stands in its own grounds of mature trees and a lawn, and is located 10 minutes from the city centre. Greenmount has spacious rooms and there is a warm, informal atmosphere. Although there are no en suite rooms, all the bedrooms have washbasins, and there is one enormous family room. Children are welcome and a cot is provided. The large lounge/dining room where breakfast is served has a marble Georgian fireplace rescued from an old house. It is recommended that guests leave their cars here and take the bus into town. No pets and no smoking.

OWNER Gladys Duggan   OPEN Closed at Christmas   ROOMS 1 double, 1 twin, 2 family   TERMS B&B IR£20; single supplement

DUBLIN 4

Ariel House
52 Lansdowne Road, Dublin 4, Co. Dublin
Tel: 01 668 5512 Fax: 01 668 5845

Ariel House is an attractive Victorian mansion in an excellent residential neighbourhood, very conveniently located for access to the city centre. Very high standards pervade throughout the house, which cleverly combines the graciousness of a bygone era with all-modern comforts. This is a family-run enterprise, and the O'Briens take great pride in their house. They are constantly upgrading and refurbishing the accommodation. It has an informal and friendly atmosphere, and the elegant drawing room and small wine bar are relaxing spots to recover from a day's sightseeing. The comfortable bedrooms, which vary in size, each have TV, hairdryer, trouser press, iron and ironing board, telephone and tea and coffee making facilities. Breakfast (an extra charge) is served in the old dining room and its conservatory-style extension, which overlooks the garden. No pets. Smoking is permitted in the wine bar and drawing room. Visa, Mastercard, Access accepted.

OWNER Michael O'Brien OPEN Closed Christmas & New Year's
ROOMS 12 double, 11 twin, 2 family, 1 triple, 2 suites; 26 bath, 2
showers en suite TERMS IR£39.50–80; reduction for children; single
supplement IR£15 MEALS Continental breakfast IR£5; Irish breakfast
IR£5

Beaufort House

25 Pembroke Park, Dublin 4, Co. Dublin
Tel: 01 668 9080 Fax: 01 660 9963

This rather unassuming 1890s house in a quiet residential street is quite delightful. It is light and bright, the welcome warm, the service excellent, and the owner professional and friendly. It has been attractively decorated and furnished throughout, with all shapes and sizes of rooms, including a big family room at the top of the house. The bedrooms are equipped with every convenience, including hairdryers, trouser presses, telephones, TVs, personal computer modems and tea and coffee making facilities. Additionally, a laundry service is offered as well as temporary membership at a local health club – visitors pay the guest fee only. Breakfast, and light meals all day long until 10.30 p.m. are available in the attractive conservatory-type room off the sitting room, offering an unusual selection of healthy food. Kate, who is enjoying a complete career change from merchant banking, loves to cook and look after her guests. Under the same ownership are service apartments and a car rental company that specialises in exotic makes of cars. No pets. Smoking in designated rooms only. All major credit cards accepted.

OWNER Kate Mullally OPEN All year ROOMS 3 double or twin, 1
family, 1 single TERMS B&B IR£29–42; reduction for children; single
supplement IR£16 MEALS Light meals all day till 10:30 p.m.

Cedar Lodge

98 Merrion Road, Dublin 4, Co. Dublin
Tel: 01 668 4410 Fax: 01 668 4533

This turn-of-the-century, stucco house is set back off Merrion Road opposite the British Embassy, where frequent buses run to the city centre. Guests are accommodated in a newer wing of the house that has been very well designed, providing spacious en suite bedrooms that are attractively decorated and have TVs, hairdryers, telephones and tea and coffee making facilities. The breakfast room, with separate tables, is also in this part of the house. Mary Doody is a very friendly lady, and you can be assured of a warm welcome at Cedar Lodge. There is a large garden at the back of the property. No pets. Smoking in designated rooms only. Visa, Mastercard, American Express accepted.

OWNER Mary & Gerard Doody OPEN All year ROOMS 10 double, 3 family, 3 triple; all en suite TERMS B&B IR£40–55; reduction for children; single supplement

Elva
5 Pembroke Park, Ballsbridge, Dublin 4, Co. Dublin
Tel: 01 660 2931 Fax: 01 660 5417

An impressive Victorian residence in a central location, just five minutes from the town centre. The house continues to maintain its high standards; it is freshly decorated and spotlessly clean. There is a good bus service into town; guests with a cars would find it less stressful to leave the car at the B&B and take the bus. The front door has some beautiful stained-glass work and leaded windows, and other original features include decorative ceiling cornices and fireplaces in the bedrooms and lounge. There are antique furnishings throughout the house and the atmosphere is warm and friendly. Pleasant and personal attention guaranteed.

OWNER Sheila Matthews OPEN February 1 – November 30 ROOMS 1 double, 1 family; all en suite TERMS B&B IR£25–30; single supplement IR£15

Glenogra Guesthouse
64 Merrion Road, Dublin 4, Co. Dublin
Tel: 01 668 3661 Fax: 01 668 3698 E-mail: glenogra@indigo.ie

Glenogra House is a beautifully appointed Georgian residence in an excellent location, close to the city centre, DART and all amenities. The house has been furnished to a high standard of comfort in pleasing fabrics and colours. The good-sized bedrooms all have TVs, telephones, hairdryers and tea and coffee making facilities. The dining room, where breakfast only is served, is quite ornate with pillars, a decorative ceiling and a fireplace. Mr and Mrs McNamee offer all the facilities of a hotel, combined with the warmth and personal service of a private residence. No pets and no smoking. Mastercard, Visa, American Express accepted.

OWNER Seamus & Cherry McNamee OPEN Closed Christmas & New Year's ROOMS 7 double, 2 twin, 1 single; all en suite TERMS B&B IR£35–40; reduction for children; single supplement IR£10–15

Glenveagh
31 Northumberland Road, Dublin 4, Co. Dublin
Tel: 01 668 4612 Fax: 01 668 4559

Glenveagh is an impressive Victorian house retaining many original features, including beautiful cornices and a ceiling rose. There are antique furnishings, including a grandfather clock in the hallway. The well-appointed bedrooms are decorated and furnished to a high standard, providing all the comforts of a first-class hotel in an inviting atmosphere. Improvements are continually ongoing, the kitchen has now been moved upstairs, and two additional bedrooms have been added. The house is spacious, beautifully maintained, extremely comfortable, and retains the warmth and friendliness of a private house. Joe and Bernadette are a gracious couple who enjoy welcoming people to Dublin and are happy to offer advice on what to see. Freshly prepared breakfasts are presented on fine china at separate tables in the elegant dining room, which has a fireplace, soft, restful wallpapers and matching curtains. The lounge has soft furnishings and a fireplace. A quiet spot in which to relax after a busy day, with plenty of information provided for guests. Glenveagh is delightful in every way, a good choice for visitors wanting first-class accommodation in a convenient location. There is an excellent bus service to town, and the house is minutes from the DART station. There are several venues for evening meals within walking distance. Visa, Access accepted.

OWNER Joe & Bernadette Cunningham OPEN All year ROOMS 5 double, 3 twin, 3 family; all en suite TERMS B&B from IR£35; reduction for children; single supplement (seasonal)

Haddington Lodge
40 Haddington Lodge, Dublin 4, Co. Dublin
Tel: 01 660 0974

A Georgian house in a good location, 15 minutes' walk from the town centre. Mary Egan has been running her B&B for over 12 years and the house has recently been freshly decorated with soft pastels and new carpets installed. Each bedroom has an electric blanket, and some rooms overlook a pretty courtyard with shrubs and trees. Ground floor rooms are available. Haddington Lodge started life as two separate houses, but they were cleverly converted to one house 12 years ago, when Mary Egan opened up the premises for business. The lounge area is quite small, and leads onto the dining room, which has a soft yellow and orange décor. Breakfasts only are served, and vegetarians catered for if pre-arranged. There is a self-catering unit available.

OWNER Mrs Mary Egan OPEN February 1 – December 1 ROOMS 1 double, 3 twin, 1 family; all en suite TERMS B&B IR£23.50–25; single supplement (seasonal)

Merrion Hall
54–56 Merrion Road, Dublin 4, Co. Dublin
Tel: 01 668 1426 / 668 1825 Fax: 01 668 4280

This substantial Victorian brick-built house is set back off the main road, opposite the Royal Dublin Showgrounds (RDS) in the

heart of Ballsbridge, one of Dublin's elegant suburbs, a few kilometres from the city centre. The rooms are spacious and comfortable, and the Sheerans are welcoming, caring hosts. The house recently underwent a complete refurbishment and upgrading of the rooms, and eight further bedrooms opened in the new extension. The en suite bedrooms all have TVs, telephones, tea and coffee making facilities, and some have trouser presses. The dining room, where a buffet-type breakfast is served, has a bay window overlooking the garden, and the large, comfortable drawing room has high ceilings with the original plasterwork. The centre of Dublin can easily be reached by the DART railway, or regular bus service. No pets. Smoking in the lounge and designated bedrooms. Visa, Mastercard accepted.

OWNER Paul & Elizabeth Sheeran   OPEN Closed at Christmas ROOMS 23 twin/double/single/family; all en suite   TERMS B&B IR£27.50; reduction for children; single supplement IR£20

Merrion Lodge
148 Merrion Road, Dublin 4, Co. Dublin
Tel: 01 269 1565 Fax: 01 283 9998

Built in 1921, this brick and stucco house stands in its own grounds, with an extensive rear walled garden. It is in an elegant, residential neighbourhood, very handy to the Royal Dublin Showgrounds (RDS). It is just off the busy Merrion Road, 3 km from the city centre, which is easily reached by regular bus service, or by the DART railway, which is a five-minute walk away. The bedrooms are comfortable and well equipped, with telephones, TVs, hairdryers and tea and coffee making facilities. The pleasant lounge/breakfast room has a bay window. No pets. Smoking in bedrooms only. All major credit cards accepted.

OWNER Phil & Kevin Downing OPEN All year ROOMS 2 double, 2 twin, 2 family; all en suite   TERMS B&B IR£25–45; reduction for children; single supplement IR£15

Belcamp Hutchinson

Carr's Lane, Malahide Road, Bagriffin, Dublin 7, Co. Dublin
Tel: 01 846 0843 Fax: 01 846 5703

This superb, ivy-clad Georgian house is hidden away down a narrow lane off the main Malahide road. It is named after Francis Hely-Hutchinson, third Earl of Donoughmore. The house has been renovated with the utmost care, preserving its features and elegance, whilst introducing the best of twentieth-century comforts. It stands in seven hectares of fields and gardens, including a walled garden and a maze (yet in its infancy). The house is superbly furnished and extremely comfortable, and has an easygoing, relaxed atmosphere. Each spacious bedroom has been decorated with a different colour scheme and has a hairdryer, TV, telephone and tea and coffee making facilities. Dinner for parties of 12 or more can be booked in advance and is served, as is the copious breakfast, at the enormous table in the elegant dining room. The large, long drawing room has an honesty bar, and the owners are very proud of their latest addition – a downstairs loo. The attractive little seaside village of Malahide is close by, Dublin can easily be reached by bus, and it is only a few minutes' drive to the Airport. Belcamp Hutchinson is a peaceful and relaxing place to stay, on arrival or departure from Ireland, or as a base for visiting Dublin. Neither pets nor smoking are allowed in the dining room. Visa, Access, Mastercard accepted.

OWNER Doreen Gleeson & Karl Waldburg OPEN Closed at Christmas
ROOMS 3 double, 3 twin, 2 single; all bath & shower en suite TERMS
B&B IR£42; reduction for children by arrangement MEALS Dinner for
parties of 12 to 24

DUBLIN 9

Iona House

5 Iona Park, Dublin 9, Co. Dublin
Tel: 01 830 6217

This attractive red brick residence was built at the turn of the
century and is situated in one of Dublin's unique Victorian
quarters. Jack and Karen Shouldice bought the property in 1963,
which they have refurbished to provide comfortable
accommodation with a taste of luxury. The décor and furnishings
are rich and tasteful, and several original features remain, such as
attractive coving, a ceiling rose and a marble fireplace. Fine prints
adorn the walls, and the spacious lounge, with a predominantly
green décor, is available to guests, as is a furnished patio. The
bedrooms are of a good size, well-appointed and colour-
coordinated. Breakfasts are served in the dining room, which has
booth-style tables, and there are several venues for evening meals
within walking distance. The house is well situated for the airport
and convenient to the city centre.

OWNER Jack & Karen Shouldice OPEN All year ROOMS 4 double, 4
twin, 2 single; all en suite TERMS B&B from IR£30; reduction for
children; single supplement (seasonal)

Moyne Guest House

17 Botanic Road, Dublin 9, Co. Dublin
Tel: 01 830 9337

Mrs Susan Forde has been in business for 24 years offering good
value accommodation. Many of her visitors return; advance
reservations are advised. Susan is interested in crafts: one of her
tapestries hangs in the lounge, and her embroidered cushions
reflect a Celtic design. The house is immaculate and the bedrooms
have country diary bedspreads. Substantial breakfasts are served;
guests help themselves to starters, followed by a traditional cooked

breakfast. Vegetarians can be catered for if pre-arranged. Botanic House is across the road, the city centre bus stop is a two-minute walk, and the airport is 9 km. Plenty of establishments within walking distance serve evening meals.

OWNER Mrs Susan Forde OPEN All year ROOMS 2 double, 2 twin, 1 single, triple; 3 en suite TERMS B&B IR£16–18; reduction for children; single supplement IR£5–10 (seasonal)

DÚN LAOGHAIRE

Chestnut Lodge
2 Vesey Place, Monkstown, Dún Laoghaire, Co. Dublin
Tel: 01 280 7860 Fax: 01 280 1466

This delightful Regency terraced house has a pleasant, walled back garden and faces a wooded park. The house has beautifully proportioned rooms, with high, ornate ceilings. It is elegantly furnished, comfortable and well equipped, and has a delightful host who used to work in television. The en suite bedrooms all have hairdryers, trouser presses and telephones, and breakfast, which includes homemade preserves and bread, is beautifully presented in the dining/sitting room. There is also a separate drawing room. Chestnut Lodge is located between Salthill and Dún Laoghaire, with excellent access into central Dublin on the swift DART train service. It can be highly recommended both as a touring point f rom Dún Laoghaire, or as a Dublin base. No pets and no smoking. Mastercard, Visa accepted.

OWNER Nancy Malone OPEN Closed at Christmas ROOMS 2 double, 2 twin; all en suite TERMS B&B IR£30–35; reduction for children; single supplement IR£10

Rosmeen House
13 Rosmeen Gardens, Dún Laoghaire, Co. Dublin
Tel: 01 280 7613

This turn-of-the-century, Spanish-style villa is set in its own grounds in a quiet cul-de-sac, minutes from the ferry, bus and train terminals. The good size bedrooms are prettily decorated and have comfortable beds. There is one ground floor en suite room. Joan Murphy and her sister Maureen are friendly hosts, and serve a good breakfast in the dining room. There is also a well furnished, comfortable lounge. No pets. No smoking in the dining room or lounge.

OWNER Joan M. Murphy   OPEN February – December   ROOMS 3 double, 1 twin, 1 single; 2 en suite   TERMS B&B IR£20–22.50; reduction for children; single supplement

GLASNEVIN

Egan's House
7/9 Iona Park, Glasnevin, Dublin 9, Co. Dublin
Tel: 01 830 3611 Fax: 01 830 3612 E-mail: eganshouse@tinet.ie

Egan's House is an attractive red brick turn-of-the-century house that has been refurbished to a high standard. It started out as two separate houses, which have been tastefully converted to provide comfortable accommodation. The bedrooms have good-sized bathrooms, quality furnishings and are individually decorated in soft shades and rich colours of blue, grey, green and wine. There are 12 ground floor bedrooms. The house is impeccably maintained and retains many original features, including covings and fireplaces. Two lounges provide comfortable areas in which to relax, and are furnished in keeping with the character of the house, with rich green velvet curtains. The house is situated in a quiet residential area, 1.6 km from the city centre, the bus stop is just a few minutes' walk; guests who have a car would be well advised to leave it behind and take the bus. All major credit cards accepted.

OWNER John & Betty Egan   OPEN All year   ROOMS 25 double/twin/family; all en suite TERMS B&B IR£27–31; reduction for children; single supplement (seasonal)

KILLINEY

Druid Lodge
Killiney Hill Road, Killiney, Co. Dublin
Tel: 01 285 1632 Fax: 01 284 8504

Built in 1832, this delightful family home stands in an old-fashioned garden with beautiful views over Killiney Bay. The main rooms have lovely carved pine door surrounds, painstakingly stripped by the owners, as was the staircase. The McClenaghans have lived here 18 years and brought up six children. The two front bedrooms are enormous, with two or three beds apiece, and they have cleverly hidden, small en suite bathrooms which in no way detract from the original shape of the rooms. Smaller rooms on the ground floor do not have sea views, but are comfortable, and all rooms have TVs. Guests eat breakfast at one large table in the dining room, and there is a lovely, comfortable drawing room. No pets and no smoking. Killiney Hill Road is above the centre of Killiney and Druid Lodge is located between Druid's Chair Pub and Killiney Avenue. It is a 10-minute walk from the DART station, with trains running every 15 minutes into central Dublin. Visa, Mastercard accepted.

OWNER Ken & Cynthia McClenaghan   OPEN Closed at Christmas
ROOMS 2 double, 2 family; all en suite   TERMS B&B IR£30–35;
reduction for children

SANTRY

Ivylea
220 Swords Road, Santry, Dublin 9, Co. Dublin
Tel: 01 842 1000 / 3457

A modern, clean and cosy property on the main airport road, 2.5 km from the airport and 3.2 km from the city centre. There are plenty of buses from the house to town and the airport. Tressa Brazil keeps the house spotlessly clean and she is as busy as ever, advance reservations are recommended. The bedrooms are fresh and bright and have comfortable beds. There is a shopping complex and leisure centre in the area. There is an enclosed car park for guests' use.

OWNER Tressa Brazil   OPEN All year   ROOMS 1 double, 2 twin, 1
single; 3 en suite   TERMS B&B from IR£18; reduction for children;
single supplement IR£5

COUNTIES LOUTH AND MEATH

The Boyne Valley cuts right through the centre of this area – one of the most historic and evocative places in Irish history, and for thousands of years the centre of political power. Innumerable remains from every century lie scattered across this fertile, green valley.

Dominating the town of Trim are the ruins of King John's Castle, the largest Anglo-Norman castle in Ireland, dating from 1172. The Duke of Wellington's family came from here, as did the family of Bernardo O'Higgins, a prominent figure in Chilean history.

Apart from a few earthworks, there is not much left to see at the Hill of Tara, the seat of Ireland's kings since prehistoric times. Imagination is needed to conjure up the sight of great buildings and a mass of warriors and nobles who inhabited this place in days gone by.

At the attractive village of Slane, the old castle overlooks the river, and a little farther along the valley is Brugh na Boinne (the Palace of the Boyne), an enormous cemetery with graves dating back to the Neolithic era, the main sites of which are at Newgrange, Knowth and Dowth.

The pretty village of Kells, which is in the Blackwater Valley, was the site of the settlement of the Columban monks, who moved here from Iona in 807. St Columba's house still stands, and in the church is a copy of the famous Book of Kells.

Monasterboice and Mellifont are the sites of the two ancient ecclesiastical centres, and at Drogheda, in the Church of St Peter, one can see the preserved head of St Oliver Plunkett, former Archbishop of Armagh.

The Cooley Peninsula is an attractive and unspoilt area with lovely views, and the old town of Carlingford has lots of historical sites, including King John's Castle.

ARDEE

Red House

Ardee, Co. Louth
Tel: 041 685 3523 Fax: 041 685 3523

This attractive, red brick Georgian house, just off the main Dundalk to Ardee road, is approached through park-like grounds. It was once the home of the politician Chichester Fortescue (Lord Carlingford) and the Countess Waldegrave, a famous hostess. It is a relaxed, informal place with very friendly owners and a welcoming atmosphere. The house is grand and elegant, including a large entrance hall, formal dining room, comfortable drawing room and enormous bedrooms. Outside, one end of the stable courtyard has been turned into a swimming pool and sauna, and beyond is a hard tennis court that is floodlit at night. Guests have access to Slane Castle to fish for salmon and trout on the River Boyne, and racing, foxhunting, shooting and golf are all within easy access. Pets outside only. Smoking is permitted downstairs. Mastercard, American Express accepted.

OWNER Linda Connolly OPEN January 15 – December 15 ROOMS 1 double, 2 twin, 1 family; 1 en suite TERMS B&B IR£35–45; reduction for children; single supplement IR£10 MEALS Dinner IR£22.50

CARLINGFORD

Jordan's Townhouse

Carlingford, Co. Louth
Tel: 042 937 3223 Fax: 042 937 3827

The entrance to Jordan's Restaurant is off Newry Street in the centre of the attractive little medieval town of Carlingford, which is set at the foot of Slieve Foy on the shores of Carlingford Lough. The restaurant has justifiably earned a reputation for being one of Ireland's top eating establishments. With either of the genial and hardworking hosts, Harry or Marian Jordan, cooking and directing operations, the food features freshly caught local seafood, lamb from Carlingford's mountain slopes and locally grown vegetables. The restaurant stretches through the older, cosier room into a newer addition, beyond which a bridge leads to the Townhouse (the bedroom wing), formerly a row of seventeenth-century cottages. The rooms are especially large and simply furnished with antique pine, and each one has a sea view, en suite bathroom, telephone, hairdryer, TV, trouser press and mineral water. Residents have use of a comfortable sitting room and there is separate access to the bedroom wing. There are five golf courses nearby, an adjoining tennis court, historic sites to see and lovely walks. All major credit cards accepted.

OWNER Harry & Marian Jordan OPEN Closed January 6 – 25 ROOMS 5 double or twin; all en suite TERMS B&B IR£42.50; reduction for children; single supplement IR£5 MEALS Dinner

Shalom
Ghan Road, Carlingford, Co. Louth
Tel: 042 937 3151 E-mail: shalombandb@tinet.ie

Shalom is located in an attractive garden with a goldfish pond and adjoining crazy putting course. It is close to the shore near the outer end of the harbour. It was built as a family home and added on to a couple of times. It is an interesting house with all sorts of angles and strange-shaped rooms decorated in unusual, strong colours. Three rooms are in a garden annex, motel-style, with sliding doors out to a sun-filled patio. The two dining rooms, where breakfast only is served, are on the upper floor to take advantage of the sea view. All rooms have tea and coffee making facilities and TVs. No pets in the house.

OWNER Kevin & Jackie Woods OPEN Closed December 20–30 ROOMS 3 double, 2 family; all en suite TERMS B&B IR£17; single supplement IR£6

Viewpoint
Omeath Road, Carlingford, Co. Louth
Tel: 042 937 3149 Fax: 042 937 3149

Enjoying spectacular views of the town and harbour and across to the Mourne Mountains, Viewpoint is a modern house standing above the road on the edge of Carlingford. All the bedrooms are motel-style, with their own entrances and en suite shower rooms, and most have a view. They are comfortably furnished with modern fittings. The large breakfast room with separate tables takes full advantage of the view, and visitors are invited to use the owner's sitting room. No pets. No smoking in the dining room. Visa, Mastercard accepted.

OWNER Marie & Paul Woods OPEN Closed at Christmas ROOMS 6 double, 2 twin, 2 family; all shower en suite TERMS B&B IR£21; single supplement IR£7

DROGHEDA

Harbour Villa
Mornington Road, Drogheda, Co. Louth
Tel: 041 983 7441

Harbour Villa is an attractive, vine-covered old country house on the banks of the River Boyne, just 1.5 km from town. Eileen Valla took over the house in 1997 and offers the same warm welcome her predecessor did. The gardens are most attractive, and there is a garden house containing a sun lounge where guests can relax. The bedrooms are small, clean and simply furnished, and the comfortable lounge has the original marble fireplace. No pets. No smoking in the dining room.

OWNER Eileen Valla OPEN May – October ROOMS 2 double, 1 twin, 1 single TERMS B&B IR£17–18; single supplement

The Glebe House
Dowth, Drogheda, Co. Louth
Tel: 041 983 6101

This attractive, whitewashed, small country house is covered in wistaria, clematis and honeysuckle. Surrounded by a pretty garden, and with lovely views over the tennis court to distant hills, the Glebe House is set in the heart of the Boyne valley, between Newgrange and Drogheda. Mrs Addison is a delightful, welcoming person, who apart from her bed & breakfast business, specialises in small functions and private dinner parties. The reception rooms are welcoming and warm, with fireplaces in both the large formal drawing room and the small, cosy study/sitting room. The bedrooms are pretty and comfortable. Dinners are available if arranged in advance. Cream teas are served to the public. There are restrictions on smoking. For those who wish to improve their art skills, there are art workshops. All major credit cards except American Express accepted.

OWNER Elizabeth Addison OPEN All year ROOMS 5 double or twin; all en suite TERMS B&B from IR£25 MEALS Dinner IR£18

DULEEK

Annesbrook
Duleek, Co. Meath
Tel: 041 982 3293 Fax: 041 982 3024

An impressive gate and a long wooded drive bring you to Annesbrook, an interesting house, the core of which is seventeenth-century with additions of different periods. The pedimented portico of the house and the ballroom were added on to impress George IV when he came here in 1821, and the front entrance hall is beautifully proportioned with a lovely winding staircase. Another distinguished visitor was William Thackeray. However, the formal hospitality of those days has been replaced by a relaxed and welcoming family atmosphere. All of the bedrooms are spacious and comfortable, with folders detailing events of local interest and suggested walks and drives to local attractions. Each bedroom has tea and coffee making facilities and hairdryers. The reception rooms have big log fires. Evening meals must be ordered prior to 11:30 a.m. and feature home-grown organic vegetables picked fresh daily from the walled garden. There is a wine licence. Smoking in the sitting room only. No pets. The house can be found 7 km north of Ashbourne.

OWNER Kate Sweetman OPEN May 1 – September 30 ROOMS 5 double/twin/family; all en suite TERMS B&B IR£27–35; reduction for children; single supplement IR£8 MEALS Dinner IR£18

DUNSHAUGHLIN

Gaulstown House
Dunshaughlin, Co. Meath
Tel: 01 825 9147 Fax: 01 825 9147

This small, attractive, whitewashed early-nineteenth-century farmhouse overlooks a golf course and stands in a small garden. Gaulstown House is located in a rural, peaceful spot and is surrounded by fields of grazing sheep and horses. There is an extensive range of farm buildings to the rear of the house. Mrs Delany is a most friendly lady who has won all kinds of prizes for her baking. Evening meals might well include home-reared lamb. The house is immaculately kept, the rooms are fresh and bright, and there is a comfortable drawing room. No pets and no smoking. Visa, Access accepted.

OWNER Kathryn Delany OPEN April 1 – September 30 ROOMS 3 double/twin/family TERMS B&B IR£20; single supplement IR£5 MEALS Dinner IR£14; high tea IR£9

The Old Workhouse
Dunshaughlin, Co. Meath
Tel: 01 825 9251 Fax: 01 825 9251 E-mail: comfort@a-vip.com

As its name implies, this was a workhouse first used in 1841, and later used as various factories. It is an imposing building which over the last 10 years has been lovingly restored by the Colgans. It stands just off the main road, about 1 km outside Dunshaughlin. There is still a wing to be renovated, and the derelict buildings to the rear of the house belong to the local authority. It is a very interesting building; it was used by the administrators of the workhouse, and the immense, lovely drawing room with a high beamed ceiling on the first floor was the board room. The house has been furnished with old pieces, some quite heavy and big, and there are three large, comfortable, ground floor bedrooms. Guests also have use of a small, cosy sitting room with TV. Meals are served at one table in the large entrance hall area; dinner is by arrangement. The bedrooms have TV on request, hairdryers, bathrobes, tea, coffee and mineral water; three are en suite and one has a private bathroom. Proximity to the main road makes it somewhat noisy, alleviated by new double-glazed windows. Glebeland and Glebewood Gardens are nearby, there is an old famine graveyard at the back of the house up the hill, and Dublin is only 20 minutes away by car. Smoking in the sitting room only. All major credit cards accepted.

OWNER Niamh Colgan OPEN Closed at Christmas ROOMS 3 double, 1 twin; 3 en suite TERMS B&B IR£30–35; reduction for children by arrangement; single supplement IR£10 MEALS Dinner by arrangement IR£22

KELLS

Lennoxbrook
Carnaross, Kells, Co. Meath
Tel: 046 45902

Lennoxbrook is a substantial farmhouse standing just off the main road. The back part of the house is over 200 years old, and the surrounding farmland is let out. The house is cosy, the bedrooms are plain but comfortable and dinner is available if booked in advance. Guests may use a laundry room. Pets outside only. Smoking is permitted in the drawing room. Lennoxbrook is 5 km north of Kells on the N3. Visa accepted.

OWNER Pauline Mullan OPEN Closed at Christmas ROOMS 2 double, 1 twin, 1 single; 2 en suite TERMS B&B IR£20–22; single supplement IR£5 MEALS Dinner IR£12

NAVAN

Gainstown House
Navan, Co. Meath
Tel: 046 21448

This attractive country house dating from the early nineteenth-century stands in peaceful lawned gardens surrounded by 80 hectares of farmland. Pleasantly decorated, the drawing room with open fireplace leads off the large entrance hall. Breakfast and evening meals and high tea by arrangement, are served in the dining room. A patio at the rear of the house overlooks the garden.

There are bicycles for hire, and fishing, golf, swimming and riding are all available locally. Pets are allowed in cars. Smoking is permitted only in the lounge. Gainstown House is signposted on the Navan/Dublin N3 road at the Old Bridge Inn.

OWNER Mrs Mary Reilly OPEN June – August ROOMS 1 double, 1 twin, 2 family TERMS B&B IR£19; reduction for children; single supplement MEALS Dinner; high tea

Lios na Greine
Athlumney, Navan, Co. Meath
Tel: 046 28092

Lios na Greine, meaning "enclosure of the sun," is a modern house in a sunny location. It is set back off the road 1.6 km from the town centre on the Duleek to Ashbourne airport road. The house is immaculate and decorated with matching wallpapers, fabrics and cosy duvets. One room is on the ground floor and there is a comfortable TV lounge where tea is served in the evening. Breakfast is served in the bright and cheerful dining room, and evening meals are available by arrangement. The pleasant garden is a nice spot to sit after exploring Newgrange and the Boyne Valley, which are within easy reach. No smoking. Pets are accepted in the car or garage.

OWNER Mrs Mary Callanan OPEN All year ROOMS 1 double, 1 twin, 1 family; all en suite TERMS B&B IR£17; reduction for children; single supplement IR£6.50 MEALS Dinner IR£14

TRIM

Crannmór
Dunderry Road, Trim, Co. Meath
Tel: 046 31635 Fax: 046 31635

This old country house is in a peaceful setting surrounded by pleasant gardens and 2.5 hectares of fields. It is decorated with old-fashioned farming equipment. When the Finnegans bought Crannmór 10 years ago, there was no water or electricity installed. Three of the fresh and bright guest rooms are located in what was once the stable block. They are on the ground floor level, and one is particularly suitable for disabled guests. The fourth room is on the first floor in the main part of the house. The house is full of all kinds of knick-knacks, most of which have been picked up at car boot sales, and the breakfast/sitting room is very charming with comfortable chairs, a fireplace and antique furniture. Guests also have use of a further sitting room. Crannmór is a friendly, comfortable place to stay to take advantage of all the activities and sights around historic Trim, which is only 1 km away and boasts the largest Norman castle in Ireland. One of Trim's attractions is the annual Trim Fair, "The Power and the Glory" – a multimedia exhibition explaining the background of Trim's medieval ruins. A shed containing safe storage facilities for fishing tackle, golfing gear, etc. is available for guests to use. No pets and no smoking. Visa, Mastercard accepted.

OWNER Colin & Anne Finnegan   OPEN April 1 – September 30
ROOMS 1 double, 1 twin, 2 family; all showers en suite TERMS B&B
IR£18; reduction for children; single supplement IR£6.50

COUNTY WICKLOW

Lying just to the south of Dublin, this is an area of hills and mountains, lakes and streams – a pleasant, peaceful place of escape after the bustle of the city.

From Dublin one comes first to Bray, a large seaside resort, and then to Enniskerry. Here one can visit the gardens of Powerscourt Estate. The house, which had been one of the most beautiful in Ireland, was destroyed in the 1950s, leaving only the shell still standing.

Glendalough is a beautiful, scenic place in the mountains, set between two small lakes near the ruins of St Kevin's Kitchen, the church and the cathedral founded by St Kevin in 520. Just beyond is the small twelfth-century priory of St Saviour. The county town, Wicklow, is on the coast, and farther south is Arklow, a popular resort and fishing centre.

At Blessington is Russborough House, a beautiful Palladian-style house, containing a marvellous art collection, and the Poulaphouca Reservoir, which has been formed by damming the River Liffey.

ANNAMOE

Carmel's Bed & Breakfast
Glendalough, Annamoe, Co. Wicklow
Tel: 0404 45297 Fax: 0404 45297

The house was built by the Hawkins in 1970 and has been added on to a few times, most recently to enlarge the lounge/dining area and a couple of the bedrooms. Carmel's is a warm and welcoming house, set back off the main road in half a hectare of immaculately kept garden, where everyone is treated as a family friend and plied with cups of tea or coffee on arrival. All the bedrooms, which are all en suite and with hairdryers, are on the ground floor. Mr and Mrs Hawkins are local people, willing to assist with sightseeing and local events. The Glendalough Fun Park is close by, and hiking and walking can also be enjoyed. Pets are allowed outside. Smoking is permitted in the lounge only. The house is signposted from Laragh and is 3 km from Glendalough.

OWNER Carmel Hawkins OPEN March – end October ROOMS 2 double, 1 twin, 1 family; all en suite TERMS B&B IR£18; reduction for children; single supplement

ARKLOW

Ballykilty Farmhouse
Coolgreany, Arklow, Co. Wicklow
Tel: 0402 37111 Fax: 0402 37272

This 200-year-old house stands in a lovely garden with a tennis court in peaceful countryside. It is part of an 80-hectare dairy farm with 100 milking cows. Mrs Nuzum is a friendly lady and the house has a warm and welcoming atmosphere. There are two cosy sitting rooms, with open fires each side of the front door, and one has a TV. The dining room was the original kitchen and still has the old beams and cooking pots. There are no tea and coffee making facilities in the rooms, but tea is readily available on request. Babysitting can be arranged. No pets. This is a good base for exploring Powerscourt and Mount Usher gardens, Avondale House and Forest Park, Russborough House, Castleruddery Transport Museum, and the Vale of Avoca. Ballykilty can be found on the road between Coolgreany and Arklow, 5 km from Arklow. Visa, Mastercard accepted.

OWNER Mrs A. Nuzum   OPEN March 1 – November 1   ROOMS 3 double, 2 twin, 1 family; 5 en suite   TERMS B&B IR£20; reduction for children; single supplement IR£6

Fairy Lawn
Wexford Road, Arklow, Co. Wicklow
Tel: 0402 32790

This brick and plaster house, set back off the main road, is located 1.5 km from Arklow on the N11 road to Gorey. The comfortable bedrooms are regularly redecorated and are simply furnished. There's a comfortable guest lounge with a TV, and breakfast only is served in the dining room. Mr Kelly is a keen gardener, maintaining the well landscaped gardens and colourful window boxes. Visa, Mastercard, Eurocard accepted.

OWNER Rita Kelly OPEN All year ROOMS 2 double, 1 twin, 1 family; 3 en suite   TERMS B&B IR£17.50; reduction for children; single supplement IR£6.50

Moneylands Farm
Arklow, Co. Wicklow
Tel: 0402 32259 Fax: 0402 32438 E-mail: mland@tinet.ie

This small farm is located down a quiet country lane on the outskirts of Arklow and has sea views. There is a lovely ground floor family room which has a small sitting area and French doors that open on to the garden. The comfortable lounge leads through to the large conservatory, where breakfast is served. Evening meals are served if arranged in advance. Mr and Mrs Byrne are a kindly couple. They have made many additions to the farm, including an indoor heated swimming pool, a gym, a sauna and a tennis court, which are available both to bed & breakfast guests as well as to those staying in the self-catering courtyard of stone-built coach houses. Moneylands Farm is 1 km south of Arklow on the N11. Mastercard, Visa, American Express accepted.

OWNER Michael & Lillie Byrne   OPEN February 1 – December 1 ROOMS 1 double, 2 twin, 1 family; 3 en suite   TERMS B&B IR£25; reduction for children; single supplement IR£6.50   MEALS Dinner IR£15

Plattenstown House

Arklow, Co. Wicklow
Tel: 0402 37822 Fax: 0402 37822

This old farmhouse was built in 1853 for Lady Jane O'Grady. It is set in 20 hectares of farmland, supporting cows and goats, and has a lovely, peaceful, mature front garden. The attractive, whitewashed farm buildings are at the back of the house. The comfortable drawing room is for nonsmokers, while smokers can use the small sitting room with fireplace and TV. Additionally, there is a conservatory and bicycles to use. There are beaches 5–7 km away and pleasant forest walks. No pets. Plattenstown House is 5 km from Arklow on the Coolgreaney road. Visa, Mastercard, Eurocard, Access accepted.

OWNER Mrs Margaret McDowell OPEN March 1 – October 31 ROOMS 2 double, 1 twin, 1 family; 3 en suite TERMS B&B IR£23–25; reduction for children; single supplement IR£6 MEALS Dinner IR£18; light meal £10

ASHFORD

Ballyknocken House

Glenealy, Ashford, Co. Wicklow
Tel: 0404 44627 / 44614 Fax: 0404 44627

Ballyknocken House, dating from 1880, has been in the Byrne family for the last 60 years, 30 of those belonging to Charlie and Mary Byrne. It is set in a pretty wooded valley below Carrick Mountain. The 190-hectare sheep farm is run by Charlie and Mary. Mary, a kind, welcoming hostess, has been running her bed & breakfast business for 20 years. The house is warm and comfortable, with a turf fire in the sitting room. The large, simply furnished bedrooms are all en suite (three with baths) and have tea and coffee making facilities. Five-course dinners, by arrangement, using local farm produce are served in the rather dreary dining room at individual tables, and packed lunches are also available. Ballyknocken House is an ideal spot for walking holidays; week-long and three-day packages are organised by Mary. There is a hard tennis court for guests' use. No pets. Smoking in the lounge only.

The house can be found 4 km from Ashford. Visa, Mastercard accepted.

OWNER Mary Byrne OPEN March – November ROOMS 3 double, 4 twin; 3 with bath, 4 with shower en suite TERMS B&B IR£18; reduction for children; single supplement IR£7 MEALS Dinner IR£13; packed lunch

AVOCA

Keppel's Farmhouse
Ballanagh, Avoca, Co. Wicklow
Tel: 0402 35168

Built around 1880, Keppel's Farmhouse is set in quiet countryside with beautiful views over the Vale of Avoca. A new wing, with a large dining room where evening meals are served, a lounge and two bedrooms upstairs, was added later. The bedrooms are spacious, clean and bright and full of fresh country air; all have hairdryers and en suite facilities. Guests are welcome to walk around the farm, watch the cows being milked and observe the famous Avoca handweavers nearby. Avoca is the setting for the BBC TV series *Ballykissangel*. No smoking and no pets. Visa, Mastercard, Access, Eurocard accepted.

OWNER Charles & Joy Keppel OPEN Easter – October 1 ROOMS 2 double, 2 twin, 1 family; all en suite TERMS B&B IR£20; reduction for children; single supplement IR£8

BLESSINGTON

The Manor

Manor Kilbride, Blessington, Co. Wicklow
Tel: 01 458 2105 Fax: 01 458 2607

This delightful, rambling house was built in 1830 around a much older building, which had been here since Cromwell's time. It is set in 16 hectares of gardens and trees and has a small river and private lake stocked with brown trout, and, for the more energetic, a heated indoor swimming pool. The drawing room is completely panelled, and the dining room, which is part of the older house, has also been restored. The paintings in these rooms date from 1840. There are three most attractive self-catering cottages converted from old farm buildings. Pets outside only. Smoking only in reception rooms. The Manor is just 28 km from Dublin. From Blessington travel 7 km north on the N81, take the Sallygap turn and turn left at the Sallygap sign – the entrance gates are 50 m on the right. Visa, Mastercard, American Express accepted.

OWNER Charles & Margaret Cully OPEN April 1 – October 1 ROOMS 5 double; 3 (bath) en suite TERMS B&B IR£45–55; reduction for children by arrangement; single supplement by arrangement MEALS Dinner IR£21

DUNLAVIN

Grangebeg House

Dunlavin, Co. Wicklow
Tel: 045 401367 Fax: 045 401367

Grangebeg stands in a park-like setting on a quiet country lane about 1.5 km from Dunlavin. It probably dates from the first half of the eighteenth-century and, when acquired by Aine McGrane's father in the 1930s, was twice as big as it is today. Although half the house was pulled down in the 1940s, today it has a neat, square and complete look to it, with a front porch and classical lines. Aine McGrane was born here, and now that her six children have moved away she has plenty of room for guests. The eldest daughter runs the riding centre, with stables at the back of the house, and there is a cross-country course. The house is decorated in an individual style with flamboyant wallpapers and matching curtains and chair covers. There's a formal dining room, a smaller dining room off the kitchen, a pleasant drawing room with open fire and a smaller TV room. Guests are welcome to use the tennis court, and there is coarse fishing on the 1.6-hectare lake in the grounds. Rathsallagh Championship Golf Course is a seven-minute drive away. Grangebeg House is a delightful, friendly place, very handy for the Punchestown Races and only 45 minutes from Dublin Airport. Visa, Mastercard, Access accepted.

OWNER Aine McGrane OPEN Closed at Christmas ROOMS 4 double, 1 twin; all en suite TERMS B&B IR£35; single supplement IR£10

Rathsallagh House
Dunlavin, Co. Wicklow
Tel: 045 403112 Fax: 045 403343

Set in 214 hectares of beautiful, mature parkland, the house is reached up a majestic, long, sweeping driveway across the Rathsallagh Championship Golf Course which, were it not for the odd sign to stop and watch for golfers, one would hardly be aware of. The original house was built in the early 1700s and was burnt down in the rebellion of 1798. Not being able to afford to rebuild the house, the family moved into the Queen Anne stables, which now form Rathsallagh House. Its long rooms and comparatively lower ceilings give it a relaxed, country house feel, in comparison to the more formal, high ceilinged ornate Georgian houses. It is built around a courtyard, the bedrooms arranged off one side of the long, narrow corridors. Some rooms are very spacious with lovely parkland outlooks and are comfortably and unfussily furnished. They have every amenity including hairdryer, iron and ironing board, telephone, TV, tea and coffee making facilities and mineral water. The food at Rathsallagh is an experience – beautifully presented dishes are served in the light panelled dining room, and there is an extensive buffet at breakfast time and excellent menus in the evening using organically produced food, fresh fish and game when in season. There are any number of activities within the estate for guests to enjoy, including golf, tennis, croquet, snooker, swimming in the indoor pool, sauna and massage. Arrangements can be made for riding, shooting, deer stalking and archery. All major credit cards accepted.

OWNER Joe & Kay O'Flynn   OPEN Closed at Christmas   ROOMS 6 double, 11 double or twin; all en suite   TERMS B&B IR£55–95; reduction for children; single supplement IR£30–50

Tynte House
Dunlavin, Co. Wicklow
Tel: 045 401561 Fax: 045 401586

Built in the early 1800s, Tynte House is a tall, whitewashed building standing right in the middle of town. In its later days it was a pub until 1930. John Lawler's father bought the house and there was still a lot of work to be done on it when John and Caroline took it over. It has been furnished and decorated appealingly in keeping with its style and age. The bedrooms, some of which are on the second floor, have telephones and tea and coffee making facilities and they are unfussily furnished and decorated. There is a cosy snug room, and the dining room is in two different areas – separate tables in a darker, inner room, and one big table in a large, bright room with a sitting area at one end. Caroline is friendly and welcoming and also provides two self-catering mews cottages in the courtyard, which were originally stables and lofts. There is a hard tennis court, a children's playground and golf courses and riding nearby. Visa, Mastercard accepted.

OWNER John & Caroline Lawler   OPEN Closed Christmas & New Year's   ROOMS 6 twin or double, 2 family; all en suite   TERMS B&B IR£17; reduction for children; single supplement IR£5.50   MEALS Dinner IR£12.50

ENNISKERRY

Ferndale
Enniskerry, Co. Wicklow
Tel: 01 286 3518 Fax: 01 286 3518 E-mail: ferndale@tinet.ie

This attractive, 160-year-old house stands right in the centre of Enniskerry and has been in Noel Corcoran's family for a good part of its life. He and his wife, Josie, took it over a few years ago and did up the whole house, almost to the extent of rebuilding it.

There is a relaxing drawing room, and elegant bedrooms with brass and old iron beds, all of which are en suite and have TVs, hairdryers and tea and coffee making facilities. The dining room, with one large table covered with a white linen tablecloth, is in the basement and leads into the conservatory, which in turn has doors out to the pleasant terraced rear garden with a gazebo. Beyond is the car park. Only breakfast is served. No pets. Smoking is permitted in the conservatory. Dublin is only 19 km away, served by a regular bus service, and Ferndale is close to Powerscourt.

OWNER Josie & Noel Corcoran OPEN April 1 – October 31 ROOMS 2 double, 1 twin, 1 family; all en suite TERMS B&B IR£20–25; reduction for children by arrangement; single supplement

GREYSTONES

Springmount House
Newtownmountkennedy, Greystones, Co. Wicklow
Tel: 01 281 9195

Springmount, an attractive classical Georgian house, is part of a 60-hectare working farm and is set in a pretty garden. It was recently taken over from Mr Foley by his son and daughter-in-law, who are a very pleasant, friendly young couple with two small children. The house has been pleasantly furnished with large, old pieces, and there are good views from the bedrooms, which are both en suite. Breakfast only is served. No pets. No smoking in the bedrooms. Springmount, which can be found 500 m from the church in the Wicklow direction, is well placed for Powerscourt House and Gardens, Glendalough and Avoca.

OWNER Pauline Short Foley OPEN April – November ROOMS 2 double; 2 showers en suite TERMS B&B IR£18–22; reduction for children; single supplement

RATHDRUM

Avonbrae Guesthouse

Rathdrum, Co. Wicklow
Tel: 0404 46198 Fax: 0404 46198

Avonbrae House stands just off the road on the edge of the village of Rathdrum and has wonderful views of the Wicklow hills. This area is a walker's paradise and the Geoghegan family provide detailed maps and are happy to discuss walking itineraries and arrange for guided hill-walking tours. There is a grass tennis court and an indoor heated swimming pool for guests' use. There is free fishing for brown trout close by. The house is comfortable with small, simply furnished bedrooms. Transport to and from Rathdrum railway station, or bus, can be arranged. Visa, Mastercard accepted.

OWNER Paddy Geoghegan OPEN March 1 – November 30 ROOMS 1 double, 3 twin, 2 double & single; all showers en suite TERMS B&B IR£25; reduction for children; single supplement IR£6

RATHNEW

Hunter's Hotel

Newrath Bridge, Rathnew, Co. Wicklow
Tel: 0404 40106 Fax: 0404 40338

This attractive, long, low building, covered with climbing plants, was originally an old coaching inn. Built in 1720, it stands on what used to be the main road, though now it is 1 km off the new Dublin road, 5 km outside Wicklow. Owned and run by the Gelletlie family, it has been in the same ownership since 1840. It is comfortable and old-fashioned, combining a lot of old-world charm with modern comforts. Several rooms overlook the beautiful, colourful garden, and others on the ground floor are suitable for disabled guests. Tables and chairs are dotted around the garden, which lies along the banks of the River Vartry, a delightful place for afternoon tea or a pre-lunch or dinner drink. The garden room is available for small conferences or private parties. Smoking in public lounges only. Mount Usher Gardens are nearby. All major credit cards accepted.

OWNER The Gelletlie Family OPEN All year ROOMS 16 double or twin; all en suite TERMS B&B IR£60 MEALS Lunch; dinner; afternoon tea

REDCROSS

Saraville
Redcross, Co. Wicklow
Tel: 0404 41745

Right in the middle of the little village of Redcross, Saraville is a small, modernised house with some farm buildings at the back. The Flemings, a young couple with two small children, farm in a small way and keep horses. The house is immaculately clean, the cooking fresh and wholesome, with freshly squeezed orange juice for breakfast and homemade food using local produce available by request for dinner and lunch. Children are very welcome, the hostess is charming and the atmosphere is friendly and relaxing.

OWNER Henry & Sarah Fleming OPEN March 17 – September 30 ROOMS 3 double, 1 twin; 2 en suite TERMS B&B IR£15–17; reduction for children; single supplement IR£6.50 MEALS Dinner IR£13; lunch and packed lunches IR£6.50

WICKLOW

Lissadell House
Ashtown Lane, Wicklow, Co. Wicklow
Tel: 0404 67458

Built in the Georgian style, Lissadell is a modern house surrounded by its own grounds on the outskirts of Wicklow, and is part of a mixed farm. The Klaues, who built the house themselves, are a most friendly couple, and the house has a welcoming, warm atmosphere. The rooms are plainly decorated and furnished, and there is an elegant sitting room and dining room where home-cooked meals are served. Both rooms have French windows that open onto the lawn and garden. Pets outside only. Smoking is permitted in the lounge.

OWNER Patricia Klaue OPEN March 1 – November 1 ROOMS 4 family; 2 en suite TERMS B&B IR£18; reduction for children; single supplement IR£8 MEALS Dinner IR£16

Silver Sands
Dunbur Road, Wicklow, Co. Wicklow
Tel: 0404 68243

This modern, friendly bungalow is on the coast road just outside the town centre. It has a reputation for its warm welcome and has lovely sea views. The bedrooms are on the small side, immaculately clean and simply furnished. They have hairdryers, TVs and tea and coffee making facilities, and three are on the ground floor. Guests share the family lounge and breakfast is served in the bright dining room overlooking the sea. Mr and Mrs Doyle are a down-to-earth, friendly couple, always willing to help plan outings to local events and places of interest. Babysitting is available. Smoking only in the lounge. Pets outside.

OWNER Mrs Lyla Doyle OPEN All year ROOMS 1 double, 1 twin, 3 triple; 3 en suite TERMS B&B IR£19; reduction for children; single supplement IR£6

*The South
and the Southwest*

COUNTY CORK

Ireland's largest county is like a miniature of the whole country in terms of its history and scenery. It has a spectacular coastline alternating between long, sandy beaches and wild, rugged cliffs, high, rocky mountains, corn-covered farmland and subtropical gardens.

Cork is a bustling, cosmopolitan, friendly city founded by St Finbar in the sixth century on some dry land in the Great Marsh of Munster – Cork meaning "a marsh." The appearance of much of the city is nineteenth-century, with elegant, wide streets. Cork is a city of bridges. The city extended up a hill, on the north side of which is the Tower of Shandon, with its two faces and famous chime of bells. The French spires of St Finbar's Cathedral dominate the city. The cathedral is built on the site of Finbar's monastery.

The famous Blarney stone-kissing – it gives you the gift of the gab – is at the castle, one of the largest and finest tower houses in Ireland.

Nineteenth-century Cóbh, with its Gothic cathedral, is Cork's harbour, some 24 km from the city. Beyond, westward along the coast, is Kinsale, an attractive old town, popular with yachtsmen, and packed with people enjoying its many restaurants and old buildings. There are marvellous cliffs at the Old Head of Kinsale and the remains of a fifteenth-century castle, plus a lovely sandy beach at Garretstown.

Youghal, which is a most attractive seaside town, has many interesting things to see, including the Clock Gate and St Mary's Collegiate Church, and is known for its association with the potato. Sir Walter Raleigh is said to have planted the first potato in his garden during the time he was mayor of the town. Nearby is Shanagarry with its pottery, where William Penn lived, and Ballycotton, a small fishing village.

The coastal scenery west of Skibbereen is particularly beautiful, and the view from Gabriel Mountain, which can be easily climbed, is spectacular. Garnish Island has a wonderful garden, which can be visited most days. Bantry House at Bantry is a most interesting house to visit and has a superb view; and Castle Hyde, a Georgian house close to Fermoy and former home of Douglas Hyde, first

President of the Irish Republic, is one of the most beautiful houses in Ireland. Macroom is set in glorious countryside, and the road across the pass of Keimaneigh and through the forest of Gougane Barra is particularly beautiful.

BALLYCOTTON

Spanish Point Seafood Restaurant
Ballycotton, Co. Cork
Tel: 021 646177 Fax: 021 646179

It is the food and the splendid location just above the sea that attract visitors to Spanish Point Seafood Restaurant. It was originally a nuns' holiday home and was bought and renovated by the Tattans in 1992. The staff and atmosphere are friendly and there is excellent food prepared by John Tattan using fish caught by his own trawler. The restaurant extends into a larger, built-on conservatory overlooking the sea and the cosy sitting room has an open fire and a small bar. All the comfortable bedrooms have some sort of a sea view as well as hairdryers, telephones, TVs and tea and coffee making facilities. Spanish Point Seafood Restaurant is located on the edge of Ballycotton, which is a great area for walking, swimming, bird-watching or angling.

OWNER John & Mary Tattan OPEN All year ROOMS 3 double, 2 double & single; all en suite TERMS B&B IR£20; reduction for children; single supplement IR£5 MEALS Dinner; lunch May – September

BANDON

Butlerstown House
Butlerstown, Bandon, Co. Cork
Tel: 023 40137 Mobile: 087 2203672

Butlerstown House is an outstanding example of Georgian craftsmanship, with beautifully proportioned rooms, ornate plasterwork and a lovely bifurcated staircase. Built at the end of the eighteenth-century, it stands in park-like grounds, approached along an avenue of trees with views over rolling Irish countryside and the distant Dunmanway Mountains. Lis and Roger have done an outstanding job furnishing and decorating their lovely home, which they were well qualified to do as Roger restores furniture and Lis used to do upholstery. The four guest bedrooms each have unique features – the Tudor room has a four-poster bed and one twin room has French antique beds and a particularly lovely bathroom with a fireplace. The beautifully proportioned drawing room has comfortable furniture and French doors leading out to the garden. The "Butlerstown table" in the dining room is where an extensive breakfast menu is served. Butlerstown House offers guests peace, tranquillity and comfort; there are no TVs in the house. The sea is only 2.5 km away. The house can be found about a kilometre outside Butlerstown. Smoking in study only. All major credit cards accepted.

OWNER Elisabeth Jones & Roger Owen OPEN March 15 – December 15 ROOMS 1 double, 2 twin, 1 four-poster; 3 en suite TERMS B&B IR£35; single supplement IR£10

Glebe Country House
Ballinadee, Bandon, Co. Cork
Tel: 021 778294 Fax: 021 778456 E-mail: glebehse@indigo.ie

Set next to the church in the centre of Ballinadee, Glebe Country House is a very pretty Georgian rectory, which was carefully renovated by the Brackens, and then redecorated after extensive damage during the 1997 Christmas storm. The bedrooms are spacious and attractively decorated and furnished and some have views of the river. All have hairdryers, irons, telephones and tea and coffee making facilities. Guests have the run of the house, which includes a large drawing room with television and open fire, and the dining room where good home-cooked dinners are served featuring organically home-grown salads and herbs. Gill Bracken is a bright, cheerful person, and the atmosphere is friendly and informal. The attractive garden contains a croquet lawn and "fun" grass tennis court. Three self-catering units are available. Ballinadee is a 15-minute drive from Kinsale. There are several nearby golf courses, and river fishing and sea angling can be arranged. Visa, Access, Mastercard accepted.

OWNER Gill Bracken   OPEN All year   ROOMS 2 twin, 2 double & single; 2 with bath, 2 with shower en suite   TERMS B&B IR£22.50–27.50; reduction for children; single supplement IR£7.50   MEALS Lunch IR£5; table d'hôte dinner IR£16.50

St Anne's

Clonakilty Road, Bandon, Co. Cork
Tel: 023 44239 Fax: 023 44239

This attractive Georgian house was in pretty bad shape when Anne Buckley bought it. She has done a great job renovating the house, which now offers bright and attractively furnished bedrooms. Both the dining room, where breakfast only is served, and the sitting room have their original fireplaces. Anne, who is an ex-school teacher, is very charming and attentive to the needs of her guests. Pets to be kept in the car, and smoking is only permitted in the lounge. St Anne's is 1 km from Bandon on the N71 to Clonakilty. Visa, Mastercard, Access accepted.

OWNER Anne Buckley   OPEN All year   ROOMS 1 double, 3 family, 1 single; all en suite   TERMS B&B IR£17; reduction for children; single supplement IR£5.50

BANTEER

Clonmeen Lodge
Banteer, Co. Cork
Tel: 029 56238 Fax: 029 56294

Clonmeen Lodge is a most attractive, small, Georgian stone-built house set in its own grounds on the Blackwater River. The comfortable, plainly furnished bedrooms are mostly in the rambling back part of the house, which was built on in different periods. A popular place to gather is the rather strange bar room which has a tiled floor and is decorated with all kinds of knick-knacks and sporting pictures. Catherine O'Leary is a bright, gregarious lady who offers good home-cooked evening meals using home-grown produce. Horseback riding is available at Clonmeen and the area has three golf courses as well as the possibility of shooting, fishing and fox hunting. There are two well converted self-catering units in part of the old farm buildings, which are also sometimes used by overnight guests. The house is signposted from Banteer. All major credit cards accepted.

OWNER Gerry & Catherine O'Leary OPEN Closed at Christmas
ROOMS 3 double, 1 twin, 2 single; 5 en suite TERMS B&B IR£30–35; reduction for children; single supplement IR£5 MEALS Dinner IR£18

BANTRY

Bantry House
Bantry, Co. Cork
Tel: 027 50047 Fax: 027 50795

Bantry House, overlooking Bantry Bay, is one of the finest stately mansions in Ireland. Purchased by the White family in 1739, it is furnished with the most wonderful collection of pictures, furniture and works of art. The White family were also responsible for laying out the formal gardens. Both the east and west wings of Bantry House provide newly refurbished en suite accommodation, all with telephones, hairdryers and tea and coffee making facilities. Residents have use of a sitting room, billiard room and a balcony TV room overlooking the Italian garden with its fountain, parterres and "stairway to the sky." There is a wine licence, and guests are welcome to help themselves to drinks from the bar. Bantry House is open to the public and overnight guests are admitted at no extra charge. There is also a tennis court, tea room and craft shop on the premises. Evening meals are sometimes available, but must be booked by noon. Smoking is permitted in the bar and lounge. Pets are allowed outside. Visa, American Express, Mastercard accepted.

OWNER Egerton & Brigitte Shelswell-White OPEN March 1 – October 31   ROOMS 9 double/twins/family/single; all en suite   TERMS B&B IR£60–70; reduction for children; single supplement IR£10   MEALS Dinner IR£25

Dunauley
Bantry, Co. Cork
Tel: 027 50290 Fax: 027 50290

Dunauley stands in a spectacular position with magnificent views of Bantry Bay and the Caha Mountains. It is located above the town of Bantry in its own garden. Rosemary McAuley is a warm and welcoming host and serves a wonderful breakfast, including freshly squeezed orange juice and drop scones, in the spacious lounge-cum-dining room, which takes full advantage of the view. There are three bedrooms on the ground floor, and they are furnished simply and comfortably. There is also a self-catering unit available. No smoking. No pets. Upon arriving in Bantry, follow signs for the hospital until you see Dunauley signposted.

OWNER Rosemary McAuley OPEN May 1 – September 30 ROOMS 1 double, 2 twin; all en suite   TERMS B&B IR£20–25; reduction for children; single supplement IR£5

Grove House
Ahakista, Bantry, Co. Cork
Tel: 027 67060

This 250-year-old whitewashed stone farmhouse is set amidst beautiful scenery on the Sheep's Head Peninsula. It is an idyllic setting, perfect for nature lovers, with beautiful walks, bird-watching and a private beach for swimming or boating (a boat is provided); with advance notice, bicycle hire can also be arranged.

There is a huge old log fireplace, and the dining room has been extended to include a conservatory with a stone floor that also enjoys the lovely view. Down-to-earth Mary O'Mahoney is a good cook, using home-grown vegetables from the garden and, when the fishing is good, fresh seafood. Light meals, as well as evening meals, can be provided upon request. Honey fresh from the hive, soda scones and home-baked breads are all on the menu here. Pets outside only. Smoking by arrangement. Grove House is signposted in Durrus, 8 km away.

OWNER Mary O'Mahoney   OPEN May 1 – October 1   ROOMS 2 double, 1 twin, 1 family, 1 single; 2 en suite   TERMS B&B IR£18; reduction for children; single supplement IR£6 MEALS Evening meals

Hillcrest House
Ahakista, Durrus, Bantry, Co. Cork
Tel: 027 67045

Hillcrest is an attractive, old stone dairy farm that was renovated a few years ago, and stands in a lovely position on top of a hill with wonderful views over the coast. Mrs Hegarty previously lived in a bungalow on the farm, where she also did bed & breakfast. An extension has been built onto the house, linking it with the old barn, which now houses the large games room. There are flagstone floors, peat fires and quite spacious rooms, simply furnished and decorated. Fresh farm produce is used for evening meals and breakfast, as is home baking. Babysitting can be provided. Pets are allowed outside only. There are smoking restrictions. Hillcrest is a five-minute walk to a sandy beach; there is good sea fishing and mountain walking behind the house, and the new Sheep's Head Way walking path runs by the property. It is signposted from Durrus 12 km away.

OWNER Mrs Agnes Hegarty OPEN April 1 – November 1 ROOMS 1 double, 1 twin, 1 family, 1 triple; 3 en suite   TERMS B&B IR£18; reduction for children; single supplement IR£6   MEALS High tea IR£10.50; dinner IR£13.50

The Mill
Glengarriff Road, New Town, Bantry, Co. Cork
Tel: 027 50278   Fax: 027 50278

Tosca and Kees Kramer fell in love with Bantry while on an Irish holiday from their native Holland, so they stayed and made Ireland their home. The Mill is a chalet-style house, set back from the road in attractive, landscaped gardens 1 km from the town centre. The Kramers have recently made extensive improvements to the house. This included making all bedrooms en suite and adding a conservatory furnished with cane furniture, where guests can sit and relax. Most of the bedrooms are on the ground floor and have hairdryers and TVs. Kees Kramer is not only a craftsman, making all the wardrobes, cabinets and dining room tables, but also an artist. A selection of his work can be found around the house. The Mill offers a laundry service and there are bicycles for hire. There are plenty of excellent pubs and restaurants in the area, and close by there are golf, fishing and horseback riding. No pets and no smoking. The house is on the N71 in the direction of Glengarriff. Visa accepted.

OWNER Tosca & Kees Kramer OPEN March – November ROOMS 4 double, 1 twin, 2 family, single; 7 en suite   TERMS B&B IR£20; reduction for children; single supplement IR£15

BANTRY BAY

Ballylickey Manor House
Ballylickey, Bantry Bay, Co. Cork
Tel: 071 50071 Fax: 071 50124

On the boundary of Cork and Kerry, amidst sheltered lawns, flower gardens and parkland and bordered by sea, river and mountains, stands Ballylickey House, commanding a magnificent view over Bantry Bay. Built some 300 years ago by Lord Kenmare as a shooting lodge, Ballylickey has been the home of the Graves family for over four generations. Robert Graves, the poet, was an uncle of the present owner. The house was burnt down in recent years, but was rebuilt incorporating the best of the old features with a new standard of comfort. This elegant residence is exquisitely decorated with many pieces of antique furniture. One

of the main features of a stay at Ballylickey is the food, which is superbly prepared and presented, and served with great elegance in the attractive dining room. The bedrooms are luxurious and all have TVs, phones, hairdryers and trouser presses. The suites include a bedroom, drawing room and bathroom. Some of the rooms are in the manor house, and others are delightful garden cottages around the swimming pool and gardens. A restaurant by the pool is open to non residents. The 4 hectares of grounds include another Georgian home for self-catering, and two rookeries, which are believed to bring a special blessing to a house. There are two golf courses nearby and miles of mountainous coastline. No pets. No smoking in the restaurant. The house is between Bantry and Glengarriff on the N71. Visa, Mastercard, American Express accepted.

OWNER Mr & Mrs Graves OPEN April – November ROOMS 6 double, 7 suites; 13 en suite TERMS B&B IR£60–100; reduction for children by arrangement MEALS Dinner IR£28; lunch à la carte

BLARNEY

Ashlee Lodge
Tower, Blarney, Co. Cork
Tel: 021 385346 Fax: 021 385726

Taken over by Anne and John O'Leary during 1997, Ashlee Lodge has been refurbished and upgraded with all rooms having

hairdryers, TVs, telephones and tea and coffee making facilities. It is a modern whitewashed bungalow with a porticoed front porch standing in the village of Tower, 3 km from Blarney. Ashlee Lodge is professionally run and immaculately clean and has a pleasant open plan sitting/dining room with cathedral ceilings and a fireplace. Visa, Mastercard accepted.

OWNER Anne & John O'Leary   OPEN January 5 – December 20
ROOMS 2 double, 1 twin, 1 triple, 2 double & single; 5 en suite   TERMS
B&B IR£20; reduction for children; single supplement IR£6   MEALS
Dinner IR£15

Traveller's Joy
Tower, Blarney, Co. Cork
Tel: 021 385541

Traveller's Joy is an unassuming little bungalow set in a pretty garden, but what makes it special is the friendly welcome from warm-hearted Gertie O'Shea and the atmosphere of a home away from home. The rooms are basic and spotlessly clean and there is a cosy guest lounge with TV, off of which is the small breakfast room where breakfasts "to last you the day" are served. The O'Sheas are happy to offer advice on local sightseeing and where to find the best traditional entertainment. Traveller's Joy is in the village of Tower, 3 km from Blarney. Visa, Mastercard, American Express accepted.

OWNER Sean & Gertie O'Shea   OPEN February 1 – December 20
ROOMS 1 double, 1 twin, 1 family, 1 single; 2 en suite   TERMS B&B
IR£17–18; reduction for children; single supplement IR£5   MEALS Light
meals; dinner

BUTLERSTOWN

Sea Court
Butlerstown, Co. Cork
Tel: 023 40151 Fax: 023 40218

Set in 4 hectares of wooded parkland, Sea Court is a handsome Georgian country house, built in 1760 by the Longfield family. David Elder, an American, acquired it on a visit to Ireland some 15 years ago – a daunting project as he spends the greater part of the year practising law in Kentucky, and the house was in serious need of repair. Restoration took place, gradually but meticulously, and eventually it was opened up to overnight visitors during the summer, and for self-catering parties at other times of the year. It has been furnished simply with antiques and has comfortable bedrooms, all with their own or en suite bathrooms, one of which used to be the Edwardian ballroom wing, and four have sea views. Breakfasts are quite a feast and include scones made from the owner's own recipe. Evening meals are available if ordered in advance. Pets are allowed outside only. Smoking is not permitted in the bedrooms. Sea Court lies between Courtmacsherry Bay and Dunworley Bay and is within walking distance of the Coolim Cliffs, said to be the second highest in Ireland. Timoleague with its monastic ruins is 7 km away and Kinsale is a 40-minute drive.

OWNER David Elder OPEN June 8 – August 20 ROOMS 3 double, 2 twin, 1 family; 5 en suite TERMS B&B IR£23.50; reduction for children MEALS Dinner IR£18.50

CASTLELYONS

Ballyvolane House
Castlelyons, Co. Cork
Tel: 025 36349 Fax: 025 36781 E-mail: ballyvol@iol.ie.

In a beautiful parkland setting, Ballyvolane is a gracious, beautifully restored country house. It is surrounded by its own farmland, wooded grounds (quite spectacular in the bluebell season), formal terraced gardens and three recently restored lakes

stocked with trout. It was built in 1728 on the site of an older house and later altered to the Italianate style. Guests experience here a blend of elegance, informality and charming hosts. Jeremy and Merrie Green have done a superb job, gradually furnishing and restoring the house, which offers six very comfortable and spacious bedrooms, all with hairdryers and TVs, and one of the bathrooms has a wonderful old bathtub, encased in wood and raised on two steps. The lovely pillared hall has a baby grand piano and plenty of comfortable chairs in front of the open fire. Beautifully presented delicious food is served in the elegant dining room at the long dining room table, the open fire is lit both in the evening and at breakfast time, and guests serve themselves drinks from the honesty bar by the sitting room. Salmon fishing is available by arrangement on Ballyvolane's own stretch of the River Blackwater; there is trout fishing in the lakes and a croquet lawn. There are signs for the house on the N8 at the River Bride in Rathcormac. All major credit cards accepted.

OWNER Jeremy & Merrie Green OPEN All year ROOMS 4 double, 2 twin; 5 en suite TERMS B&B IR£35–45; reduction for children; single supplement IR£10 MEALS Dinner IR£23

CASTLETOWNSHEND

Bow Hall

Castletownshend, Co. Cork
Tel: 028 36114

Dating from the late seventeenth-century, Bow Hall is right in the centre of the picturesque village of Castletownshend, whose one steep street leads to the harbour and sea. The Vickerys are a delightful retired couple from New York state who have lived here for 20 years and have created a charming home. The bedrooms are light and spacious, with some American furniture. Breakfast is a grand affair, with homemade sausages and pancakes a particular treat. Good home-cooked dinners are served in the dining room and the large drawing room-cum-library has floor to ceiling bookshelves at one end with a fireplace at the other; all kinds of ornaments and knick-knacks are found throughout the house. The slate-faced front of the building overlooks a very large and immaculately kept walled garden. No smoking and no pets.

OWNER Dick & Barbara Vickery OPEN Closed at Christmas ROOMS 3 double; 1 en suite TERMS B&B IR£60 (dinner included); single supplement IR£5 MEALS Dinner

CLONAKILTY

An Garran Coir

Castlefreke, Clonakilty, Co. Cork
Tel: 023 48236

The original family farmhouse is close to the old farm buildings, some 200 m up the lane, where guests like to wander and watch the cows being milked. An Garran Coir was built by the Calnans and then extended to accommodate bed & breakfast guests. It offers clean and comfortable rooms equipped with TVs and hairdryers, a smartly decorated lounge with plush red chairs, and a dining room with both a piano and a "help yourself" tea and coffee area. Evening meals using fruit and herbs from the herb garden are available by arrangement. Children are well catered for with their own play area, and they can go on for rides with a leading rein on the farm pony. Adults can use the tennis court, play croquet or take a lovely walk to the award-winning village of Rathbarry. Smoking only in reception area. Pets outside only. The farm is signposted off the Skibbereen/Clonakilty road.

OWNER The Calnan Family OPEN All year ROOMS 2 twin or double, 3 family, 1 single; 3 shower/3 bath en suite TERMS B&B IR£17.50; reduction for children; single supplement IR£5 MEALS Dinner IR£11–15

Ard Na Greine
Ballinascarthy, Clonakilty, Co. Cork
Tel: 023 39104 Fax: 023 39397

Norma Walsh must take the prize for being the most hospitable, warm-hearted and amusing bed & breakfast owner in Ireland. A stay here is truly memorable – from the simple farmhouse comfort to the copious amounts of delicious food, or just watching the cows being milked. The atmosphere is friendly and informal, and guests immediately feel at home, many returning year after year. Set in pleasant farming countryside and enjoying lovely views, Ard Na Greine is a working dairy farm well located for Kinsale and visiting the attractive south and west Cork coastlines. The bedrooms are very comfortable and equipped with TVs and hairdryers, and there is a cosy TV lounge and dining room with separate tables where guests are spoiled with Norma's wonderful home-cooked meals. Visa, Mastercard accepted.

OWNER Norma Walsh OPEN All year ROOMS 1 double, 3 twin, 2 family; 4 en suite TERMS B&B IR£18–20; reduction for children; single supplement MEALS Dinner IR£12–17

Duvane Farm
Ballyduvane, Clonakilty, Co. Cork
Tel: 023 33129

This Georgian farmhouse was built around 1870 and has been in the McCarthy family for quite a while; before that it belonged to a bishop. It is beautifully furnished and has some brass and half tester beds. The farm supports cattle, and the attractive farm buildings lie behind the house. Breakfast includes honey from the farm's own bees and good value evening meals are available by arrangement. Smoking in sitting room only. Duvane Farm can be found on the N71, 2 km west of Clonakilty. Visa accepted.

OWNER Noreen & Rensie McCarthy OPEN April – October ROOMS
2 double, 2 family; 3 en suite TERMS B&B IR£17–20; reduction for
children; single supplement MEALS Dinner IR£10–13

CONNA

Conna House
Conna, Co. Cork
Tel: 058 59419

This charming Victorian country house is set in 3.5 hectares of
mature woodland and lawns. The Verlings are an interesting
couple who have lived in many different countries. Michael is an
army officer, and Maura runs the house and is an excellent cook.
The house has been most attractively furnished and decorated.
Rugs cover polished floors, and the pretty dining room leads from
the cosy sitting room. The restored stables can be used for self-
catering. Fishing on the Blackwater and hunting can be arranged.

OWNER Michael & Maura Verling OPEN All year ROOMS 4 double or
twin; all en suite TERMS B&B IR£25; reduction for children MEALS
Dinner IR£20

CORK

Garnish House
Western Road, Cork, Co. Cork
Tel: 021 275111 Fax: 021 273872 E-mail: garnish@iol.ie

Conveniently located on the western edge of town opposite
University College Cork, Garnish House is a double fronted
Victorian town house, set back from the main road by its parking
lot. It is a comfortable house, efficiently and commercially run by
pleasant, helpful staff and offering such facilities as a night porter
and a 24-hour service for arrivals and departures. The bedrooms
vary in size, some being quite spacious, and quite a few have
jacuzzi baths. They all have en suite bathrooms, hairdryers, trouser
presses, telephones, TVs and tea and coffee making facilities, as
well as fresh fruit and flowers. Guests have use of a small TV
lounge, and breakfast with its extensive menu is served in the

dining room from 6 a.m. until 11 a.m. or midday. All major credit cards accepted.

OWNER Hansie Lucey OPEN All year ROOMS 7 double, 7 twin; 14 en suite   TERMS B&B IR£22.50–30; reduction for children; single supplement

Riverview
Douglas Village, Cork, Co. Cork
Tel: 021 893762 Fax: 021 896502 E-mail: edwardsc@tinet.ie

Riverview, which is a Georgian-style house built in the Victorian era, can be found right in the centre of Douglas village. Mr and Mrs Edwards are a charming couple who offer their guests a personal service, and the atmosphere is warm and welcoming. The lounge/dining room has the original fireplace and is interestingly furnished, and the bedrooms are a good size with comfortable beds, TVs and hairdryers. No pets. Smoking in the bedrooms only. The house is 100 m from Barry's Pub, next to the Garda Station, and about 1.5 km from the centre of Cork, which can be reached by bus.

OWNER Catherine Edwards OPEN January – December 20 ROOMS 1 double, 1 twin, 1 family; all en suite TERMS B&B IR£18; reduction for children; single supplement IR£6.50

Seven North Mall
7 North Mall, Cork, Co. Cork
Tel: 021 397191 Fax: 021 300811 E-mail: sevennorthmall@tinet.ie

This terraced, 240-year-old, listed building is in a tree-lined mall facing the river, right in the middle of Cork. When the Hegartys bought the property it was derelict, and they decided to do all the restoration work themselves. Now it is comfortable and tastefully decorated. The bedrooms are spacious and have telephones, cable TVs, trouser presses, hairdryers and tea and coffee making facilities, and overlook either the river or the rural aspect at the back of the house. Both the sitting room and breakfast room have original 1740 fireplaces. There is wheelchair access to the house, and one room is equipped for the disabled. No pets. Smoking in the sitting room only. Access, Visa, Mastercard accepted.

OWNER The Hegarty Family OPEN January 8 – December 1 ROOMS
1 double, 1 twin, 1 single, 4 double or twin; all en suite TERMS B&B
IR£27.50–45; single supplement IR£10

FERMOY

Ghillie Cottage

Kilbarry Stud, Fermoy, Co. Cork
Tel: 025 32720 Fax: 025 33000 E-mail: flyfish@tinet.ie

Ghillie Cottage takes its name from the previous owner, who was
ghillie to the Duke of Devonshire, owner of nearby Lismore
Castle. Built around 1903, it is a converted "high cottage" – an
original council cottage built on half a hectare of land. The cottage
lies on a minor country road overlooking the River Blackwater
with 10 hectares of land stretching up the hillside behind. Kilbarry
is a working stud farm, crossing traditional Irish cobs with
thoroughbred mares and supporting three stallions. There are
livery stables for visiting riders and horseback riding can be
arranged. As well as, or perhaps above, the interest in horses is
Doug and Joy's passion for fishing. Doug is a fly fishing instructor
and guide and can arrange fishing on the Blackwater. The décor of
the attractively furnished small house reflects these interests. There
is an informal and relaxed atmosphere, and guests share the TV
lounge with the owners. Good home-cooked evening meals are
available by prior arrangement and packed lunches can be ordered.
Mastercard, Visa accepted.

OWNER Joy Arnold & Doug Lock OPEN All year ROOMS 2 twin, 1
single TERMS B&B IR£20–25 MEALS Dinner IR£17.50; packed
lunches

GLENGARRIFF

Cois Coille

Glengarriff, Co. Cork
Tel: 027 63202

This modern house stands in a commanding position overlooking
Bantry Bay and Garnish Island and is set in a lovely hillside

garden. It is a peaceful spot by the woodlands of Glengarriff, within walking distance of the village. The Barry-Murphys are kind and welcoming, and offer comfortable accommodation and an extensive breakfast menu. The attractive bedrooms are all now en suite. No smoking. Pets to be kept in the car. Cois Coille is on the Bantry road on the edge of the village.

OWNER Rita Barry-Murphy   OPEN April 1 – October 31   ROOMS 2 double, 2 twin, 2 family; all en suite   TERMS B&B IR£18; reduction for children; single supplement IR£6

GOLEEN

Fortview House
Gurtyowen, Toormore, Goleen, Co. Cork
Tel: 028 35324

Although built only a few years ago by the Connells, Fortview House has an air of rustic charm. It is a small, stone-built farmhouse on a working dairy farm in an excellent location for exploring the Mizen Head, Sheep's Head and the Beara Peninsula. The interior of the house is very attractive. It is fresh and bright and quite simply but comfortably furnished with pine floors, antique country pine furniture, brass and iron beds and comfortable sofas in the sitting room, where drinks are available by donation. The dining room has a tiled floor, wood-burning stove and white tablecloths; excellent breakfasts are served which include freshly squeezed orange juice and pancakes. Evening meals are available by arrangement. No pets. No smoking in the bedrooms. Fortview House can be found 10 km from both Schull and Goleen.

OWNER Violet Connell   OPEN March 1 – November 1   ROOMS 1 double, 1 family, 1 single, 2 triple; all en suite   TERMS B&B IR£25; reduction for children; single supplement IR£6.50   MEALS Dinner IR£15–20

Glenlohane

Kanturk, Co. Cork
Tel: 029 50014 Fax: 029 51100 E-mail: hidden.ireland@indigo.ie

Glenlohane is a superb Georgian country house set in beautiful park grounds with some wonderful old trees and views to the distant mountains. The present owners are direct descendants of the family who built it in 1741. Desmond lived and worked in the United States and Melanie is American, and between them they have combined the very best of modern comforts with the character and atmosphere of the past. Glenlohane is an informal house with good food and log fires to relax in front of. The large, comfortable drawing room features a square bay window, a superb full-length mirror, baby grand piano, grey marble fireplace and interesting pictures and furniture. There is also a small study filled with books, a dining room and a country kitchen. A traditional stable yard is attached to the house, where visitors' horses can be housed by arrangement. There are plenty of animals around, and the farm includes sheep and cattle. Guests are welcome to watch the daily farm activities. With notice, riding, or hunting with the Duhallow Hunt, the oldest pack of hounds in Ireland, can be arranged. Fishing is available only 1 km away on the River Blackwater, and there are a variety of golf courses and lovely walks nearby. To reach Glenlohane from Kanturk take the R576 towards Mallow. Bear left on the R580 towards Buttevant, then take the

first right towards Ballyclough. Look for the first residential entrance on the left after 2.2 km – there is no sign. Visa, Mastercard, American Express accepted.

OWNER Desmond & Melanie Sharp Bolster   OPEN Closed at Christmas   ROOMS 4 double or twin; all en suite   TERMS B&B IR£45–50; reduction for children by arrangement; single supplement IR£10   MEALS Dinner IR£25

KINSALE

Leighmoneymore
Dunderrow, Kinsale, Co. Cork
Tel: 021 775312 Fax: 021 775692

Reached via a series of country lanes and a long driveway, Leighmoneymore was built in 1912 as the dower house to the adjoining old farmhouse (now derelict). It stands in pretty countryside on the banks of the tidal Bandon River, and is surrounded by its own land with grazing pedigree cattle and sheep. The bright, fresh bedrooms have plain wooden floors and are simply but attractively furnished and decorated. They have tiled en suite bathrooms. They all have hairdryers, telephones and TVs; the three ground floor bedrooms have en suite bathrooms with bathtubs, and the two upper bedrooms have showers. Tea or coffee can be served at any time. The house has an interesting wooden archway to the staircase, a small sitting room and dining room. Breakfast is served either here or in the conservatory. No pets. Leighmoneymore is located between Innishannon and Kinsale. Visa, Mastercard accepted.

OWNER Michael & Dominique O'Sullivan-Vervaet OPEN March 15 – October 31 ROOMS 3 double, 2 double/single; all en suite TERMS B&B IR£18–22.50; reduction for children; single supplement IR£10

O'Connor's
Scilly, Kinsale, Co. Cork
Tel: 021 773222 Fax: 021 773222 E-mail: ocbb@iol.ie

The O'Connors virtually rebuilt this attractive, 200-year-old stone-built house, which stands on the edge of Kinsale, right on one of the roads into town. Designed for self-contained comfort, the renovation has resulted in four very comfortable rooms, two on the first floor, and two on the second floor, each one having splendid views over the harbour to Charles and James Forts on the other side of the channel. The top two rooms have the best views, but are smaller, whilst the first floor rooms have extra-large bathrooms and conservatory type sitting areas. Pretty much anything a guest might need can be found in the bedrooms, including breakfast served in the room, if so desired. The alternative is a rather boring breakfast room sandwiched between the kitchen and the owner's lounge. There is also a patio for sitting outside. No smoking and no pets. All major credit cards accepted.

OWNER Denis & Geraldine O'Connor   OPEN Closed at Christmas & New Year's   ROOMS 4 twin or double; all en suite   TERMS B&B IR£43–48; reduction for children; single supplement IR£33–38

Perryville House
Kinsale, Co. Cork
Tel: 021 772731 Fax: 021 772298

This spectacular house stands right in the centre of Kinsale on the quay overlooking the marina and the colourful streets of the medieval fishing port. Laura Corcoran, who previously owned Albany House in Dublin, bought Perryville House in a very run-down state and transformed it into a place of elegance and comfort, opening for business in 1997. The house is run with a quiet air of friendly professionalism. It has lovely furniture and tasteful décor, the Hessian covered floors offsetting colourful rugs. The bedrooms, which are luxuriously appointed, come in every shape and size, some overlooking the harbour, some in a newer wing, but even the smallest room is a good size. They all have TVs, hairdryers, telephones and mineral water and the majority have separate bathtubs and showers in the en suite bathrooms. The drawing room, where morning coffee and afternoon tea are served daily, is comfortable and elegant, and the large, open reception area is another place to sit and relax. Substantial buffet-style breakfasts are available in the dining room, including home-baked breads and preserves, local cheeses and fresh fruit. No pets, no smoking and no children under 12. All major credit cards accepted.

OWNER Laura Corcoran OPEN March 1 – October 31 ROOMS 3 twin, 22 twin or double; all en suite TERMS B&B IR£45–100; single supplement IR£20–30

MACROOM

An Cuasan
Coolavokig, Macroom, Co. Cork
Tel: 026 40018

This small country house is in a peaceful position and stands in a lovely mature garden. It is comfortable and clean, and has a relaxed atmosphere. Two of the en suite rooms are on the ground floor, and all rooms have hairdryers. The large conservatory is used both as a lounge and to accommodate the overflow from the dining room. The patio is a nice spot to sit on sunny days, and angling facilities are provided – a shed for the tackle and refrigeration of bait. An Cuasan is a good spot for visiting Kerry and western Cork, and for riding, fishing and walking. The house can be found 9 km west of Macroom on the N22. Visa, Eurocard, Access, Mastercard accepted.

OWNER Sean & Margaret Moynihan OPEN May 1 – October 31 ROOMS 2 double, 3 twin, 1 family; 5 en suite TERMS B&B IR£17.50; reduction for children; single supplement IR£6.50 MEALS Evening snack

MALLOW

Longueville House
Mallow, Co. Cork
Tel: 022 47156 Fax: 022 47459 E-mail: longueville@msn.com

This impressive, listed Georgian manor house is set in beautiful park-like grounds with lovely views overlooking the Blackwater River valley, surrounded by 200 hectares of woods, farmland, a vineyard and gardens which include 1.2 hectares of kitchen gardens. Visitors flock to Longueville House primarily for its food, which mostly comes from the river, garden and farm and is under the direction of William O'Callaghan; its lovely peaceful setting;

the salmon fishing on the Blackwater, which runs through the estate; and because it is a good touring base for exploring both the south and southwest coasts. The bedrooms are supremely comfortable, ranging in shape and size, and seven have mini suites which include sitting areas and luxury bathrooms. In spite of the grandeur, the atmosphere is warm and welcoming and guests have use of the comfortable drawing room, the old conservatory and a games room with a full-size billiard table. As well as breakfast and dinner, a snack lunch is available all week. There are five non-smoking bedrooms and no smoking is permitted in the restaurant. Longueville House is 6.5 km west of Mallow on the N72. All major credit cards accepted.

OWNER The O'Callaghan Family OPEN Closed at Christmas & January
ROOMS 10 double, 10 twin; all en suite TERMS B&B IR£67–82; single
supplement IR£25–40 MEALS Dinner IR£30; light meals

MIDLETON

Ballymaloe House
Shanagarry, Midleton, Co. Cork
Tel: 021 652531 Fax: 021 652021 E-mail: bmaloe@iol.ie

Famous as one of Ireland's top restaurants and the training ground (at Ballymalaoe Cookery School) for many of Ireland's best chefs, it is undoubtedly food that lures many visitors to this lovely old family home. Set in 160 hectares of its own farmland, Ballymaloe is built around an old Geraldine castle, the fourteenth-century keep still intact. The bedrooms, which vary in size and character, are located in the main house; around the old coachyard, where there are four on the ground floor designed to take wheelchairs; in the Gatehouse, with the twin bedded room up short steep stairs, and where, in an addition, there are five newer rooms. Three small dining rooms open off the main room, and they have an interesting collection of modern Irish paintings, including works by Jack B. Yeats, brother of the poet William Butler Yeats. The Allens, in addition to Ballymaloe House, the Cookery School and the farm, also run a craft shop on the premises, and the restaurant in the Crawford Art Gallery in Cork. Facilities on the estate include a heated outdoor swimming pool (summer only), tennis court, small golf course, children's play equipment and the craft shop. Restricted smoking and no pets. Ballymaloe is 3 km outside Cloyne on the Ballycotton road. All major credit cards accepted.

OWNER The Allen Family OPEN Closed at Christmas ROOMS 33 double or twin; all en suite TERMS B&B IR£57–75; single supplement IR£20 MEALS Dinner IR£32

Barnabrow House
Cloyne, Midleton, Co. Cork
Tel: 021 652534 Fax: 021 652534

Built in 1639, with two wings added later, Barnabrow – meaning a fairy fort – stands on a hill surrounded by its own 14 hectares and enjoys pleasant country views. The house was gutted and has been most interestingly restored with the four large second-floor bedrooms having high raftered ceilings. Apart from one bedroom on the first floor, the remainder are in two ranges of converted farm buildings at the back of the house, one of which also houses the bar and restaurant above it. The house has been unusually decorated and plainly and simply furnished with a mixture of old and new, and strong, vibrant and bright colours are used on the walls, reflecting the colours of Guatemala. A lot of the interestingly shaped furniture and the flooring are made from imported teak from Botswana. The restaurant's chef spent some time at the Ballymaloe cookery school which, together with Ballymaloe House, is just down the road. Organically grown vegetables from the walled garden are a part of the delicious food on offer, and the outside terrace is used for barbecuing. The cathedral at Cloyne, 1.5 km away, was the seat of George Berkeley, the well-known philosopher after whom the Californian university was named. All major credit cards accepted except American Express.

OWNER John & Geraldine O'Brien OPEN Closed at Christmas ROOMS 11 double, 5 twin, 2 family, 1 single; all en suite TERMS B&B IR£25–45; reduction for children; single supplement IR£5 MEALS Dinner à la carte

Glenview House

Midleton, Co. Cork
Tel: 021 631680 Fax: 021 631680

Dating from 1780, this Georgian house is in a lovely rural setting, and stands in 8 hectares of grounds and gardens. When the Sherrards bought the house some 30 years ago, it was derelict, with ivy growing through the floor. They added the bow-shaped end of the drawing room that faces south, and in the course of renovation and furnishing, bought the contents of 16 houses, using what they needed and auctioning off the remainder. One of these acquisitions is the old bath, which has a brass surround. Evening meals are served in the attractive dining room, and there is a wide hall with a fireplace at one end. Visitors to Glenview find it a relaxing and peaceful place, the ideal setting in which to paint or write. The ground floor double bedroom has outside access and is suitable for the disabled. There are doors leading from the bar out onto the patio, which is a nice sunny spot to sit on fine days. Currently being built are two new self-contained units, one with a double en suite room and the other with two double en suite rooms, and both will be wheelchair accessible. There is a grass tennis court and croquet lawn. No pets. Smoking in the lounge by arrangement. The house is signposted off the L35 Midleton to Fermoy road. All major credit cards accepted.

OWNER Ken & Beth Sherrard OPEN All year ROOMS 1 double, 3 double or twin; all en suite TERMS B&B IR£40; reduction for children; single supplement IR£8 MEALS Dinner IR£20

Old Parochial House

Castlemartyr, Midleton, Co. Cork
Tel: 021 667454 Fax: 021 667429

Built in 1784 by the Earl of Shannon for his land agent, this very attractive house stands in a small garden in the village of Castlemartyr. Later the house belonged to the Catholic Church and was home to the Bishop of Cloyne. It was in really bad shape when the Sheehys bought it in 1996, and they have done a splendid restoration job, furnishing and decorating the house with taste and care. There are pine floors and open fires in both the small sitting room and dining room. The dining room has one table, and local pottery is used for serving breakfast. The spacious bedrooms are all en suite with hairdryers, TVs, tea and coffee making facilities and fresh flowers. The old conservatory off the sitting room is reputed to have one of the oldest vines in Ireland, which in summer is laden with fruit, and honey comes from home beehives. The garden is currently being restored. Kathy and Paul Sheehy are a very welcoming young couple with two small children. Bicycles and packed lunches are available. No pets and no smoking in bedrooms. Visa, Mastercard accepted.

OWNER Kathy & Paul Sheehy OPEN Closed December 20 – January 2 ROOMS 2 (four-posters) double, 1 double or twin; all en suite TERMS B&B IR£30–40; reduction for children; single supplement IR£10 (high season only) MEALS Packed lunches

MILLSTREET

Ballinatona Farm

Millstreet, Co. Cork
Tel: 029 70213 Fax: 029 70940

Not your typical farm, this is a most unusual and wonderful place, set in beautiful countryside, with outstanding views of mountains, moors and farmland. But what makes it such a special place is cheerful, welcoming Jytte Storm, who immediately makes her guests feel at home. Jytte's Danish origins have a big influence on the décor and the house, which she and her husband originally built 20 years ago, and then added on to. Ballinatona was meant to be for their retirement, which is a pretty active one, what with running a 40-hectare dairy farm and a six-bedroom guesthouse. It seems every room in the house was built to take advantage of the best views. The sitting room, conservatory and dining room are all bright with large windows, as is the honeymoon suite reached up a very narrow spiral staircase. The décor and furnishings are simple, clean cut and very bright. Ballinatona Farm is a walker's dream – from the doorstep there are wonderful hikes, including this most remote and beautiful part of the Blackwater Way, which is part of the coast to coast walk and runs the other side of Clara Mountain, one of the viewpoints from the house. Flexible evening meals are available if arranged in advance. Smoking is only allowed in the conservatory. Excellent value are the tiny chalets in the grounds, which offer basic accommodation; they have no inside water, but do have fridges and small cookers. Water and a toilet are available outside. They can be rented by the night and cost from IR£5 per person. Visa, Mastercard accepted.

OWNER Jytte Storm OPEN March – October ROOMS 1 double, 2 twin, 1 single, 2 triples; all en suite TERMS B&B IR£17–25; reduction for children; single supplement

SCHULL

Stanley House
Colla Road, Schull, Co. Cork
Tel: 028 28425

Although it has a modern look, Stanley House is actually a renovated old farmhouse about 1 km from Schull. Surrounded by 3 hectares of fields with deer and colourful gardens, it is in a wonderful position overlooking Schull harbour, Roaring Water Bay with its many islands and Mount Gabriel. Nancy Brosnan has been doing bed & breakfast for 17 years, and has a far-flung circle of guests who return again and again to this home away from home. Maeve Binchy is among her regular visitors and she has written: "This is my fifth visit to the gleaming place where all the guests stare in wonder at the sparkling surfaces and shining windows and wonder do folk from another world come and do the housework at night." The small dining room has separate tables where breakfast is served. The comfortable TV lounge has a sun porch beyond which is the terrace – a great place to sit and take in the views. The Brosnans have quite a presence in Schull, with Nancy's husband running the Spar Supermarket and her son managing the restaurant and bar. They also have four houses for self-catering, including a thatched cottage. It is a lovely walk into the village, which runs the length of one main street; there are ferries to the islands two or three times a day in summer; bicycles can be hired, or, for the energetic, a climb to the top of 412 m Mount Gabriel is well worth it for the wonderful view. Visa, Mastercard, Eurocard accepted.

OWNER Nancy Brosnan OPEN March 1 – October 31 ROOMS 2 double, 1 twin, 1 family; all en suite TERMS B&B IR£17; reduction for children; single supplement IR£8

YOUGHAL

Aherne's
163 North Street, Youghal, Co. Cork
Tel: 024 92424 Fax: 024 93633 E-mail: ahe@iol.ie

The Fitzgibbon family have owned Aherne's for three generations. The inn started life as the family's pub and small grocery store that made sandwiches. It is the present generation of the family that made the transformation from sandwiches to a restaurant, and later built on an entire wing for accommodation. Located in the heart of the historic walled port of Youghal, Aherne's is a renowned seafood restaurant serving freshly caught local fish, including lobster, prawns, crab, salmon, oysters and sole. The restaurant is decorated in warm, glowing colours, and there are two small, cosy bars with prints and pictures. The bedrooms are exceptionally large, have very big beds and are restfully decorated. They each have en suite bathroom, TV, trouser press, telephone and hairdryer. The drawing room has an open fireplace, books and antique furniture, and the bright dining room in the new wing is where residents are served breakfast. River and deep-sea fishing, horseback riding and hill walking are activities that can easily be undertaken from Youghal. No pets and some restriction on smoking. The restaurant is open from 10:30 a.m. to 10:30 p.m. Access, Visa, Diners, American Express accepted.

OWNER The Fitzgibbon Family OPEN Closed at Christmas ROOMS 12 double or twin; all en suite TERMS B&B IR£55–65; reduction for children; single supplement IR£20–30 MEALS Dinner IR£30; lunch IR£17

Ballymakeigh House
Killeagh, Youghal, Co. Cork
Tel: 024 95184 Fax: 024 95370

The friendliest of welcomes, superb food and comfortable rooms make Ballymakeigh House a delightful place to stay. The 250-year-old farmhouse is located in the rich farmlands of east Cork and guests are welcome to walk around the intensive dairy farm and watch the cows being milked. For the energetic there are bicycles available, a full-size hard tennis court and horseback riding with a variety of courses on offer. The conservatory has been extended and offers lots of sunny sitting space, and the bedrooms are constantly being upgraded and are equipped with every comfort. Margaret won the AA Landlady of the Year Award in 1997 and has written a book containing some of her favourite recipes, *Through my Kitchen Window*. Copies are available for sale at the house. Her meals are imaginative and beautifully presented, featuring fresh vegetables, herbs and fruit from the garden, and fresh cream and milk from the farm. Vegetarian and special diets are catered for, and there is a wine licence. The Brownes are currently building an equestrian centre, learning centre and restaurant 3 km from the house. This is a marvellous spot in peaceful and tranquil surroundings, convenient to beaches, Fota Wildlife Park, Trabolgan Leisure Centre and Blarney Castle. No smoking in certain rooms. Pets outside only. Ballymakeigh is signposted at the Old Thatch pub in the village of Killeagh on the N25. Visa, Mastercard, Access accepted.

OWNER Margaret Browne OPEN February 1 – November 15 ROOMS 3 double, 2 twin, 1 family; all en suite TERMS B&B IR£30; reduction for children; single supplement IR£10 MEALS Dinner IR£22.50–25

COUNTY KERRY

Every tourist wants to visit Kerry to see for him- or herself the beauty of the landscape. The sea surrounds most of the county and it is the mixture of water and light that makes Kerry such a special place. There is an inconsistency in the weather – wind and rain from the Atlantic, misty drizzle or bright light and sunshine – making each day or part of a day different from the next and projecting a constantly changing pattern over the mountains, lakes and streams. Each type of weather brings its own peculiar beauty to the landscape.

The Killarney area is the most famous of Irish places of beauty. The town caters to large numbers of tourists and is full of hotels, yet the lakes, mountains and woods of the surrounding countryside remain unspoiled. Close to Killarney is the ruined fourteenth-century Ross Castle. From here one can hire a boat to Inisfallen Island and visit the ruins of the twelfth-century Augustian Inisfallen Abbey. Muckross House is now a folk museum and has the most beautiful garden. From the Gap of Dunloe there is a marvellous view of the Black Valley. This is where huge torrents of water poured through the Gap at the end of the ice age.

The Ring of Kerry is a famous scenic drive around the Iveragh Peninsula. Killorglin is known for its annual horse and cattle fair, Puck Fair, held for two days in August, a great event with pagan origins, when a wild mountain goat is captured and enthroned in the centre of the town. Waterville is the principal resort on the Ring of Kerry, and at Cahirsiveen one can see the magnificent police barracks, which were meant to have been built in the north-west frontier of India, but the plans got mixed up. At Ballinskelligs, which is an Irish-speaking area, there are the ruins of a monastery and a fine beach with wonderful views. The Skelligs are rocky islands off the extreme western part of the Ring of Kerry, which can be visited. It is wonderful place for birds, notably kittiwakes, guillemots, petrel, shearwater and fulmar. One can also see the ruins of the old monastery that stands 183 m above the landing place and is approached by long flights of stone steps. There are also beehive huts, stone crosses, the Holy Well, oratories and cemeteries to see. This is a beautiful, peaceful spot in fine weather, but terrifying in a storm.

The Dingle Peninsula is made up of mountains, cliffs, glacial valleys, lakes and beaches, West of Dingle, the scenery is wild and beautiful. Some 2,000 prehistoric and early Christian remains have been discovered, and a little old Gaelic culture can be observed at the tip of the peninsula. The little village of Ventry was the scene of a legendary battle, and at Fahan lies the greatest collection of antiquities in Ireland: stone beehive huts, cave dwellings, standing and inscribed stones and crosses, souterrains, forts, cahers and a church. There are spectacular views around Slea Head, especially of the Blasket Islands and scattered rocks, all part of an exploded volcanic area, and it was around here that the film *Ryan's Daughter* was made. Beyond Ballyferriter, a mostly Irish-speaking village that attempts to preserve its Gaelic culture, is Gallaurs, the most perfect example of early Irish building and dry-rubble masonry.

The principal town of Kerry is Tralee, a trading and industrial centre. At Ardfert, the cathedral, which was built in 1250 and has the ruins of its Franciscan Friary, is the most striking building.

ANASCAUL

Four Winds
Anascaul, Co. Kerry
Tel: 066 9157168

Kathleen O'Connor has been running her B&B for about 17 years; she enjoys meeting people and sharing her house and is an accommodating host. There are views of the Anascaul Mountains and Dingle Bay and Ross Beigh from the house. The simply furnished rooms are fresh and bright. There is a unique chaise-longue in the hallway. Anascaul is the birthplace of the Antarctic explorer Tom Crean and the well-known sculptor Jerome Connor. Tasty freshly prepared breakfasts are served in the cosy dining room and there is also a comfortable TV lounge. There are plenty of activities for the visitor, including walks, fishing, sandy beaches, mountain climbing and archaeological sites. The house is situated on the Dingle/Tralee Way Walk. Drying facilities available.

OWNER Kathleen & P. J. O'Connor OPEN All year ROOMS 1 double, 2 twin, 1 family; 3 en suite TERMS B&B IR£17; reduction for children; single supplement IR£4

BALLYBUNION

The 19th Green
Golf Links Road, Ballybunion, Co. Kerry
Tel: 068 27592 Fax: 068 27830

An immaculate bungalow in a superb location overlooking Ballybunion Golf Course – a two-minute walk to the first tee and a good seven iron to the club house: a golfer's paradise. The bedrooms are furnished with rich wood, pretty pastel fabrics and lace curtains. The sitting room is pleasantly furnished and there is a conservatory for guests' use. Breakfast is plentiful and is available as early as 6 a.m. Owners Mr and Mrs Beasley are a most accommodating couple who go out of their way to ensure their guests have everything they need. Tea or coffee is offered upon arrival. Garden furniture is available on fine days. Children are welcome during the month of August; the house is not suitable for children at other times. Breakfast only is served, but there is no shortage of restaurants and pubs for other meals in Ballybunion. Five minutes from sandy beaches, salmon fishing, cliff walks and seaweed baths on the beach.

OWNER Mrs Mary Beasley OPEN All year ROOMS 2 double, 1 twin, 1 family, single, triple; 5 en suite TERMS B&B from IR£20; reduction for children; single supplement IR£10

The Country Haven
Car Ferry Road, Ballybunion, Co. Kerry
Tel: 068 27103

This superb Georgian-style house is ideally situated just 3 km from the golf course and a 10-minute drive from the Tarbert car ferry. The driving range with 12 all-weather indoor bays will enable you to practice your golf and enjoy panoramic views of the Atlantic Ocean at the same time. Mrs Eileen Walsh is a friendly lady with a good sense of humour, who takes excellent care of her guests.

The house sits on a 65-hectare farm, and there are 7.5 hectares of young forest and a 6.5-km designated walk. The spacious bedrooms are of a very high standard, tastefully decorated with every comfort. There is a ground floor room with a small conservatory. A honeymoon suite is also available. Full Irish breakfast is offered with homemade scones, breads and marmalade; early breakfast prepared for golfers. The house has antique furniture throughout and most bedrooms have sea views. Guests will be extremely comfortable here, and have easy access to two golf courses and the scenic countryside. Visa accepted.

OWNER Mrs Eileen Walsh OPEN Easter – October 31 ROOMS 1 double, 3 twin, 1 family; all en suite TERMS B&B IR£20; reduction for children; single supplement IR£5

CAHERDANIEL

Moran's Farmhouse
Bunavilla, Caherdaniel, Co. Kerry
Tel: 066 9475208

Moran's is a modern bungalow with the most spectacular views, overlooking Derrynane and the Atlantic, and just five minutes' walk to the sea. There are two clean sandy beaches where guests can swim, hike, boat or just relax and enjoy the beautiful scenery. The house is simply furnished and has a pleasant, welcoming atmosphere. All bedrooms are on the ground floor. Moran Farm is a working farm of sheep and cows. Home-cooked wholesome evening meals are available by arrangement. Nancy Moran is happy to assist visitors in every way to ensure they have a comfortable stay, and to give advice on what to see and do in the area. Daniel O'Connell's House and Gardens and wonderful walks are close by.

OWNER Nancy Moran OPEN January 20 – December 1 ROOMS 2 double, 1 twin, 1 family; all en suite TERMS B&B IR£17; reduction for children; single supplement IR£13 MEALS Dinner

The Old Forge

Rathfield, Caherdaniel, Co. Kerry
Tel: 066 947 5140 Fax: 066 947 5140

The Old Forge is surrounded by 12 hectares of rugged land in a remote spot, and offers panoramic views of the Caha Mountains and Kenmare Bay. The property extends down to the sea, where there is a rocky cove for swimming, windsurfing and fishing. A restaurant and coffee shop are in operation during the summer months, and the Old Forge has been restored to a museum. The Fitzmaurices are a good team: Reg cooks breakfast and Cathy cooks dinner, which is served in the dining room overlooking the view. Dinners should be ordered in advance and light meals to full dinners are served; vegetarians can be catered for with advance notice. The rooms are clean and simply furnished. Trips to the Skelligs and fishing excursions can be arranged. Safe, sandy beaches are close by as are an ancient fort, hill walking and golf. Visa, Mastercard accepted.

OWNER Cathy Fitzmaurice OPEN All year ROOMS 3 double, 2 twin, 1 family; all en suite TERMS B&B IR£17; reduction for children; single supplement IR£6.50 MEALS Dinner

CAHIRSIVEEN

The Final Furlong

Cahirsiveen, Co. Kerry
Tel: 066 947 2810 Fax: 066 947 2810

This immaculate, warm bungalow sits in a tranquil location on the banks of the River Fertha Estuary, and enjoys lovely views. It is part of a 40-hectare farm with a Suckler Cow herd and a Sport Horse Enterprise. Approved riding stables offer beach gallops and horseback riding in secluded areas of the Ring of Kerry. Guests can also view the ruins of the old Union Workhouse, and a detailed history is available. The rooms are immaculately maintained and attractively decorated. Breakfasts, and prearranged four-course dinners, are served on a large refectory table in the dining room. Kathleen O'Sullivan is an excellent cook (seafood is a specialty) who enjoys chatting with guests and provides information on the area. Her motto is, "You may come as a stranger, but we hope you will leave as a friend." Group rates are available and special offers can be had in May, June and September/October. Deep-sea angling packages as well as trips to Skellig Rock from a nearby pier are offered. Visa, Mastercard, Access, Eurocard accepted.

OWNER Kathleen O'Sullivan OPEN All year ROOMS 1 double, 1 twin, triple family, double/single; all en suite TERMS B&B IR£17; reduction for children; single supplement IR£5 MEALS Dinner

Glenville Farmhouse
Gleesk, Kells, Cahirsiveen, Co. Kerry
Tel: 066 947 7625 Fax: 066 947 7625

Situated in a delightful position, midway between Glenbeigh and Cahirsiveen on the main Ring of Kerry Road, Glenville is a spacious new country house, with panoramic views of Dingle Bay. The rooms are well-appointed, with an attractive bright décor. There is a comfortable TV lounge. Tasty breakfasts are served in the dining room that overlooks the bay and the mountains. For evening meals, the Thatch Tavern very close by serves a good pint of Guinness, and there is dancing and good *craic*. A restaurant is within a five-minute drive. There is hill walking on the farm, and fishing trips on Skellig Bay can be arranged. The famous 18-hole champion course at Waterville is just 19 km away. Visa, Mastercard, Access, Eurocard accepted.

OWNER Marion O'Grady OPEN April 1 – September 30 ROOMS 1 double, 2 twin, 1 family; 3 en suite TERMS B&B IR£17; reduction for children; single supplement IR£5

CARAGH LAKE

Glendalough
Caragh Lake, Co. Kerry
Tel: 066 976 9156 Fax: 066 976 9156

Glendalough House is a charming Victorian residence just a short distance from the shores of Caragh Lake. It is a warm country house with mature gardens and views of the lake and Ireland's highest mountain range, the McGillycuddy's Reeks. It is furnished with antiques and there are several old paintings. An ideal spot for those looking for peace and tranquillity, the house is approached by a long private gravel drive, bordered with trees, shrubs and wildflowers. There is a garden inhabited by a colourful peacock and peahen. Candlelit dinners featuring Caragh salmon and succulent mountain lamb are served in the elegant dining room. There is a conservatory and also a mews that comprises two double en suite bedrooms with a private living room and south-facing terrace. Glendalough is truly a house for all seasons: there are several championship golf courses where tee times can be arranged, there is trout and salmon fishing, wonderful walks, and it is an excellent base from which to tour the Ring of Kerry and the Dingle Peninsula. Visa, Mastercard, American Express accepted.

OWNER Josephine Roder Bradshaw   OPEN March 1 – November 30
ROOMS 4 double, 3 twin; 6 en suite   TERMS B&B IR£45–50; single
supplement IR£10–15 MEALS Dinner

DINGLE

Ard na Greine
Spa Road, Dingle, Co. Kerry
Tel: 066 915 1113 Fax: 066 915 1113

This warm and inviting bungalow in a quiet location is just a five-minute stroll to the town centre. Mary Houlihan wanted to ensure that her guests had everything they could need, and she has certainly accomplished her goal. All the bedrooms, which are on the ground floor, are equipped with satellite TV, teamakers, electric blankets, hairdryers, irons and ironing boards, direct dial phones, and bath/shower combinations; the latest additions are fridges. The orthopedic beds have Dorma-designed duvets, and the rooms are bright and attractive. There is a breakfast menu featuring smoked herring, salmon, home-baked breads, Irish cooked breakfast, etc. You certainly won't need lunch. An added bonus is the delightful owner, Mary Houlihan. The house is extremely good value and there is a home-away-from-home atmosphere. The beautiful shamrock/harp tapestry displayed in the dining room was hand-made by Mary's sister. Visa, Mastercard accepted.

OWNER Mary & Michael Houlihan OPEN All year ROOMS 2 double,
1 twin, 1 family; all en suite TERMS B&B IR£17–20; single supplement
IR£8–10

Duinin House

Conor Pass Road, Dingle, Co. Kerry
Tel: 066 915 1335

Duinin, meaning "little fort," is a friendly ranch-style bungalow
with beautiful views of the sea and mountains. There is a large
front garden with a manicured lawn and lots of pretty flowers and
shrubs. Guests enjoy tea outside on warm days, or in the
conservatory that overlooks Dingle Harbour and Valley. The
comfortable lounge has a VCR that guests may use, plus an
additional lounge for reading or just relaxing in after a busy day.
All of the bedrooms are on the ground floor, with modern
furnishings, large, fitted wardrobes and chairs. The front
bedrooms have lovely views. The extensive breakfast menu, with
fresh baked breads, is served in the sunny dining room overlooking
the harbour. Golf, fishing, boat trips, beaches, hillwalking and
excellent pubs and restaurants are close by. Visa, Mastercard.

OWNER Anne & Pat Neligan   OPEN February 1 – November 30
ROOMS 3 double, 2 twin; all en suite TERMS B&B IR£17–19; single
supplement IR£8

Greenmount House

Gortnora, Dingle, Co. Kerry
Tel: 066 915 1414 Fax: 066 915 1974

Greenmount House, also known as Curran's Bed and Breakfast,
stands in an elevated site overlooking Dingle town and the
harbour. A special feature are the wonderful breakfast feasts: guests
help themselves from an enormous buffet choice of fruits, cereals,
home-baked bread, muffins, fresh juices, puddings, and other
delights, followed by tasty omelettes or a traditional Irish
breakfast. An added bonus is that it is served in a lovely
conservatory/dining room that overlooks the bay. Little wonder
the establishment was awarded the Certification of Merit Award.
The house has been extended, all the rooms are of a high standard,
and there are six newly developed superior rooms. Each has a full

bathroom, large sitting area, many more extras, and sea views. There are two lounges for guests' use. John and Mary Curran are from local, long established families, and will provide guests with an unlimited amount of knowledge on the area. Plenty of written information is also provided. Local amenities include golf, fishing, horseback riding and trips to see Fungi the Dolphin, whom you might even see from your bedroom window. Visa, Access accepted.

OWNER John & Mary Curran OPEN All year ROOMS 12 double/twin/family; all en suite TERMS B&B IR£17–22 standard room, IR£20–25 superior room; reduction for children; single supplement IR£15

The Lighthouse
High Road, Dingle, Co. Kerry
Tel: 066 915 1829

This pleasant two-storey spacious house stands in its own grounds overlooking Dingle Harbour. A galleried landing and a pine staircase lead to the spacious bedrooms, all of which have a bath/shower combination; one is on the ground floor. The bedrooms are bright and fresh; they are furnished with pine and have bright colourful duvets. The lounge and dining room overlook the view. Breakfast only is served, but there are several choices for evening meals in Dingle, which is within walking distance. The Lighthouse offers a high standard of accommodation. Mary Murphy is very helpful indeed and has information for visitors on what to see and do in this scenic area.

OWNER Mary Murphy OPEN March 1 – October 31 ROOMS 1 double, 4 double/single; all en suite TERMS B&B IR£16–18; reduction for children; single supplement IR£6

DINGLE PENINSULA

Barnagh Bridge
Camp, Dingle Peninsula, Co. Kerry
Tel: 066 713 0145 Fax: 066 713 0299

Barnagh Bridge stands in an elevated position in well-landscaped gardens overlooking Tralee Bay and the Maharee Peninsula. The house was designed by architect Michael Williams and is delightful in every way. Just about everything has been thought of for guests' comfort. The house offers all the facilities of a hotel, with warm attentive hosts, at modest prices. The spacious bedrooms, each with an individual wild flower theme, have high standards of décor and furnishings; all have great views. Heather Williams takes great pride in her cooking, which includes a daily breakfast special, featuring tasty dishes such as mushrooms, kippers, smoked trout, French toast, a wide choice of cereals and fruit, yoghurts, fresh squeezed orange juice, homemade jams and marmalade. A traditional Irish breakfast is also on the menu. The lounge leads out to a patio area and the gardens, which guests are welcome to enjoy on fine days. The ambience is warm and informal, and Heather Williams is very helpful and accommodating. This is a perfect combination for folks looking for a taste of luxury in a beautiful "get away from it all" setting. Visa, Access accepted.

OWNER Heather Williams OPEN March 15 – November 7 ROOMS 2 double, 3 twin; all en suite TERMS B&B IR£18.50; reduction for children; single supplement IR£10

GLENBEIGH

Mountain View
Mountain Stage, Glenbeigh, Co. Kerry
Tel: 066 976 8541

This soft green bungalow lives up to its name: the setting is spectacular – it stands in an elevated position with magnificent views all round. The bedrooms are colourful and immaculately maintained; three are on the ground floor. The TV lounge overlooks the view. Breakfast and dinners, if ordered in advance, are served in the bright dining room. Owner Anne O'Riordan is a very helpful, accommodating lady who has been in business for three years. Lassie, the sweet collie, is friendly. Beaches are close by, and there are mountain and hill walks, fishing and horseback riding in the area, and the Kerry Way Walk is close by.

OWNER Mrs Anne O'Riordan OPEN March 15 – October 31 ROOMS 2 double, 2 single; all en suite TERMS B&B IR£17; reduction for children; single supplement IR£5 MEALS Dinner

GLENCAR

Blackstones House
Glencar, Co. Kerry
Tel: 066 976 0164 Fax: 066 976 0164

This spacious award-winning old-style farmhouse is situated at the foot of Carrantuohill, Ireland's highest mountain, beside Blackstone Bridge, Licken Wood, overlooking the Caragh River. Walkers will be interested to know it is on the Kerry Way Walk. The bedrooms, which have floral fabrics and pine furniture, are in the oldest part of the house and are clean and cosy. The sitting room has antique pine furniture and comfortable easy chairs. Breakfast and pre-arranged four-course evening meals are served; wild salmon and home-produced lamb are often on the menu. The setting is superb, and kindly Breda Breen makes guests feel immediately at home. She offers a hot drink upon arrival. The perfect spot for nature lovers, outdoor activities include nature walks (guides can be arranged), mountain and hill walking, fishing, rock climbing and canoeing. Also of interest are the ruins of an old smelting works, which can be seen in Blackstone. Visa, Access, Eurocard accepted.

OWNER Padraig & Breda Breen   OPEN February 15 – October 31
ROOMS 1 double, 2 twin, 2 family, 1 single; 5 en suite   TERMS B&B
IR£17.50; reduction for children; single supplement IR£6.50   MEALS
Dinner

KELLS

Glenville House
Gleesk, Kells, Ring of Kerry, Co. Kerry
Tel: 066 947 7625

Glenville is a spacious, new country house set in a delightful position with panoramic views of Dingle Bay. The rooms are well-appointed with an attractive décor – one has a sitting area – and all are on the ground floor. There is a comfortable TV lounge, which has a wood- and peat-burning stove, and leads out to a patio area. An enjoyable breakfast is served in the dining room, which overlooks the bay and mountains. Full evening dinners are not available, but light snacks, such as mackerel salad, prawn cocktail, and sandwiches are available by request. There is hill walking on the farm, and fishing trips on Skellig Bay can be arranged. The famous 18-hole champion course at Waterville is just 19 km away. Marion O'Grady is an excellent host and guests are well taken care of here. Information on local activities are provided and this is a good base from which to explore this beautiful region.

OWNER Marion O'Grady   OPEN April 1 – October 31   ROOMS 1 double, 1 twin, 2 double/single; 3 en suite   TERMS B&B IR£17; reduction for children; single supplement IR£5   MEALS Light snacks

KENMARE

Ardmore House
Killarney Road, Kenmare, Co. Kerry
Tel: 061 41406

This luxurious farmhouse is set in beautiful, scenic countryside overlooking the sea. It is warm and inviting and Kathy Mullen is a delightful and pleasant host. Guests here are assured of true Irish hospitality. The immaculate bedrooms are well decorated and have comfortable beds. There are two lounges, one with a TV and an open fire and one quiet lounge for chatting and/or reading. Seafood is a specialty for evening meals, and light meals are also available. Dinners must be ordered in advance. Lake and deep-sea

angling, pony trekking, beautiful walks and golf are all available in the area. Scenic farm walks to the cliff and picnic areas can also be taken. Visa, Access, Mastercard accepted.

OWNER Toni & Tom O'Connor   OPEN March 1 – November 30 ROOMS 2 double, 1 twin, 3 double/single; all en suite   TERMS B&B IR£20; reduction for children; single supplement IR£5

Muxnaw Lodge
Castletownbere, Kenmare, Co. Kerry
Tel: 064 41252

This interesting, eighteenth-century house stands in a lovely position set in 1.5 hectares of beautiful landscaped grounds, with an all-weather tennis court. The house has an informal, lived-in atmosphere, and is decorated with Laura Ashley wallpapers, a Waterford crystal chandelier, antique furnishings and many items of interest. The comfortable TV lounge has the original fireplace and window shutters. The spacious bedrooms are refurbished in keeping with the character of the house, which has lovely views, original fireplaces and antique furniture; one bedroom has a brass bed. Telephones are available on request. Evening meals are available by arrangement; vegetarians can be catered for with advance notice. There is no licence, but guests may bring their own wine. A peaceful and relaxing house, this is a wonderful base for touring this beautiful area. It's a pleasant 10-minute stroll into town over the bridge.

OWNER Mrs H. Boland OPEN All year ROOMS 3 double, 2 twin; all en suite   TERMS B&B IR£22.50; reduction for children; single supplement from IR£3 (seasonal) MEALS Dinner

O'Donnells of Ashgrove
Ashgrove, Kenmare, Co. Kerry
Tel: 064 41228

O'Donnells of Ashgrove is a charming, peaceful house set in tranquil surroundings of pasture and woodland with a view of the Caha Mountains. Lynne O'Donnell is a friendly lady who welcomes guests as friends into her home. In the evening, guests are welcome to relax in the armchairs in front of the fire, or, if preferred, to join the family in their spacious and elegantly furnished TV lounge. There are many antique pieces around and the house is tastefully furnished. Breakfasts are served in the Jacobean-style dining room with its exposed beams, stone fireplace and log fire. Light snacks are available and tea and coffee can be requested at any time. There is one ground floor room with bath and shower. Of special interest are the stone circle, Kenmare town, sea trips around Kenmare Bay and the Gleninchiquin Amenity Area. Terry O'Donnell loves to fish, and is a local award-winning fisherman. He would be delighted to take small groups up to eight on fishing trips; packed lunches, evening meals and accommodation can be arranged for an inclusive price. The fishing is great and the company friendly.

OWNER Mrs Lynne O'Donnell OPEN May 1 – October 31 ROOMS 2 double, 1 twin, 1 family; 3 en suite TERMS B&B IR£20; reduction for children; single supplement IR£6

Whispering Pines
Bellheight, Kenmare, Co. Kerry
Tel: 064 41194

Whispering Pines is a delightful place to stay, located a two-minute walk from the town centre, and a five-minute walk from the golf course. This modernised period home with spacious gardens is set back off the road and is quiet and peaceful. The bedrooms are attractively decorated with matching fabrics and duvets. The charming owners, John and Mary Fitzgerald, make this a wonderful place to stay; nothing is too much trouble, and they are happy to give advice on what to see and do in the area. An ideal location for touring the scenic Ring of Kerry. Pets outside only. Smoking restricted. Private parking.

OWNER John & Mary Fitzgerald OPEN March 1 – November 1 ROOMS 2 double, 2 twin, family; all en suite TERMS B&B IR£20; reduction for children; single supplement IR£10

KILGARVAN

Sillerdane Lodge
Coolnoohill, Kilgarvan, Co. Kerry
Tel: 064 85359

This inviting bungalow is in an "away from it all" spot, surrounded by beautiful scenery. The bedrooms, all on the ground floor, are light and bright; all have a bright pastel décor. Breakfasts are served in the conservatory-style dining room overlooking the view; the lounge has an open fire. This is wonderful walking country and there is a swimming pool (heated in summer) for guests' use. Evening meals are available with everything prepared from fresh produce and local ingredients. The reputedly highest pub in Ireland is close by.

OWNER Joan McCarthy OPEN May 1 – September 30 ROOMS 2 double, 2 twin, 1 family; all en suite TERMS B&B IR£17; reduction for children; single supplement IR£3 MEALS Dinner

KILLARNEY

Crystal Springs
Ballycasheen, Killarney, Co. Kerry
Tel: 064 33272

This luxurious two-storey residence stands in its own grounds with a fountain, and although it's within walking distance to town, the adjacent fields are dotted with sheep, and a river runs by the property. The entrance to the reception area has stained-glass windows and a gas fireplace. Eileen Brosnan is a welcoming host who goes out of her way to ensure visitors are well looked after. The beautifully coordinated bedrooms (three are on the ground floor) have pine furnishings; one spacious deluxe room has creamy peach décor, a king-size bed and two singles. All the curtains and bed covers are made by Eileen, who has a flair for décor, evidenced by the tasteful appointed rooms throughout the house. The lounge has a marble fireplace and a fine display of flags from around the world showing where visitors travelled from, as well as some interesting lamps and old Killarney pictures. There is free fishing for brown trout, and rods and tackle are available. Visa, Mastercard accepted.

OWNER Eileen Brosnan   OPEN All year   ROOMS 2 double, 4 double/single; all en suite   TERMS B&B IR£19; reduction for children; single supplement IR£6

Fair Haven
Cork Road, Killarney, Co. Kerry
Tel: 064 32542

Fair Haven is a comfortable, warm country house set in half a hectare of land in peaceful, scenic surroundings. The simply furnished bedrooms are spotlessly clean. The lounge has open fires and teamakers, and guests may help themselves at any time at no extra charge. There's a separate bright dining room where freshly cooked breakfasts are served. Ann Teahan is an extremely friendly lady who has been welcoming visitors since 1984. Fair Haven was named after the hometown of an American who was the first guest. For guests who would enjoy a rest from driving, Ann Teahan can arrange tours of the Ring of Kerry and Dingle Bay at a modest charge. Buses collect guests at the door. Reservations can also be made for the Killarney Manor House Banquet, an excellent evening of food and entertainment which started in 1990. Golf and fishing are nearby. The postal address for Fair Haven is Fair Haven, Lissivigeen (N22), Killarney.

OWNER Anne & Jim Teahan   OPEN May 1 – October 25   ROOMS 2 double, 2 twin, 1 family; all en suite   TERMS B&B IR£17; reduction for children; single supplement IR£4

Kathleen's Country House
Tralee Road, Killarney, Co. Kerry
Tel: 064 32810 Fax: 064 32340

Kathleen's Country House is a delightful, family-run guest house where traditional hospitality and courteous personal attention are assured. The house is extremely well maintained and stands in 1.2 hectares of mature gardens, just 1 km north of Killarney. Kathleen's love of art reflects the décor; there is a splendid display of original oil and watercolour paintings, and inspirational verse decorate the walls. The well-appointed bedrooms are elegantly furnished in antique pine with orthopedic beds. Breakfasts only are served in the spacious dining room at separate tables overlooking the garden. Kathleen's combines the facilities of a first-class hotel with the comforts and warmth of an Irish home. The house motto is "Easy to get to, hard to leave," and is endorsed by the many visitors who return again and again. There are three 18-hole golf courses, plus two 9-hole courses within a five-minute drive, and fishing, lovely country walks, cycling and swimming are all available close by. Special group rates upon request.

OWNER Kathleen O'Regan Sheppard ROOMS 6 double, 10 twin, 1 family; all en suite TERMS B&B IR£28.50–42; reduction for children; single supplement from IR£5

Knockcullen
New Road, Killarney, Co. Kerry
Tel: 064 33915

Knockcullen, which means "hill on top," is an immaculate family home in a private location off the main road, situated two minutes' walk from town and the National Park. Marie O'Brien has been in business for 10 years; she started when the family had grown and she needed to do something to fill in her time and her home. It has become a popular venue, and many guests return often for her special hospitality and the warm and welcoming atmosphere. The house is an ideal base for touring this scenic area. Breakfasts only are served, but there are lots of good pubs and restaurants close by. Marie is interested in walking and mountain climbing and is pleased to assist guests with information and/or planned itineraries.

OWNER Marie O'Brien OPEN March 17 – November 31 ROOMS 3 double with shower, 2 twin; 4 en suite TERMS B&B IR£16; reduction for children; single supplement IR£2

Linn
Aghadoe Heights, Killarney, Co. Kerry
Tel: 064 33828

A dormer bungalow surrounded by scenic countryside, Linn overlooks Killarney's lakes and mountains. The bedrooms are spotlessly clean and nicely decorated; all have pine orthopedic beds. Tea making facilities are on the landing and hairdryers are available on request. Carmella Sheehy is an enthusiastic lady who decided to open up her home when her children were young; B&B allowed her to stay home with her children and still have the opportunity to meet people. There's a comfortable lounge with a TV, and a large, furnished patio area and a spacious garden for guests' use. This is a peaceful area and golf, fishing and horseback riding are all available close by. For visitors wanting a rest from driving, local tours can be arranged. All major credit cards accepted.

OWNER Carmella Sheehy OPEN March 1 – November 30 ROOMS 2 double, 1 twin, 2 family; all en suite TERMS B&B IR£17; reduction for children; single supplement IR£5

Lohan's Lodge
Tralee Lodge, Killarney, Co. Kerry
Tel: 064 33871

Lohan's Lodge stands back off the road and is surrounded by a beautiful, well tended garden. Two of the nicest things about the Lodge are the owners, Cathy and Mike Lohan; they are a delightful, warm and friendly couple who love what they do – guests are treated more like friends. The bedrooms, all on the ground floor, are average in size and are colour-coordinated. Most have views of the gardens, which guests are encouraged to enjoy, and the patio is furnished. Electric blankets are provided for cool nights. There is an extensive menu for breakfast, which is served in the dining room on separate tables, and there is an elegant, spacious lounge, which has cathedral ceilings and is warmed by a gas fire. This is wonderful spot for visiting Killarney, a three-minute drive away, after which guests can return to the tranquillity and comfort of Lohan's Lodge. Visa, Mastercard accepted.

OWNER Cathy & Mike Logan OPEN March 5 – November 5 ROOMS 2 double, 1 twin, single, 2 double/single; all en suite TERMS B&B IR£17.50; reduction for children; single supplement IR£7.50

The 19th Green

Fossa, nr. Killarney, Co. Kerry
Tel: 064 32868 Fax: 064 32737

The 19th Green is an immaculate, well maintained property situated in quiet and peaceful countryside, just a five-minute drive from Killorgin and Ring of Kerry Road. High standards prevail here. The house is efficiently run, and the large bedrooms are tastefully decorated with comfortable beds. The spacious lounge has an open fire in a stone fireplace and overlooks the mountains. Situated across the road are Killarney's two 18-hole championship courses, sited in mature woodlands. Tee times can be arranged, part of the service extended by the accommodating owners, Timothy and Bridget Foley. Tours can also be arranged for the Ring of Kerry, Dingle Peninsula, Blarney Castle, etc. Timothy and Bridget are proud of the personal attention guests receive here and make every effort to ensure that guests feel welcome and comfortable. They are pleased to offer advice on the wide range of restaurants in Killarney. Visa, Access, Mastercard accepted.

OWNER Timothy & Bridget Foley   OPEN March 1 – November 15
ROOMS 5 double, 5 twin, 3 family; all en suite TERMS B&B IR£20–27; reduction for children; single supplement negotiable

Villa Marias

Aghadoe Heights, Killarney, Co. Kerry
Tel: 064 32307

A dormer bungalow in a peaceful and quiet location, Villa Marias is five minutes' drive from the scenic Aghadoe Heights area. The house is immaculate, the bedrooms well-appointed and comfortable. There is a separate TV lounge with an open fireplace, over which is displayed a fine Waterford crystal sword. Mary Counihan has been established for 12 years, prior to which she was in the catering industry; she went into the B&B business to maintain her contact with people. Mary is a wonderful host: her first concern is her guests' comfort, and a warm friendly welcome is extended to everyone. Guests are greeted with a cup of tea or coffee and biscuits upon arrival, even though teamakers have been installed in the bedrooms. Well located and convenient for all local amenities.

OWNER Mary Counihan OPEN April 1 – October 31 ROOMS 3 double,
1 twin; 2 en suite TERMS B&B IR£15–17; reduction for children; single
supplement IR£5

KILLORGLIN

The Grove Lodge
Killorglin, Co. Kerry
Tel: 066 976 1157 Fax: 066 976 2330

This gracious country house stands in 1.2 hectares of mature
gardens and woodlands on the banks of the River Laune, and has
south-facing views of the McGillycuddy Reeks mountains. The
rooms are spacious and the reception lounge has an antique cast-
iron fireplace, fully restored from a rusty condition. The luxurious
bedrooms are tastefully appointed. They each have coordinated
floral bedding and curtains (one has a lace-canopied four-poster
bed) and four have their own balconies. The Lodge is delightful in
every way: there are high ceilings, a galleried landing, a colourful
patio area and a conservatory. Breakfasts are excellent, guests can
help themselves to yoghurt, cereal, fruit and juices followed by
pancakes or a traditional Irish breakfast. A superb place to stay
when visiting this beautiful region of Ireland, the location is idyllic
and the welcome is wonderful. Blennerville Windmill Centre,
Crag Cave and Killorgan Golf Club are all within driving distance.
Visa, Access, Mastercard accepted.

OWNER Fergus & Delia Foley OPEN All year ROOMS 5 double, 1
twin, 4 family; 6 en suite TERMS B&B IR£25–28; reduction for
children; single supplement IR£5

LISPOLE

Devane's Farmhouse
Lisdargan, Lispole, nr. Dingle, Co. Kerry
Tel: 066 915 1418

A warm welcome awaits you at this family-run farmhouse, a
working dairy farm of 16 hectares nestled at the foot of the
mountain with beautiful views all around. The Farmhouse is very

popular with walkers and tourists, as it is situated on the Dingle Way Walk. The bedrooms are clean, if a little small, but the owners are so hospitable, offering tea and home-baked bread and cake to guests, that room size seems unimportant. There is an extra cot available. Tea makers are in the TV lounge and hairdryers, irons and a trouser press are available on request. Dinner is by advance arrangement only, but there are several establishments for evening meals in Dingle, which is just 5 km away. Guests return here year after year, and visitors new to the property sometimes book in for a night and end up staying for a week or more. Guests are welcome to enjoy the daily farm activities, watch the sheep grazing or walk in this beautiful area. The farmhouse is located on a small side road, but don't give up; just when you think you have passed it, the farm comes into view.

OWNER Mary Devane OPEN April 1 – November 1 ROOMS 3 double, twin, 1 family; 3 en suite TERMS B&B IR£17.50; reduction for children; single supplement IR£7.50 MEALS Dinner

LISTOWEL

Ceol na h'Abhann
Tralee Road, Ballygrennan, Listowel, Co. Kerry
Tel: 068 21345

Ceol na h'Abhann, which means "Music of the River," is aptly named. This charming thatched house stands on the bank of the River Feale, in a lovely garden with a huge chestnut tree. This is an idyllic setting and guests lucky enough to book in here will not be disappointed. Niall and Kathleen Stack, the delightful owners, originally had the house built as a retirement home, but missed contact with people, and bed & breakfast seemed a fun thing to do. It was hard work, but enjoyable; successful from the beginning, many guests return for the special hospitality extended here. The immaculately kept bedrooms are individually decorated and have rich, tasteful furniture; they are reached by a staircase with an old cast-iron railing. One bedroom is on the ground floor. Excellent breakfasts are served in the bright dining room, and there is a lounge and sunny conservatory for guests' use. On fine days guests can stroll along the river bank or, for the less energetic, seating is provided. Listowel is within walking distance and there are several venues for evening meals.

OWNER Niall & Kathleen Stack OPEN April 1 – October 31 ROOMS 2 double, 2 twin, 3 family; 3 en suite TERMS B&B IR£15–21; single supplement IR£6 (high season)

RING OF KERRY

Cul Draiochta
Clogherbrian, Fenit Road, Ring of Kerry, Co. Kerry
Tel: 066 947 3141

Cul Draiochta means "Magic Nook" in Irish, and this *is* a magical area of the Ring of Kerry. Situated at the foot of the Bentee Mountains overlooking Valentia Harbour, the house was designed as a bed & breakfast and was built to ensure that guests have every comfort. The well-appointed good-sized bedrooms are light and airy. They have cherrywood furniture, pink candystriped duvets, and are attractively decorated with coordinated fabrics; all have orthopedic beds and overlook the view. Owners Ian and Ann Nugent are from a farming family in North Kerry and are very hospitable. They have been in business for just over three years, and have built up a fine reputation for offering very good value accommodation. Tea or coffee is offered upon arrival and other times on request. Excellent breakfasts and table d'hôte dinners are served in the conservatory-style dining room overlooking the view, and packed lunches can be provided upon request. Vegetarian meals are also available with advance notice. The lounge is very comfortable and has multichannel TV. Routes for walkers are provided. This is an ideal spot for nature lovers.

OWNER Ian & Ann Nugent OPEN All year, including Christmas ROOMS 2 double, 2 twin, family; 3 en suite TERMS B&B IR£15–17; reduction for children; single supplement IR£3–5 MEALS Dinner, packed lunches

Avonlea House

Sneem, Co. Kerry
Tel: 064 45221

Avonlea is an immaculate, comfortable home in a secluded spot close to the village. Mrs Hussey began her bed & breakfast business after a friend asked her to take her overflow guests during high season. Mrs Hussey enjoyed the experience so much that she decided to do B&B full time. A most accommodating host, she is assisted by her children during the summer holidays. The modern bedrooms are warm and comfortable. The TV lounge, with a real fire, has a piano that guests may play. The house is situated just two minutes' walk from the village, which has several good restaurants and local pubs with entertainment during the season. Advance reservations recommended during high season. Visa accepted.

OWNER Mrs Maura Hussey OPEN Easter – October 31 ROOMS 2 double, 2 twin, 1 family; all en suite TERMS B&B IR£15–17; reduction for children; single supplement IR£2

Derry East Farmhouse

Sneem, Co. Kerry
Tel: 066 45193 Fax: 066 45193

Derry East is a working beef-suckling farm. This is a botanist's paradise, with its wild mountain landscape background. Derry East has its own hard tennis court and a private fish pond stocked with trout. Guests are welcome to use the facilities and to take farm walks. The bedrooms are warm and comfortable, and there is a bright, colourful dining room, where dinners, if arranged in advance, are served featuring home-grown vegetables, with vegetarian and special diets catered for. An ideal spot for a relaxing holiday. Mrs Teahan is a caring and considerate host, offering guests a truly warm welcome, ably assisted in the summer by her children, who are happy to play Irish music for her guests.

OWNER Mrs Mary Teahan OPEN Easter – November 1 ROOMS 1 double, 2 twin, 1 family; all en suite TERMS B&B IR£17.50–20; reduction for children; single supplement IR£10–12.50 MEALS Dinner

Hillside Haven

Tahilla, Sneem, Co. Kerry
Tel: 064 82065

This country house stands in an elevated position set in mature gardens with a magnificent view of the sea, mountains and glorious countryside. The bedrooms, all on the ground floor, are spotlessly clean and comfortable. This is very much a family-run establishment with traditional hospitality and friendly, accommodating owners. Tasty evening meals are served (if pre-arranged) featuring traditional dishes, Irish stew, bacon and cabbage, home-baked breads and desserts; vegetarians are catered for. Breakfasts are served in the dining room, or, if guests prefer, outside in good weather. Light snacks are available on request. Walking is one of Helen Foley's hobbies, and she would be pleased to arrange walking holidays for small groups, and to outline local walks for individual walkers. Complimentary tea and coffee is available at any time.

OWNER Maurice & Helen Foley OPEN April 1 – October 30 ROOMS 2 double, 2 family; all en suite TERMS B&B IR£18; reduction for children; single supplement IR£5 MEALS Dinner, snacks

The Old Convent House

Pier Road, Sneem, Co. Kerry
Tel: 064 45181 Fax: 064 45181

Visitors enjoy the old-world atmosphere of the Old Convent House, set in its own grounds on the estuary of a river. The house was built in the middle of the last century as a convent for the Presentation nuns, who taught in the local school until 1891. Since that time it has been in the hands of the O'Sullivan family, who have been careful to preserve the character of the house while offering modern comforts. There are two lounges – one for reading or chatting with other guests, the other a very spacious lounge, and a conservatory. Guests are welcome to make use of the large gardens, and there is access to the river. Fishing enthusiasts may take trips out on the Bay from Oysterbed Pier, and Sneem with its gaily painted houses is just a pleasant three-minute stroll

away. Alice O'Sullivan is an enthusiastic walker and can provide walking maps and assist guests with walking itineraries.

OWNER Alice O'Sullivan OPEN All year ROOMS 2 double, 2 twin, 2 family; all en suite TERMS B&B IR£17; reduction for children; single supplement IR£17

TRALEE

Brianville
Clogherbrian, Fenit Road, Tralee, Co. Kerry
Tel: 066 712 6645

A luxurious modern bungalow situated in half a hectare of landscaped grounds, Brianville stands back off the road behind a beautiful stone wall entrance, with views of the mountain. The well furnished lounge has a fireplace, TV and piano. The rooms are well maintained, tastefully furnished and have comfortable beds. There is a lovely antique grandfather clock in the hallway. This is very much a family-run establishment and the owners are helpful and provide literature on what to see and do in the area. All rooms are on the ground floor. There are some excellent seafood restaurants nearby, and golf, fishing, windsurfing and sailing are also within easy reach.

OWNER Mrs Joan Smith OPEN All year ROOMS 2 double, 1 twin, 1 family, 1 single, triple; 4 en suite TERMS B&B IR£17; reduction for children; single supplement IR£5

Castlemorris House

Ballymullen, Tralee, Co. Kerry
Tel: 066 718 0060 Fax: 066 712 8007

Castlemorris House, a beautiful ivy-clad nineteenth-century Victorian house, stands in its own grounds on the edge of town. It was built in 1870 by the local regiment of the British Army and used by the commanding officer as his private residence. The house was purchased by the charming owners, Paddy and Mary Barry, in 1997. They have lovingly restored the residence, which is under a preservation order, carefully combining old-world charm with modern comforts. Many original features remain, such as stained-glass windows and casement shutters. The coving and fireplaces were removed and reinserted after restoration. This is a lovely old house – a warm and simple elegance pervades, the ambience is unpretentious, and the Barrys are charming hosts. The spacious bedrooms, three with original fireplaces, have king-size beds and are furnished in keeping with the character of the house; two have sloping ceilings and beams, and there several interesting antique pieces about. The peaceful drawing room has an open fire, which is lit at the first sign of a chill in the air. Mary is a trained chef and takes pride in her cooking. Imaginative breakfasts and candlelit dinners are served at separate tables in the dining room. Meals must be ordered in advance and vegetarian and special diets are catered for. There is plenty to interest the visitor, including *Siamsa Tíre* (the National Folk Theatre), and Irish music can be heard at local pubs. An Equine Centre is within walking distance of the house. Visa, Mastercard accepted.

OWNER Mary & Paddy Barry OPEN All year ROOMS 3 double, 3 twin; all en suite   TERMS B&B IR£30; single supplement IR£10   MEALS Dinner

The Fairways

Kerries, Fenit Road, Tralee, Co. Kerry
Tel: 066 712 7691

The Fairways is in a tranquil spot with beautiful views of Tralee Bay and the Slieve Mish Mountains and overlooks cattle grazing pastures and a 9-hole golf course. The light and airy modern country house is impeccably maintained and well-appointed. The bedrooms are large and tastefully decorated, two are on the ground floor. There is an excellent choice for breakfast: guests can have just about anything they want, including yoghurts, fruits, cereals, homemade brown bread and/or a traditional cooked breakfast. Evening meals are not available, but there are some excellent restaurants in Tralee. An ideal spot for golfers and tourists, fishing, sailing and beaches are all close by. Visa, Mastercard, Eurocard accepted.

OWNER Marion Barry OPEN March 1 – October 31 ROOMS 2 double, 1 twin, 1 family; all en suite TERMS B&B IR£17.50; reduction for children; single supplement IR£6.50

WATERVILLE

Seaview
Toor, Waterville, Co. Kerry
Tel: 066 947 4297

Seaview is situated in a "top of the world" location and has panoramic views of the Ballinskeeligh Bay, the Ballinskeeligh Mountains and Hogs Head. The house is clean and modestly furnished and the family suite is ideal for a family or friends travelling together. This is a friendly, informal house, the welcome is warm, and the owners are very happy to sit and chat with guests. Complimentary tea or coffee is offered on arrival. There is a cosy conservatory which overlooks the view, and there is a good supply of games and books around. Guests are also welcome to share the family lounge. Breakfasts only are served, but Margaret Curran is happy to give advice on places serving evening meals.

OWNER Margaret Curran OPEN March 1 – October 31 ROOMS 1 double, 1 twin, 1 family; all en suite TERMS B&B IR£17.50; reduction for children; single supplement IR£5

Sunset House
Waterville, Co. Kerry
Tel: 066 947 4258

This attractive bungalow overlooks Ballinskeeligh Bay on the edge of town. The house is clean and pleasantly furnished with a spacious dining room and a lounge with TV and piano. There is a pretty furnished patio for guests' use. Mrs Fitzgerald began offering bed & breakfast over 16 years ago, adding more rooms for the many guests looking for accommodation. However, she still has to turn people away; advance reservations are recommended, particularly during high season. Evening meals are not available, but accommodating Mrs Fitzgerald would be happy to recommend local eating places serving good food at reasonable prices. Golf, horseback riding and the beach are close by.

OWNER Mrs Patricia Fitzgerald OPEN All year ROOMS 1 double, 7 twin; 4 en suite TERMS B&B IR£15–17; reduction for children; single supplement IR£3

COUNTY WATERFORD

Waterford is probably best known for its crystal factory, which has regular hours for visits. Situated in the southeast of the country, it is reputedly one of the sunniest spots in Ireland. Waterford has a pretty coastline and a more rugged interior, with good farmland. The Nire Valley is good for walking and pony trekking, and has wonderful views.

Waterford city has much of interest to visit. Reginald's Tower, a massive circular fortress, is now the civic museum. Christ Church Cathedral, built in 1779; the French church; the Chamber of Commerce, a lovely Georgian building; and the City Hall, which houses two old theatres, are all worth seeing. The International Festival of Light Opera is held in Waterford in September.

Dunmore East, Tramore, Annestown and Dungarvan are all pleasant seaside spots, particularly Dunmore East, which resembles a Devon fishing village. Farther south is the Irish-speaking village of Ring, where Irish scholars go to study.

St Declan's Oratory, built in the ninth century, and St Declan's Well and Temple Disert, can be found at Ardmore. The cathedral, which dates back to the twelfth century, is known for its sculptured figures.

Seven kilometres from Cappoquin is the Cistercian Abbey of Mount Melleray. The Abbey maintains the tradition of monastic hospitality, so it is quite in order to accept a meal if it is offered to you.

Lismore, which was at one time a great centre of learning, was built by King John in 1185 and once belonged to Sir Walter Raleigh. The gardens are open to the public. The medieval Cathedral of St Cathach is most attractive, and was restored in 1633.

ANNESTOWN

Annestown House
Annestown, Co. Waterford
Tel: 051 396160 Fax: 051 986474 E-mail: annestownhouse@tinet.ie

Annestown House has been in the Galloway family since 1830. The grounds stretch down to a wonderful sandy beach, and there are lovely sea and river views. It is a wonderful, old, long narrow house that was originally three or four houses. One end of the building at one time was the curate's house and the other end housed the village shop. The interior of this lived-in family home, with old family portraits and lots of prints, is on many different levels. It rambles from the billiard room, lined with old books and an open fire, to the small, cosy sitting room and comfortable drawing room. At one time there used to be a restaurant in the house and evening meals, served either at one big table or separate tables, are still available if arranged in advance. The bedrooms, four of which have sea views, all have telephones and tea and coffee making facilities. John and Pippa are a delightful, easygoing and interesting couple, and are happy to suggest excursions and activities ranging from golf to hill walking to just exploring the beautiful rugged coastline. Close at hand, Annestown has both a croquet lawn and a grass tennis court. No pets. No smoking in the bedrooms. The house is in the centre of the village.

OWNER John & Pippa Galloway OPEN March – November ROOMS 5 double or twin; all en suite TERMS B&B IR£30; single supplement IR£10 MEALS Dinner

Guesthouse of the Yr in '99

BALLYMACARBRY

Hanora's Cottage Guesthouse

Nire Valley, Ballymacarbry, Co. Waterford
Tel: 052 36134 Fax: 052 36540

An absolute haven of peace and tranquillity, Hanora's Cottage nestles at the foot of the Comeragh Mountains, beside the Nire Church and old schoolhouse, with the Nire River running alongside. The little cottage was built for Seamus' great grandparents in the late 1800s, and Seamus and Mary, the fourth generation of the family, bought it in 1967 as a two-bedroom cottage. It has come a long way since then, and it seems the Walls are always adding on and making improvements! Currently the house has six spacious, very comfortable bedrooms with every possible amenity. Some have jacuzzi baths and two have king-size beds, and they all have hairdryers, telephones, TVs and tea and coffee making facilities. Breakfasts at Hanora's have to be seen to be believed. Before leaving for work, Seamus bakes all the bread, which could include eight or nine different loaves, not to mention rolls, scones, muffins, etc. There is an exotic array of fruits, Mary's special porridge together with every kind of cereal, several whole local cheeses and smoked salmon, not to mention a choice of cooked breakfasts. It is just as well there are a variety of activities available for guests – guided or do-it-yourself walks both strenuous and gentle in the Comeragh Mountains; golf (Seamus is past Captain of Clonmel Golf Club, and held the course record for 11 years); and riding and bicycling. Having worked off breakfast, there's Eoin Wall's dinner to look forward to. Eoin, Seamus and Mary's son, trained at Ballymaloe Cookery School and has worked in some renowned restaurants. Later in the evening join the locals at one of the pubs for traditional music, singing and dancing. A stay at Hanora's will be an experience not easily forgotten. No pets. Smoking in the lounge only. The house is signposted at Ballymacarbry. Access, Visa, Mastercard accepted.

OWNER Seamus & Mary Wall OPEN Closed at Christmas ROOMS 2 double, 2 twin, 2 king size; all en suite TERMS B&B IR£35–40; reduction for children; single supplement IR£10 MEALS Dinner from IR£20

CAPPOQUIN

Aglish House
Aglish, Cappoquin, Co. Waterford
Tel: 024 96191 Fax: 024 96482 E-mail: aglishhouse@tinet.ie

This seventeenth-century house is on a working dairy farm in the Blackwater Valley, lying between the Knockmealdown Mountains and the sea. Aglish House is very much a family home, with six children and five dogs, and has a relaxed, informal atmosphere and friendly hosts. Families are particularly welcome. The bedrooms have telephones and TVs, and dinner, by arrangement, is served in the dining room. Golf, deep-sea fishing, pony trekking and bike hire can be arranged locally. No smoking in the bedrooms. The house can be accessed off the N25 or N72. Visa, Mastercard accepted.

OWNER Tom & Terry Moore   OPEN February 1 – December 31
ROOMS 2 double, 2 family; 3 en suite   TERMS B&B from IR£30; reduction for children; single supplement IR£10 MEALS Dinner IR£20

Finisk Valley Riding School
Kilmolash Bridge, Cappoquin, Co. Waterford
Tel: 024 96257 Fax: 024 96257

The house was built about 15 years ago and is placed between a pretty stream and the stables for the riding centre on the other side. Joe and Maura White's daughter runs the centre, which caters for beginners, advanced riders and trekking groups. There are 20 horses, a large outdoor floodlit arena, and livery is also available. The house is comfortable and simply furnished with a small dining room, a comfortable sitting room with TV and three en suite bedrooms. No pets and no smoking. The Riding School is signposted on the N72 8 km away.

OWNER Joe & Maura White OPEN March 1 – September 30 ROOMS 3 double; all en suite   TERMS B&B IR£17.50; reduction for children; single supplement

Richmond House
Cappoquin, Co. Waterford
Tel: 058 54278 Fax: 058 54988

This substantial house was built in 1704 by the Earl of Cork and Burlington and stands in well maintained parkland. It is a peaceful, comfortable country house, beautifully furnished and decorated with spacious, bright rooms. Paul Deevy trained as a chef at Ballymaloe, and the restaurant at Richmond House has won several awards for the excellence of its cuisine. Dinner is served in two elegant dining rooms, which are open also to non residents. Guests have use of both a small sitting room with a lovely marble fireplace and a conservatory overlooking the garden. The comfortable bedrooms are furnished in keeping with the style of the house and have telephones, TVs, trouser presses and tea making facilities. Arrangements can be made for salmon fishing on the Blackwater, and trout fishing on the Blackwater, Suir and the Bride. Deep-sea and coarse fishing are also available. Other amenities nearby include pony trekking, walking, mountain rambling and golf. No pets. Richmond House is 1 km outside Cappoquin on the N72 Dungarvan road. Visa, Access, Diners Club, American Express accepted.

OWNER Paul & Claire Deevy OPEN February – December ROOMS 5 double, 3 twin, 1 single; all en suite TERMS B&B IR£35–50; reduction for children; single supplement IR£15 MEALS Dinner IR£27

CHEEKPOINT

Three Rivers Guesthouse
Cheekpoint, Co. Waterford
Tel: 051 382520 Fax: 051 382542

The Three Rivers Guesthouse is in a superb location at the end of a promontory overlooking three rivers – the Suir, the Barrow and the Nore. The cheerful, welcoming owners come from a hotel management background and run the guesthouse in a professional manner. The en suite bedrooms all have telephones and are simply furnished, most having a sea view through rather small windows. The lounge, furnished with wicker chairs, has a bay window to take advantage of the view, and the restaurant is light and bright and overlooks the estuary. The Powers specialise in golfing holidays and can arrange tee times. They can also arrange equestrian holidays and outdoor activities. The small village of Cheekpoint has two seafood restaurants with great views which are within walking distance. Smoking in the lounge only. Visa, Mastercard, Diners Club, American Express accepted.

OWNER Stan & Mailo Power OPEN Closed December – January ROOMS 7 double, 2 single, 3 double/double, 2 double/single; all en suite TERMS B&B IR£22.50–30; reduction for children; single supplement IR£10 MEALS Snacks from IR£2

CLONMEL

Cnoc-na-Ri
Nire Valley, nr. Clonmel, Co. Waterford
Tel: 052 36239

Cnoc-na-Ri, meaning "hill of the kings," is a small country home set in a peaceful, quiet spot in the Comeraghs in the heart of the Nire Valley. It has a welcoming, friendly atmosphere and lovely views. Richard and Nora added a wing to their house especially to cater for visitors. The rooms are very comfortable and well equipped with hairdryers, TVs and tea and coffee making facilities, and two have views. Nora, an excellent cook, provides a wide menu for breakfast, and evening meals are served, with advance notice, at separate tables in the dining room, which overlooks the nicely landscaped garden and patio. The patio is a lovely place to sit and absorb the peace that surrounds Cnoc-na-Ri. Richard and Nora can provide walking maps and packed lunches, and if needed a local guide is available. Golf, riding and fishing are also popular pastimes in this area, and traditional music and dance is usually to be found in one of the local pubs. No pets. Smoking only in the lounge. The house is 5 km from Ballymacarbry.

OWNER Richard & Nora Harte OPEN Closed at Christmas ROOMS 2 doubles, 2 triples; all en suite TERMS B&B IR£22.50; reduction for children; single supplement IR£6.50 MEALS Dinner IR£16

DUNGARVAN

Ballyquiry Farm

Dungarvan, Co. Waterford
Tel: 058 41194 Fax: 058 41194

Ballyquiry Farm is a 300-year-old building, with a front façade
dating from the Georgian period, and it stands in a wonderful spot
with superb views. It is part of a mixed farm, with the farm
buildings being to the rear of the property. In 1940 it was bought
by the Kiely family for IR£1,200. The accommodation is simple,
and is especially suited to families. The two family rooms each
have two bedrooms, and all the bedrooms have TVs. It is an
immaculately clean home, the reception rooms having newly
installed reproduction plasterwork. Dinner and high tea are
available if arranged in advance. No pets and no smoking. Signs to
Ballyquiry can be found travelling south from Dungarvan near the
sign for Youghal Helvic Ring.

OWNER Kathleen Kiely OPEN April 1 – October 31 ROOMS 2 double,
2 twin, 2 family; 4 en suite TERMS B&B IR£18.50; reduction for
children; single supplement IR£6 MEALS Dinner; high tea

The Castle Farm

Cappagh, Dungarvan, Co. Waterford
Tel: 058 68099

Mountain Castle was the principal seat of the McGraths of
Sliabh gCua, one of the two Gaelic families that owned land in
this county before the arrival of Cromwell. The accommodation is
in a restored wing of the fifteenth-century castle, which stands in
lovely countryside with fine views. The oldest section, with the
original archway, contains the attractive, long, narrow dining
room with its 1.25-m-thick stone walls. Joan Nugent is a very
friendly, welcoming lady who has recently done up a lot of the
house with tasteful decoration. It is very comfortable and has a
welcoming sitting room, where tea and scones are served on
arrival. Dinner is available on request, featuring fruit, vegetables,
herbs and meats from the family farm, and at breakfast guests are
served farm milk and homemade jam. Guests can help themselves
to tea or coffee in the kitchen. There is a hard tennis court, and

fishing on the River Finisk, which flows through the farm. The farmhouse is set on 49 hectares of dairy land, and organised farm groups are accepted. Pets outside only. Smoking is permitted in the TV lounge. The Castle Farm can be found down a lane beside the pub in Millstreet. Visa, Mastercard, Eurocard accepted.

OWNER Joan & Emmet Nugent OPEN April 1 – November 1 ROOMS 2 double, 1 twin, 2 family; all en suite TERMS B&B IR£23; reduction for children; single supplement IR£6 MEALS Dinner IR£14

DUNMORE EAST

Church Villa
Dunmore East, Co. Waterford
Tel: 051 893390

This whitewashed period house, one of a row of cottages opposite the Church of Ireland and adjacent to the Ship bar and restaurant, is right in the centre of the attractive village of Dunmore East. The new owners have enlarged and redecorated most of the rooms, all of which have TV, and some have their original fireplaces. There is a guest lounge with TV, and breakfast is served in the conservatory. There are plenty of eating places in Dunmore East, including the restaurant next door. Church Villa is 10 minutes from the beach and fishing harbour, and close to the park where there are caves to explore. No pets. No smoking in the dining room.

OWNER Phyllis & Ed Lannon OPEN Closed at Christmas ROOMS 6 double/twin/single/family; all en suite TERMS B&B IR£17; reduction for children; single supplement IR£20

TRAMORE

Cliff House
Cliff Road, Tramore, Co. Waterford
Tel: 051 381497 Fax: 051 381497 E-mail: cliffhouse@tramore.net

Cliff House, built by its owners, stands in landscaped gardens overlooking the sea. It has a welcoming, family atmosphere, friendly and professional owners and panoramic views. Most of the well-appointed and spotlessly clean bedrooms overlook

Tramore Bay. Two are on the ground floor, and they have TVs and hairdryers. A recent addition to the house is the large, relaxing conservatory, overlooking the Bay, which has proved very popular with guests. Tea and coffee making facilities are on hand here. Cliff House is within walking distance of the town centre and adjacent to the new leisure centre. It is 10 minutes from the Waterford Glass Factory. No pets and no smoking. The house is off the R675 as you exit from Tramore to Dungarvan. Visa, Mastercard, Access accepted.

OWNER Pat & Hilary O'Sullivan OPEN Closed at Christmas ROOMS 6 double/twin/family/single; 5 en suite TERMS B&B IR£19; reduction for children; single supplement

Glenorney
Newtown, Tramore, Co. Waterford
Tel: 051 381956

This attractive-looking house on the edge of Tramore was built five years ago and has a nice front garden. It is very well cared for and has good furniture and decoration. The spacious bedrooms are clean and bright and most have a sea view, and they each have hairdryer, telephone, TV and tea and coffee making facilities. The nice, bright sitting room has a TV, open fire and piano, and double doors lead into the breakfast room, which has separate tables with linen cloths. The garden and patio area is a great place to sit and admire the view over Tramore Bay. No pets and no smoking. Glenorney is on the edge of Tramore and within walking distance of the Golf Club and beaches. Visa accepted.

OWNER Marie Murphy OPEN February 1 – November 30 ROOMS 2 double, 2 family, 1 double/single; all en suite TERMS B&B IR£20–22; reduction for children; single supplement IR£3–5

WATERFORD

Blenheim House
Blenheim Heights, Waterford, Co. Waterford
Tel: 051 874115

Blenheim House was built in 1763 and stands in 1.5 hectares of grounds, including a deer park and a children's play area. The bedrooms are spacious and comfortable, most of them with the original Georgian fireplaces. The large lounge with an open fire overlooks the grounds and is a peaceful spot to unwind in. The Waterford Glass Factory is close by, and other local activities include swimming, riding, golf and fishing. No smoking in the dining room. Blenheim House is 5.5 km from the centre of Waterford on the Passage East Road, just a seven minute drive from the ferry.

OWNER Margaret Fitzmaurice OPEN All year ROOMS 6 twin/double/family/single; all en suite TERMS B&B IR£18; reduction for children

Brown's Town House
29 South Parade, Waterford, Co. Waterford
Tel: 051 870594 Fax: 051 871923 E-mail: browns@twe.iol.ie

This modest-looking, brick-built Victorian town house is on a residential street, only a few minutes' walk into the centre. It is run by genial Les Brown; his wife, Barbara, is an accountant and financial controller for the Port of Waterford. The house was renovated some three years ago and then added on to in 1998, now providing spacious, attractive accommodation with every possible amenity. The en suite bedrooms each have hairdryer, trouser press, telephone, TV, tea and coffee making facilities and mineral water. One double room has a rooftop garden, and one is a suite. There is a small sitting room for guests' use and a dining room where excellent breakfasts are served at one table. No pets. Smoking only in the sitting room. Visa, Mastercard accepted.

OWNER Les & Barbara Brown OPEN Closed at Christmas ROOMS 2 double, 1 twin, 1 family, 1 suite, 1 double with rooftop garden; all en suite TERMS B&B IR£25–30; reduction for children; single supplement

Foxmount Farm
Passage East Road, Waterford, Co. Waterford
Tel: 051 874308 Fax: 051 854906
E-mail: foxmount@iol.ie Web Site: www.iol.ie/tipp/foxmount.htm

This lovely seventeenth-century house is set in attractive country-side surrounded by its 100-hectare farm, run by David Kent and one of his sons. The Kents are a most welcoming, friendly couple, and have been many years in the bed & breakfast business. The

drawing room is very attractive with an open fireplace, and it is a nice spot to unwind over tea or a pre-dinner drink in front of a warming log fire. The dining room, where excellent home-cooked meals using the farm's own produce – beef, lamb, wild salmon, fresh vegetables and free-range eggs – are served in a party-like atmosphere, has separate tables and a piano. After dinner it is a pleasant stroll to the atmospheric pub under the bridge. Guests are welcome to use the hard tennis court and to play table tennis. Pets outside. Smoking only in the drawing room. To reach Foxmount from Waterford, take the Dunmore East road. After 5.5 km, fork left to Passage East for just over 1 km. Right at the next Y junction, turn right just before Jack Meade's pub.

OWNER Mrs Margaret Kent OPEN March 1 – November 1 ROOMS 1 double, 4 twin, 1 family; 4 en suite TERMS B&B IR£25; reduction for children; single supplement IR£5 MEALS Dinner IR£18.50

Lakefield House
Rossduff, Dunmore Road, Waterford, Co. Waterford
Tel: 051 382582 Fax: 051 382582

This large, modern house is set in its own grounds overlooking Bellake, just below the house, and there are views to the coast at Woodstown beach about 3 km away. The surrounding farmland is mostly tillage, but there are a few goats, sheep, chickens and ducks, as well as two ponies and a donkey. Mrs Carney is a friendly lady who was previously in the hotel and restaurant management business. The house has pleasant, well furnished, comfortable rooms. Most of the en suite bedrooms have views, and they all have TVs and hairdryers. There is a patio outside the drawing room, and both dinner, by arrangement, and breakfast are served in the dining room. Smoking is allowed in designated bedrooms. Lakefield House is about 8 km from Waterford and is signposted on the Dunmore East R684 road. All major credit cards accepted.

OWNER Cally Carney   OPEN March 1 – November 1   ROOMS 5 double/twin/family; all en suite   TERMS B&B IR£20; reduction for children; single supplement IR£8   MEALS Dinner

COUNTY WEXFORD

The most southerly county and one of the main gateways, through the port of Rosslare, Wexford is also the driest and warmest part of the whole country, an area of gentle hills, fertile farmland and a coastline of sandy beaches. Much of Wexford history is associated with the Norman invasion and the 1798 rebellion.

The Wexford Opera Festival, which takes place in October, is world-renowned and features top international singers. The town throbs with an influx of opera lovers, and many fringe events take place during the festival. It is an attractive town, with narrow, winding streets, and the Maritime Museum and the twelfth-century ruins of Selskar Abbey are of particular interest.

The castle at the attractive market town of Enniscorthy now houses the county museum, with an interesting folk section. Worth a visit are the thirteenth-century castle at Ferns, the old town of New Ross, and Dunrody Abbey, dating from 1182, near Campile. Nearby at Dunganstown is the Kennedy ancestral home.

CAMPILE

Park View Farm
Campile, Co. Wexford
Tel: 051 388178 Fax: 051 388178

This 200-year-old house is set in 20 hectares beside the John F. Kennedy Park, renowned for its collection of trees and shrubs. Mike and Barbara Barrett are attentive and amusing hosts who enjoy the company of their guests. The furnishings in the lounge, dining room and three bedrooms reflect the 1960s era. All bedrooms have tea and coffee making facilities and hairdryers. Park View is a good location for bicycling holidays and is close to sandy beaches. Dinner is available by prior arrangement. Pets are allowed outside. No smoking. Park View Farm is signposted from John F. Kennedy Park.

OWNER Mike & Barbara Barrett   OPEN May 1 – September 30 ROOMS 1 double, 2 twin, 1 single; 3 en suite   TERMS B&B IR£19.50; reduction for children; single supplement IR£6.50   MEALS Dinner IR£15

ENNISCORTHY

Ballinkeele House
Ballymurn, Enniscorthy, Co. Wexford
Tel: 053 38105 Fax: 053 38468 E-mail: balnkeel@indigo.ie

Built in 1840, this impressive country house still belongs to the Maher family four generations later. It is approached up a sweeping avenue and is set in 140 hectares of farmland. Apart from the addition of such modern conveniences as bathrooms and heating, it remains much as it was built, with a distinctively Victorian flavour. The master bedroom, which has a four-poster bed, is the same shape as the drawing room below. The rooms are furnished and decorated to a high standard, and they all have

hairdryers. The Mahers are a friendly, welcoming couple, and Margaret produces delicious dinners (if booked in advance), served by candlelight in the elegant dining room. Breakfast, which is organised by John, can include hot pancakes and homemade jams. The former billiard room has reverted to the big drawing room again, and has a TV. It is the only place where guests can smoke. Visitors are welcome to walk around the farm, old walled garden and grounds, and Wellington boots can be supplied if it is muddy. There is also a croquet lawn. Pets are accepted outside. To reach Ballinkeele from the N11, turn in Oilgate at the signpost. Access, Visa, American Express accepted.

OWNER John & Margaret Maher   OPEN March 1 – November 6 ROOMS 5 double or twin; 2 bath, 3 shower en suite   TERMS B&B IR£35–45; reduction for children; single supplement IR£10   MEALS Dinner IR£22

Clone House
Ferns, Enniscorthy, Co. Wexford
Tel: 054 66113 Fax: 054 66225

This attractive, creeper-covered, 300-year-old farm house is in a quiet location on nearly 120 hectares of mixed farmland. Guests can fish on the Bann River, which runs through the property, feed the lambs, see calves born or just go for wonderful walks. The Breens bought the property about 40 years ago, and gradually did

it up. Betty is particularly gifted at landscaping and has created a lovely garden. Guests are treated as friends and enjoy such luxuries as breakfast in bed, served at any time, and delicious home-cooked food, using home-grown or reared produce. The house is very comfortable and has been attractively furnished. One of the ground floor rooms is suitable for the disabled, and another has a private balcony. There is a comfortable sitting room and dining room. There is a pony for children to ride, and baby-sitting is available. Many guests come to buy horses, others to visit a local herbalist, others to hunt and others just to relax. Pets outside only. One bedroom is for smokers, as well as the living room. Clone House is 3 km off the N11 at Ferns.

OWNER Betty Breen OPEN April – end October ROOMS 1 twin, 3 family, 1 triple; all en suite TERMS B&B IR£25; reduction for children; single supplement IR£6.50

Salville House
Enniscorthy, Co. Wexford
Tel: 054 35252

This lovely old house, built in the mid-nineteenth-century, stands in its own grounds overlooking the River Slaney and the Blackstairs Mountains. The interior is light and bright with spacious, simply furnished rooms and wooden floorboards. Salville House has a good reputation for its food, and dinner, by arrangement, is served at one long table in the dining room. Guests have use of a comfortable drawing room. The house is located just outside the cathedral town of Enniscorthy, noted for its thirteenth-century castle. There are a number of golf courses in the area, good hill walking on the Blackstairs Mountains and fine beaches along the Wexford coastline. There is also a self-catering unit available. Pets by arrangement. No smoking in the bedrooms.

OWNER Jane & Gordon Parker OPEN All year ROOMS 3 double; all en suite TERMS B&B IR£22.50; reduction for children; single supplement IR£5 MEALS Dinner IR£18

Farmhouse
Foulksmills, Co. Wexford
Tel: 051 565616

Records of this old building, originally a thatched house, go back to 1614. The Farmhouse is from a bygone era, and is part of a 60-hectare mixed farm, run by one of Mrs Crosbie's sons. She is a friendly, welcoming older lady, who was one of the founding members of the Farmhouse Association. When she started doing bed & breakfast 33 years ago she charged sixpence a night and six shillings for a week's full board. The accommodation is old-fashioned and comfortable, with compact bedrooms, some of them attic shaped. The reading room has lots of bookcases around the room and a large dining room table, and there is an attractive sitting room. The dining room with separate tables is an enormous room with a high ceiling, and was originally a farm building. Dinner is available, if booked in advance. The Farmhouse provides old-fashioned, basic accommodation with none of the modern-day extras.

OWNER Mrs J. Crosbie OPEN mid March – November 1 ROOMS 4 double, 3 twin, 1 family TERMS B&B IR£15; reduction for children MEALS Dinner IR£12

Horetown House
Foulksmills, Co. Wexford
Tel: 051 565771 Fax: 051 565633 E-mail: poloxir@iol.ie

Horetown House is a lovely, seventeenth-century Georgian manor house situated in beautiful parklands and tranquil countryside, amidst 100 hectares of mixed farming. The process of renovating the house is gradual; the latest improvements have been the addition of more en suite bedrooms and a wine bar, which is open for light meals and snacks. The entrance hall is lined with the heads of deer and other animals and the rooms have old-fashioned, functional furnishings. The bedrooms are spacious and comfortable, and guests can relax in the drawing room in front of the log fire. There's a separate TV room, and also the Cellar Restaurant – open to the public – which has a good reputation.

Lawn croquet and table tennis are available, and small conferences and business lunches can be catered for. The equestrian centre covers dressage instruction, polocrosse, escorted ride-outs and instruction for beginners, and it has two large, all-weather indoor arenas. Pets outside. Smoking only in the drawing room, restaurant and wine bar. To find Horetown House, take the right fork at the bottom of Foulksmills for approximately 1.5 km, pass a country pub and sharp bend and it is the next turn left. Visa, Mastercard, Diners Club accepted.

OWNER The Young Family OPEN Closed at Christmas ROOMS 6 double, 6 family; 9 en suite TERMS B&B IR£26.75; reduction for children; single supplement IR£5 MEALS Lunch IR£11.95; light meals; dinner IR£17–22

KILLURIN

Healthfield Manor
Killurin, Co. Wexford
Tel: 053 28253

The story runs that back in the 1400–1500s there was a plague in Wexford, and consequently the water was undrinkable. Healthfield, which has its own well, was the nearest place to the city with good water – hence the name. Built in 1820, this country house is reached up a long driveway through its 40 hectares of farmland, which supports organically reared sheep, and is bordered by mature shrubs and wonderful rhododendrons. At the top there are spectacular views over the river Slaney. The entrance to the house is through a small conservatory, and beyond is the very large drawing room. The bedrooms are incredibly spacious, some having their own sitting rooms – such as the "Five Acre Suite" – and the top floor suite has furniture made from an elm from the property, including a four-poster bed. All but one room has the lovely front view over the grounds to the river. Pets can be accommodated in the stables. Smoking is not permitted in the bedrooms. Healthfield is 8 km from Wexford, signposted on the Killurin road.

OWNER Mayler & Loretto Colloton OPEN Closed at Christmas ROOMS 4 double, twin or family; 1 en suite TERMS B&B IR£25; reduction for children; single supplement IR£5

KILTEALY

Granite Farm
Wheelagower, Kiltealy, Co. Wexford
Tel: 054 55497

This 150-year-old home is set in attractive farmland with a pretty front garden decorated with old pieces of farm equipment. It has views of the Blackstairs Mountains, where there are mapped scenic walks, and Mount Leinster, which is a favourite spot for hanggliding. The back part of Granite Farm was built on five years ago, and this is where the three simple upstairs bedrooms are located. These look out over fields of sheep. Kathleen Nolan is a pleasant, friendly lady, who likes to take the time to sit down and talk to her guests on arrival, over a cup of tea or coffee. These drinks are available at all times in the dining room, which was the original kitchen and has two old pine dressers decorated with china and knick-knacks. Evening meals are available if arranged in advance. Pets by arrangement and horses may be stabled overnight or longer. Smoking only in the lounge. Granite Farm is located on the R702. Visa, Mastercard accepted.

OWNER Kathleen Nolan   OPEN March 1 – November 1   ROOMS 2 double/twin/family, 1 single; all en suite   TERMS B&B IR£17; reduction for children; single supplement IR£5   MEALS Dinner IR£5–11

NEW ROSS

Creacon Lodge
Creacon, New Ross, Co. Wexford
Tel: 051 421897   Fax: 051 422560

This charming, long, low whitewashed house, built in the 1840s, is covered with climbing plants and is set in a very pretty, sheltered garden. Some of the attractive bedrooms are in the main house, tucked under the roof, three are in the old byre and two in the former greenhouse. All rooms have telephones and TVs. The drawing room is full of comfortable chairs and sofas and has a log fire to relax in front of with a drink before or after dinner. Of the two dining areas, one was the old kitchen and is furnished with old pieces of pine. Dinner is available if arranged in advance. The John F. Kennedy Memorial Park is a ten-minute drive away, and nearby is the Hook Peninsula, with secluded beaches and coves and the oldest lighthouse in Europe. Josephine Flood is a most imaginative and attentive host, and her slogan "Well worth the trouble of finding us" is true. No pets. No smoking in the bedrooms. To find Creacon Lodge, take the R733 signposted to John F. Kennedy Park, after 5 km turn left for the house. Access, Visa, Mastercard accepted.

OWNER Josephine Flood OPEN All year ROOMS 1 double, 1 twin, 1 single, 7 double or twin; all en suite TERMS B&B IR£35; reduction for children; single supplement IR£10 MEALS Dinner from IR£16.50

Dunbrody Country House & Restaurant
Arthurstown, New Ross, Co. Wexford
Tel: 051 389600 Fax: 051 389601

This beautiful Georgian house in a wonderful park-like setting opened as a country house hotel and restaurant in the summer of 1997. It was built in 1830 for Lord Spencer Chichester, and remained in the family until recently. Kevin and Catherine Dundon have done an outstanding job renovating the house and transforming it into an elegant and comfortable small hotel, where guests can sample the best of Irish hospitality. Kevin, a master chef, specialises in contemporary Irish cuisine. Beautifully presented dishes are served in the enormous dining room, which has well spaced out tables, and was previously both the drawing and dining rooms. There is an attractive bar, and a wonderful entrance hall. The lovely bedrooms are large and all have splendid views. They include two suites, and for those wanting a lazy morning, breakfast can be served in bed. The land around the house runs down to the river; there are horses, a nursery garden and well tended gardens containing many unusual plants and flowers. Some rooms are non-smoking. Dunbrody is on the R733, 11 km from Waterford via the Passage East car ferry and 19 km south of New Ross. Any number of special packages can be arranged, as well as conferences and weddings. All major credit cards accepted.

OWNER Kevin & Catherine Dundon OPEN All year ROOMS 2 double, 8 doubles or twins, 2 suites; all en suite TERMS B&B IR£50–55; reduction for children; single supplement MEALS Dinner

Riversdale House

Lower William Street, New Ross, Co. Wexford
Tel: 051 422515 Fax: 051 422800

This large, modern house is just three minutes from the town centre. It was built by the Foleys eight years ago and is surrounded by half a hectare of gardens. The pretty, walled rear garden originally belonged to the nearby convent. Riversdale has lovely views over the town and the River Barrow, and from the back it is particularly attractive at night, when the church is floodlit. This is a comfortable house with an upstairs lounge; the dining room and recently added conservatory are on the ground floor. The bedrooms have hairdryers, TVs and tea and coffee making facilities. Mrs Foley is a friendly, chatty lady who teaches cookery classes. No pets. No smoking. The house is signposted from the quayside.

OWNER Ann Foley OPEN All year ROOMS 2 double, 1 twin, 1 family; all en suite   TERMS B&B IR£17; reduction for children; single supplement IR£18

ROSSLARE

Churchtown House

Tagoat, Rosslare, Co. Wexford
Tel: 053 32555 Fax: 053 32555

Set in 3.25 hectares of park-like grounds, this attractive house dates from 1703. The spacious rooms have been tastefully decorated and furnished and a recent conversion has added three large, superior rooms and a single, plus a lovely garden room. One of the ground floor rooms is suitable for wheelchairs, and all bedrooms have telephones and TVs. There are two comfortable drawing rooms and three dining rooms, where evening meals are served if arranged in advance. Activities such as bird-watching, golf, fishing, swimming, walking and riding are available locally. Pets by arrangement. Smoking in the garden lounge only. Churchtown is on the R736. Visa, Mastercard accepted.

OWNER Patricia & Austin Cody   OPEN March – mid-November
ROOMS 5 double, 5 twin, 1 family, 1 single; all en suite   TERMS B&B
from IR£25; reduction for children; single supplement IR£10   MEALS
Dinner IR£19

ROSSLARE HARBOUR

Laurel Lodge
Rosslare Harbour, Co. Wexford
Tel: 053 33291

This attractive, low, modern house is down a quiet country lane in
the village of Kilrane. Laurel Lodge has recently undergone a
complete refurbishment. The en suite bedrooms are clean and
comfortable and have TVs and tea and coffee making facilities.
There is a guest lounge, and the dining room, where breakfast is
served, overlooks a small patio at the back of the house. There are
four hotels and two pubs within walking distance of the house. No
pets and no smoking. Laurel Lodge is signposted off the main road
and also in the village. All major credit cards accepted.

OWNER Mr & Mrs D. O'Donoghue   OPEN March – October   ROOMS
2 double, 2 twin; 4 en suite   TERMS B&B IR£17; reduction for children;
single supplement IR£5

TACUMSHANE

Furziestown
Tacumshane, Co. Wexford
Tel: 053 31376

This small, peaceful farmhouse is set in rural surroundings, the
whitewashed farm buildings forming an attractive courtyard
behind the house. A hectare of land supports free-range chickens
and organically grown vegetables. The house is comfortable and
has a welcoming, friendly atmosphere, and Yvonne produces
delicious breakfasts. The family room is on the ground floor with
a separate entrance, and the upstairs twin-bedded room has pretty
stencilling. The house is only 1 km from the sea, and Wexford can
be reached by a coastal path. Pets are allowed outside. No

smoking. For directions to Furziestown, it is recommended that you ask for a brochure.

OWNER Yvonne Pim OPEN April – October ROOMS 1 twin, 1 family; both en suite TERMS B&B IR£20; reduction for children; single supplement

WEXFORD

Broom Cottage
Rosslare Road, Drinagh, Wexford, Co. Wexford
Tel: 053 44434

This attractive, creeper-clad, eighteenth-century farmhouse is set back a little from the main road, and is part of a 56-hectare beef, sheep and tillage farm. Eleven hectares of the land lie around the house, which is 3 km from the centre of Wexford on the Rosslare road. Broom Cottage has been in the same family for the last 200 years and an extension was built on 25 years ago. It offers comfortable, clean, well-equipped bedrooms, and guests have use of a TV lounge and conservatory. Breakfast only is served in the dining room. The accommodation is good value and it is convenient for the Rosslare car ferry. No pets. No smoking in the bedrooms.

OWNER John & Theresa Devereux OPEN March – end October ROOMS 4 double or twin; all en suite TERMS B&B IR£17; reduction for children; single supplement

Clonard House
Clonard Great, Wexford, Co. Wexford
Tel: 053 43141 Fax: 053 43141

This elegant Georgian farmhouse, part of a 48-hectare dairy farm, is set in idyllic surroundings with a clear view of Wexford harbour. Clonard House was completely renovated and retains many of its original features, such as cornices, ceiling roses and the dining room fireplace. Since then there has been a continuous programme of updating and refurbishing to maintain its already high standard. The spacious rooms are extremely attractive, with traditional and antique furnishings, and they have TVs, hairdryers, and some have four-poster beds. The well-appointed lounge is the

perfect spot to relax in after a busy day's sightseeing. There is a games room in the basement for guests. This is a lovely, peaceful house with a lot of character (and a stairway to nowhere!). No pets. Smoking only in the TV lounge. It is signposted off the N11 ring road, 1 km away.

OWNER John & Kathleen Hayes OPEN Easter – November 6 ROOMS 3 double, 1 twin, 1 family, 1 single, 3 triples; all en suite TERMS B&B IR£20; reduction for children; single supplement IR£5

Darral House
Spawell Road, Wexford, Co. Wexford
Tel: 053 24264

This attractive-looking town house was built in 1803. It is set back a little from the road and has a small, pretty front garden. The Nolans, who are a welcoming couple, renovated the building in 1994, furnishing and decorating it very comfortably in the style of a more modern house with flowery wallpapers. It has very spacious rooms with 4.3-m-high ceilings in the dining room and lounge. Darral House has plenty of parking, and a pleasant back garden, which guests are welcome to use. The house is a few minutes' walk from the centre, and offers very good value. No pets. No smoking in the lounge or dining room. Visa, Access accepted.

OWNER Kathleen & Sean Nolan OPEN Closed at Christmas ROOMS 1 double, 3 family; all en suite TERMS B&B IR£20–22.50; reduction for children; single supplement

Killiane Castle

Drinagh, Wexford, Co. Wexford
Tel: 053 58885 / 58898 Fax: 053 58885

This eighteenth-century house is attached to the tower of a fourteenth-century castle and is part of a dairy farm. Killiane Castle is down a quiet country lane and is very handy to the Rosslare ferry, which is only ten minutes away. The Mernaghs are constantly striving to keep up standards, and regularly redecorate the house, which is attractively furnished. The first floor bedrooms are particularly large and they all have TVs and hairdryers. Coffee is available in one of the ground floor lounges and early breakfasts are available for those catching ferries. There is a hard tennis court and four self-catering apartments at the back of the house. No pets. Smoking only in one of the lounges. Killiane Castle is signposted on the N25 between Wexford and Rosslare. Visa, Mastercard, Access accepted.

OWNER Jack & Kathleen Mernagh OPEN April 1 – November 1 ROOMS 3 double, 3 twin, 2 family; all en suite TERMS B&B IR£20; reduction for children; single supplement IR£10

Newbay Country House

Wexford, Co. Wexford
Tel: 053 42779 Fax: 053 46318

Newbay Country House is a Georgian residence built in 1822 and is set in 10 hectares of lovely parkland and gardens. It was taken over early in 1997 by the Coyles, who have completely redecorated and furnished the house, giving it a different character from its previous owners. The house is comfortably furnished, and the number of bedrooms has been increased quite substantially. There is a full bridal suite and four rooms have four-poster beds. The dining room overlooks the garden and is where elegant dinners are served at two tables, as well as excellent breakfasts with homemade jams and bread. There are plans to develop the basement into a restaurant. Smoking only in the smoking room and no pets. Newbay is signposted off the N11, and is 3 km from the centre of town. All major credit cards accepted.

OWNER Des & Joan Coyle OPEN All year ROOMS 2 double, 7 twin or double, 4 four-poster, 1 bridal suite TERMS B&B from IR£28; reduction for children; single supplement IR£8 MEALS Dinner IR£20–22

The West and Northwest

COUNTY CLARE

Two hundred castles and 2,300 stone forts going back to pre-Celtic times testify to County Clare's turbulent past. Although Shannon Airport lies on the southern border, most of the county is underpopulated by tourists. The scenery varies from the barren terrain of the Barony of Burren, which in spring is covered in a profusion of northern and southern plants, to the scenic lakes and hills of Slieve Bernagh, wonderful walking country, and the towering Cliffs of Moher. Water plays an important role, the sea bordering the west, and the Shannon Estuary the south and east.

The Franciscan Ennis Friary, noted for its sculptures and decorated tombs, is one of the principal sights of the county capital Ennis, which is situated on a bend of the River Fergus.

A bridge crosses the Shannon at Killaloe. Nearby is a twelfth-century cathedral built on the site of an earlier church. It has a magnificent door and the views from the top of the square tower are splendid. Across the Shannon lies Bunratty Castle, well known for its medieval banquets. It dates from 1460 and was at one time occupied by Admiral Penn, the father of William Penn, founder of Pennsylvania. There is a Folk Park in the castle grounds, with examples of houses from the Shannon area.

The island of Iniscealta on Lough Derg can be reached by boat from the attractive village of Mountshannon. There are five old churches, a round tower, saints' graveyard, hermit's cell and a holy well.

Moohaun Fort, one of the largest Iron Age forts in Europe, is to be found at Newmarket on Fergus. Knappogue Castle, another venue for medieval banquets, and Quinn Abbey are close to Craggaunowen.

Of special interest to both botanists and historians is the Burren. Once densely populated, this savagely rocky area is rich in prehistoric and historic monuments. Look closely at its limestone and discover a wealth of exquisite, delicate plant life thriving in a myriad of tiny crevices. The Burren Display Centre explains the fauna and flora of the 500 square kilometres of the Burren and its remains of ancient civilisation. The ruined Leamaneh Castle is near Kilfenora, which is on the edge of the Burren. Between Kilfenora and Ballyvaughan is Ballkkinvarra, one of Ireland's finest stone forts, and southeast of Ballyvaughan is Aillwee Cave, which dates back to 2 million B.C.

The road from Lisdoonvarna, Ireland's foremost spa town, leads to the impressive Cliffs of Moher, which stretches for nearly 8 km. Liscannor is famous for the Holy Well of St Brigid, which is an important place of pilgrimage.

Lahinch, a small seaside resort, is best known for its championship golf course, and to the south is Spanish Point, where many ships of the Spanish Armada were wrecked.

Around the village of Quilty, seaweed can be seen drying on the stone walls. The coast south of Kilkee is every bit as spectacular as the Cliffs of Moher, with caverns and strange rock formations.

BALLYVAUGHN

Dolmen House
Tonarussa, Ballyvaughn, Co. Clare
Tel: 065 707 7202

This elegant, modern farmhouse stands in open scenic countryside and has stunning views of the Burren and Galway Bay. It is part of a working cattle farm, and there are some interesting rock formations on the land. The bedrooms are large and have dainty duvets and a light pastel décor. The dining room, where breakfasts are served at separate tables, has lace tablecloths; this room overlooks the view, as does the lounge. There are some interesting antiques about, including a grandmother clock in the hallway. Dolmen Lodge offers luxurious, high-quality accommodation at modest prices. It is a superb choice for guests touring this beautiful area. Breakfast only is served, but Ballyvaughan is only 1 km away and Philip and Mary Kyne will be happy to assist with choosing venues for evening meals, and also to give advice on what to see and do in the area.

OWNER Philip & Mary Kyne OPEN Easter – end October ROOMS 2 double, 2 twin; all en suite TERMS B&B IR£17.50; reduction for children; single supplement (seasonal)

BUNRATTY

Tudor Lodge
Hill Road, Bunratty, Co. Clare
Tel: 061 362248 Fax: 061 362569

This gracious and elegant home stands in a secluded, peaceful, wooded setting where guests awaken to the sound of birds singing. The house was in a derelict condition when it was purchased seven years ago. It has been beautifully restored into a comfortable and quite luxurious home. The tiled entryway is full of plants and the bedrooms are furnished and decorated to a high standard. The bathrooms are large and have powerful showers. There is a very comfortable lounge, with blue leather furniture, which leads out to a conservatory overlooking the well tended garden. An added bonus are the accommodating and helpful owners, Carmel and Michael Dennehey, both local people who provide lots of information for guests on what to see and do in the area. Reservations can be made for the medieval banquet at Bunratty Castle, which is within walking distance, as is Durty Nellie's pub, which serves lunch and dinner. Shannon Airport is a 15-minute drive from the house. Visa, Mastercard accepted.

OWNER Mr & Mrs Carmel & Michael Dennehy OPEN mid-February – November 31 ROOMS 2 double, 2 twin, 1 triple; all en suite TERMS B&B IR£19; single supplement IR£6

KILRUSH

Old Parochial House
Cooroclare, Kilrush, Co. Clare
Tel: 065 59059

Old Parochial House, built in 1871, was formerly the parish priest's residence, and stands in 1.25 hectares of grounds in an unspoiled area ideal for walking. The house has been tastefully restored. It has great views and all-modern comforts, yet retains the character and ambience of a bygone era. There are high ceilings, polished wood floors, original fireplaces and stripped pine doors; the house is furnished in keeping with its character, and is well maintained by Alyson O'Neill, who made all the curtains. She is an informal, congenial lady who takes excellent care of her guests. The bedrooms are large, and one of the public bathrooms has an original Victorian bath. The spacious sitting room has a bay window overlooking the view, and the dining room, where a varied breakfast is served, has an original black marble fireplace. A field on the property has been converted to a 9-hole pitch and putt course, and there is a snooker room, play room and play area, as well as a fish tackle room for lake fishing. There are also local bog walks, ring forts, ancient prayer sites and an old church close by. There are pubs and restaurants in the immediate area for meals. The stables have been converted to provide comfortable self-catering accommodation. Visa, Mastercard, Access accepted.

OWNER Alyson & Sean O'Neill OPEN April 1 – end October ROOMS 1 double, 1 twin, 2 family; 2 en suite TERMS B&B IR£18; reduction for children; single supplement IR£5–7

LISDOONVARNA

Fermona House
Bog Road, Lisdoonvarna, Co. Clare
Tel: 065 707 4243

This pleasant cream and green bungalow is set back off the road in a quiet location close to Spa Wells. It is just a five-minute walk from town. The bedrooms and en suite facilities are quite spacious, and are individually decorated in soft colours of blue and peach. There is a small, cosy TV lounge with a stereo which guests may use. The house is exceptionally well maintained and everything is spotlessly clean. Breakfasts are served at separate tables and there are several establishments in town for evening meals. Vera Fitzpatrick is an excellent host and is happy to provide information on sightseeing. Doolin, the Cliffs of Moher and the Burren, golfing, pony trekking and hill walking are all nearby. Visa, Mastercard accepted.

OWNER Vera Fitzpatrick OPEN March 1 – November 1 ROOMS 2 double, 2 twin, 1 family; all en suite TERMS B&B IR£17–18; reduction for children; single supplement IR£5

COUNTY DONEGAL

County Donegal is a large county with a spectacular variety of scenery and an indented coastline of bays, beaches, cliffs and peninsulas set against a backdrop of mountains, moors and lakes. It has many archaeological sites and much evidence of the old Irish culture and traditions. The Irish language is still spoken in areas north and west of Killybegs, an important fishing port.

Donegal takes its name from the fort the Vikings established: Dún na nGall, the Fort of the Foreigners. The town built by Sir Basil Brooke is on the estuary of the River Eske, a busy place that is good for buying tweeds. The castle with its great square tower, once the stronghold of the O'Donnells, was refurbished by Brooke in 1610.

Bundoran is one of Ireland's best-known seaside resorts with a good golf course and famous beaches. Farther north is Ballyshannon, long a centre of importance because of its river; the town winds up a steep hill above the River Erne. Rossnowlagh's beach stretches for some 4 km.

Beyond Killybegs, the coastal scenery becomes wild and spectacular. Kilcar is a centre for the hand-woven tweed industry, as is Ardara. The scenery at Glencolumbkille is magnificent, with its blend of hills and sea. Here, the late Father MacDyer organised a cooperative movement to try to keep young people from emigrating, and also established a folk museum. Portnoo and Narin are other popular seaside towns for holidaymakers.

Letterkenny is the largest town in Donegal, dominated by St Eunan's Cathedral, built in the modern Gothic style between 1890 and 1900. The winding road approaching Doocharry from Fintown is known as the "corkscrew" and brings you through the Gweebarra Glen to the sea. Aranmore Island is the most populated and largest of a series of islands. It can be reached by ferry from Burtonport, an attractive, unspoilt fishing port. Gweedore, situated in the spectacularly wild country, is a major holiday centre. From here, there is a road of remarkable scenic beauty by Loughs Nacung and Dunlewy into the Derryveagh Mountains.

Gortahork and Falcarragh are Irish-speaking areas, and are good places from which to start a climb of Muckish Mountain. Dunfanaghy has a fine beach and is a good place to explore the granite promontory of Horn Head. Between Creeslough, attractively situated on Sheephaven Bay, and Carrigart is the romantic Doe Castle, almost surrounded by the sea. Rosapenna, a resort town with a good golf course, is on the way to the beautiful Rosguill Peninsula, with wonderful views of Melmore Head, Horn Head and Muckish Mountain. Milford is a pretty town from where the Fanad Peninsula with its sandy beaches can be explored. The tranquil village of Rathmullan is beautifully situated with a sandy beach and is famous for its historical associations. The road between here and Ramelton is also in a lovely location and is a planned Planter's town, begun in the early seventeenth-century.

The Inishown Peninsula, which lies between the waters of Lough Foyle and Lough Swilly, is quite different from the rest of Donegal. The centre is very hilly, Slieve Snaght at 615 m being the highest point. From the Buncrana to Clonmany and Cardonagh road, there are fine views of sea and mountains, and a road runs right to the tip of the peninsula at Malin Head. One of the best views to be had of this part of Donegal is from the Grianan of Aileach. It is 250 m high and consists of a cashel, or stone fort, enclosed within three earthen banks. Cardonagh's chief glory is St Patrick's Cross, which dates from the seventh century, making it one of the very important Christian crosses.

Glenveagh lies in a deep gorge and is the setting for a fairytale castle, as well as wonderful gardens that were developed by Henry McIlhenny. The garden and the estate are now a national park, and Mr McIlhenny had bequeathed the castle to the nation. Gartan, Kilmacrenan and Raphoe, which has a fine old cathedral, are all associated with St Columba.

ARDARA

Rose Wood House
Edergole, Killybegs Road, Ardara, Co. Donegal
Tel: 075 41168 Fax: 075 41168

Guests continue to enjoy this two-storey house situated on the edge of Ardara. It is run in a friendly manner by Susan McConnell, who lived in New York for 11 years. Formerly a bungalow, a second storey was added to it in 1990, and the very large lounge/dining room is in this part of the house, and has lovely views of the river. Susan McConnell is an excellent host; nothing is too much trouble for her guests' comfort, and a hot drink is offered to guests upon arrival. Breakfast only is served, but there are good choices in Ardara, and Susan would be happy to make recommendations. Visa, Mastercard, Eurocard accepted.

OWNER Susan & Vincent McConnell OPEN January 1 – December 20 ROOMS 4 double, 2 twin; all en suite TERMS B&B IR£17; reduction for children

Woodhill House
Ardara, Co. Donegal
Tel: 075 41112 Fax: 075 41516 E-mail: Yates@iol.ie

Woodhill House is in a wonderful position up a valley from Ardara. It is an historic country house, and stands on a site dating from the seventeenth century, overlooking the Donegal Highlands. It was formerly the home of the Nesbitts, Ireland's last commercial whaling family. The present owners bought the house about 10 years ago and are continuing to improve the accommodation. The two front rooms are large, simply furnished and have wonderful views. There is a friendly informal atmosphere, and the house is surrounded by more than 1.5 hectares of gardens, including a walled garden, which is open to guests. The high-quality restaurant, which serves excellent French-style cuisine, is open from Easter to the end of October, and there is a licensed bar. There are several places to eat in Ardara and Irish music is often heard at most of Ardara's 13 bars. The area is well known for its Donegal tweeds and woollen goods, and also offers salmon and trout fishing, shooting, pony trekking, golf, excellent bathing beaches and of special interest, the Wildlife Reserve. All major credit cards accepted.

OWNER John & Nancy Yates OPEN Easter – October 31 ROOMS 4 double, 3 family, 2 single; all en suite TERMS B&B IR£24–32; reduction for children; single supplement IR£5 in non-single room MEALS Dinner

Bruckless House

Bruckless, Co. Donegal
Tel: 073 37071 Fax: 073 37071 E-mail: bruck@iol.ie

This classic eighteenth-century house stands in a secluded spot in an award-winning garden and cobbled yard, and is a well-known Connemara Pony Stud Farm. It offers gracious living and guests are encouraged to sit around and chat with the owners, who are happy to share their knowledge of the area. The bedrooms are large and are elegantly furnished. The spacious drawing room and dining room overlook green lawns and the sea; both have turf fires, which are lit at the first sign of a chill in the air. There are no TVs in the house, but most guests are happy with this "TV free zone." In this beautiful and unspoiled Atlantic coastal area, there are plenty of archeological sites to explore, and fishing, golf and horseback riding are available in the area. Visa, American Express, Mastercard accepted.

OWNER Joan & Clive Evans OPEN April 1 – September 30 ROOMS 2 double, 2 single; 2 en suite TERMS B&B IR£25–30

Castlereagh House

Bruckless, Co. Donegal
Tel: 073 37202 Fax: 073 37202

This very pleasant early nineteenth-century house stands in well-kept gardens with panoramic views of the Atlantic Ocean and the Blue Stack Mountains. It continues to offer the highest standard of accommodation. The house is quite luxurious, has rich red carpets, is well furnished and very comfortable. The bedrooms are tastefully decorated in soft pastel wallpapers, and one is on the ground floor. All have fine views. There is a comfortable lounge, which displays an antique sideboard. Breakfasts are served on Royal Albert china in the bright dining room. Elizabeth is a most attentive host who is always happy to give advice on what to see and do in the area and to recommend local establishments for evening meals. This is an ideal base for touring Glencolmkille, Slieve League and Glenveigh National Park. Golf, fishing, horseback riding and an Art Gallery are available within a short drive. This superb value accommodation is an excellent choice for touring this scenic area. Visa, Access, Mastercard accepted.

OWNER The Henry Family   OPEN April 1 – October 31   ROOMS 2 double, 1 twin; all en suite   TERMS B&B IR£18; reduction for children; single supplement IR£5

BUNBEG

Ard na Coille
Upper Cotteen, Bunbeg, Co. Donegal
Tel: 075 32119

A warm welcome awaits you here from owner Noreen Boyle, who has been taking excellent care of her guests for several years; she formerly ran a B&B in Galway. The house has a warm and pleasant atmosphere. It is situated in an open location close to the beach, and is ideal for the people who like the outdoors.

There is golf, walking and horseback riding close by. There is a turf fire in the lounge and breakfasts are served in a separate dining room, which has fine views. The bedrooms are spotlessly clean and one has a TV. Tea and coffee can be served at just about any time, and guests are greeted with a complimentary hot drink upon arrival. There is a restaurant within walking distance and several other options a short drive away.

OWNER Noreen Boyle   OPEN Easter – October 31   ROOMS 1 double, 1 twin, 1 family; 2 en suite   TERMS B&B IR£15–16; reduction for children; single supplement IR£3

BUNDORAN

Casa Mia
West End, Bundoran, Co. Donegal
Tel: 072 41684

Within walking distance of the beach and town this continental-style house is run by Mary Hamrogue, a friendly, bubbly lady. The bedrooms, all with Sky TV, are bright and cheery with yellow, purple and green duvets. The guest lounge is spacious and is comfortably furnished. Breakfast only is served, but there is a good choice of eating establishments in town, which is within walking distance.

OWNER Mary & Malachy Hamrogue OPEN All year ROOMS 2 double, 1 twin, 1 family; all en suite TERMS B&B IR£17; reduction for children; single supplement IR£6.50

Ceol-na-mara
Tullan Strand, Bundoran, Co. Donegal
Tel: 072 41287

Ceol-na-mara means "music of the sea," and the house is aptly named. The setting is idyllic, the house overlooks the Atlantic Ocean, horses graze in the adjacent field, and colourful potted plants and hanging baskets decorate the entryway to the house. The entry hall is very spacious, as is the guest lounge, which features a large stone fireplace, Laurel and Hardy figures decorate the mantle, and a huge teddybear relaxes in an armchair. Breakfasts are served in the adjacent elegant dining room with its unusual wooden ceilings. The bedrooms are on the ground floor and have good-sized bathrooms. Horseback riding is available at the Stracomer Silver Equestrian Centre, and golf and fishing facilities are also close by.

OWNER Marlene Fergus OPEN All year ROOMS 2 double, 2 twin; all en suite TERMS B&B IR£17.5; reduction for children; single supplement (off season only)

Conway House
4 Bay View Terrace, Bundoran, Co. Donegal
Tel: 072 41220

This Georgian-style house is conveniently located to all the amenities in this popular seaside town, including Water World. There is a relaxed and informal atmosphere. Mrs McGureen prepares the meals while Mr McGureen maintains the house and keeps it freshly decorated, and in his spare time he restores antiques. Two of the bedrooms have sea views, as does the dining room and lounge; both have original fireplaces, which are lit on chilly days. There is plenty to keep the visitor busy, and this is an ideal base from which to explore this scenic area. Horseback riding and golf are offered within a kilometre.

OWNER Dorothy McGurren OPEN March – September ROOMS 4 double, 1 family; 4 en suite TERMS B&B IR£17; reduction for children; single supplement IR£3

CARRICK

Rockville House
Roxborough Coast Road, Carrick, Co. Donegal
Tel: 073 39107 Fax: 073 39107

This friendly four-bedroom bungalow stands in an elevated position overlooking Donegal Bay. The cliffs at Bunglas, the highest marine cliffs in Europe, are 5 km away. This is a popular destination for tourists from many parts of the world, and energetic Maureen Hughes arranges walking tours in the Kilcar area. Teelin, an Irish-speaking area, lies close by and attracts people who wish to learn to speak the Irish language. The house is about a kilometre from the closest beach and from the village of Carrick. The family room has wonderful views, as does the lounge, which has a dining table at one end and sliding doors opening onto the patio. The well-appointed bedrooms are small, spotlessly clean, and are all on the ground floor. Evening meals are no longer available, but Maureen Hughes has an arrangement for meals for her guests at the village restaurant. Tasty substantial meals are served on plates made for Rockville House at a local pottery. A four-bedroom self-catering cottage is also available.

OWNER Maureen Hughes OPEN All year ROOMS 1 double, 1 twin, 1 family; 2 en suite TERMS B&B IR£16; reduction for children; single supplement IR£5

CASTLEFINN

Gortfad
Castlefinn, Co. Donegal
Tel: 074 46135

This 300-year-old Georgian house stands in its own tranquil grounds and combines old-world charm with modern comforts.

The house has been in the same family for seven generations and is furnished with old-fashioned possessions and has stained-glass windows. Dolly Taylor is a kindly, hospitable lady who has been offering her special brand of hospitality for almost 30 years; little wonder that she has guests returning year after year. Guests are usually greeted with a complimentary hot drink and home-baked scones and fruitcake upon arrival. Breakfast only is served, but there are several excellent establishments close by, and Dolly is happy to make recommendations if required. Guests can visit the tweed-weaving area of the Glenties and the 10,000 hectares of the National Park at Glenveagh Castle as well as Derek Hill's art collection at Church Hill. There are two golf courses within 10 km and salmon, trout and coarse fishing in the River Finn.

OWNER Dolly Taylor OPEN Easter – September ROOMS 3 double, 1 twin, 1 family; 4 en suite TERMS B&B IR£17.50; reduction for children

DONEGAL

Arranmore House
Killybegs Road, Donegal, Co. Donegal
Tel: 073 21242

Arranmore House stands in its own grounds in an elevated peaceful location with lovely views, yet it's only a three-minute walk to the town centre. Mrs Kenney, who hails from England, is a friendly lady who takes excellent care of her guests, and runs a comfortable house with a pleasant atmosphere. The guest lounge has an open fire and substantial breakfasts only are served in a separate dining room. The good-sized bedrooms are well furnished, are spotlessly clean, and are all on the ground floor. Guests are greeted with a hot drink upon arrival and Doreen Kenney is happy to offer assistance with local sightseeing.

OWNER Mrs Doreen Kenney OPEN Easter to mid-November ROOMS 2 double, 1 twin, 1 family, 2 single; all en suite TERMS B&B IR£15; reduction for children

Belle View

Ballyshannon Road, Lurganboy, Donegal, Co. Donegal
Tel: 073 22167

Belle View is an attractive bungalow standing in half a hectare of
grounds, in a peaceful location overlooking Donegal Bay and the
Bluestack Mountains. Mary Lawne is an attentive host who
welcomes guests with a hospitality tray featuring home-baked
scones and a hot drink. The bedrooms have comfortable beds and
good-sized bathrooms. Breakfast only is served, but there is a wide
choice of eating establishments in Donegal town. The guest
lounge, which overlooks the mountains and the bay, has an open
fire and teamakers. There are some lovely walks close by and
boating and water sports are available at nearby Lough Eske, and
there is a pitch and putt course adjacent to the house. The nearby
Donegal Craft Centre is of special interest.

OWNER Mrs Mary Lawne OPEN April – November ROOMS 2 double,
2 family; 2 en suite TERMS B&B IR£17–18; reduction for children;
single supplement IR£3

Shanveen House

Killybegs Road, Donegal, Co. Donegal
Tel: 074 21127

Shanveen House stands in an elevated position overlooking the
Blue Stack Mountains and is a three-minute walk from the town
centre. It is across from the eighteenth-century Presbyterian
church. The bedrooms are spotlessly clean and all have chairs and
individual wardrobes. Although there are only two en suite
bedrooms, another does have its own shower. There is a
comfortable lounge with Victorian furnishings, and a piano. The
atmosphere at Shanveen House is warm and pleasant and Anna
McGarrigle does everything possible to ensure her guests feel
welcome and comfortable. A waterbus tour of Donegal Bay can be
taken as well as guided tours of Donegal's Castle. For the energetic,
horseback riding and cycling are also available.

OWNER Anna McGarrigle OPEN April – end October ROOMS 2
double, 1 twin, 1 family; 2 en suite TERMS B&B IR£17; reduction for
children; single supplement IR£3

St Ernan's House Hotel

St Ernan's Island, Donegal, Co. Donegal
Tel: 073 21065 Fax: 073 22098

St Ernan's was built in 1826 by John Hamilton, a nephew of the Duke of Wellington. It is situated on what was an island; the island is now linked to the mainland by a short causeway and covers some 3.25 hectares. It is an elegant, lovely country house in a beautiful location, offering peace and tranquillity in wonderful surroundings. It was converted into a hotel in 1983 and has been in the O'Dowds' hands since 1987. The individually styled bedrooms are beautifully proportioned and very spacious; each bedroom has views of sea and countryside. Dinner featuring fresh produce is beautifully presented in the large dining room, and the elegant drawing room, with a log fire, is an informal spot in which to relax after a busy day. For guests who are seeking quality accommodations combined with peace and tranquillity, St Ernan's is an excellent choice. Access, Visa, Mastercard, Eurocheque accepted.

OWNER Brian O'Dowd OPEN Easter – October 26 ROOMS 6 double, 6 twin; all en suite   TERMS B&B IR£70–86; single supplement negotiable MEALS Dinner

DOWNINGS

Baymount Bed and Breakfast

Downings, Co. Donegal
Tel: 074 55395

Mary McBride is a local lady who was in fact born in the small house at the bottom of the road. Mary and her husband purchased this house 25 years ago. The house stands above the narrow country road and has spectacular views over the bay to the mountains. When it was built the McBrides had 12 children, many of whom have now left home, allowing the option of running a bed & breakfast establishment. The lounge, a large bright room, enjoys the same magnificent views as the dining room, which has separate tables as well as a TV and a sitting area and sliding doors onto the terrace; a great place to sit on fine days. An iron is available on request.

OWNER Mrs Mary McBride OPEN Easter – August 31 ROOMS 4 double, 1 twin, 1 single; 1 en suite TERMS B&B IR£16–17; reduction for children

DUNFANAGHY

Rosman House
Dunfanaghy, Co. Donegal
Tel: 074 36273

Rosman House, an attractive modern dormer bungalow, stands in a superb spot with spectacular views of Horn Head, Muckish Mountain and Sheephaven Bay. It has a large well-landscaped garden, and is within walking distance of the village. Roisin McHugh, formerly a teacher, takes great pride in her establishment, and her husband runs the 40-hectare dairy and sheep farm. Improvements are ongoing and the house has been freshly decorated. The spacious lounge opens onto a patio and gardens. The bedrooms are individually decorated with coordinated floral colour schemes. There are five ground floor rooms. Breakfast and pre-arranged dinners are served in the elegant dining room on separate tables, which overlook Horn Head. There are some enjoyable scenic walks close by and an 18-hole golf course. Visa accepted.

OWNER Mrs Roisin McHugh OPEN All year ROOMS 2 double, 2 twin, 2 family; 2 en suite TERMS B&B IR£18; reduction for children; single supplement IR£6.50 MEALS Dinner

DUNGLOE

Barr a' Ghaoith
Quay Road, Dungloe, Co. Donegal
Tel: 075 21389 Fax: 075 21389

Barr a' Gaoith means "top of the wind," an apt description for this house, which sits in an elevated position with panoramic views. This extremely good value accommodation is very much a family-run establishment where all the family joins in to share the work.

There is a separate dining room and a comfortable lounge with a VCR and games provided. The house is well maintained and the bedrooms are fresh and clean. Tasty freshly prepared breakfasts include home-baked bread and homemade preserves. Close by activities include angling, golf and hill walking. Tennis courts and a leisure centre are also available. Pitch and putt and deep-sea fishing can be arranged. This must be one of the best value bed & breakfast accommodations in Donegal, and it is a popular venue; early reservations are suggested.

OWNER Susan & John Gallagher OPEN All year ROOMS 1 double, 1 twin, 1 family TERMS B&B IR£12.50; reduction for children

FALCARRAGH

Sea View House
Upper Ray, Falcarragh, Co. Donegal
Tel: 074 35552

This attractive bungalow is set in 1.25 hectares of land in an elevated position, surrounded by open countryside and sweeping views of the mountains and sea. On clear days Tory Island can be seen. Jean McFadden is extremely helpful and accommodating, and guests are greeted with a complimentary hot drink upon arrival. The house is immaculate and has been upgraded: the dining room, which overlooks the view, and the lounge, which has a real fire, have new carpet and furniture. The bedrooms are of a good size and have colour-coordinated floral fabrics. All are now en suite and two have power showers. Breakfast only is served, and includes home-baked bread, but advice on local eating establishments for dinner is provided. Guests are well taken care of here. This is a wonderful spot in which to relax and to explore the local area. There are some lovely walks close by. Cots are provided.

OWNER Jean McFadden OPEN Easter – September ROOMS 3 double, 1 single; 3 en suite TERMS B&B IR£17; reduction for children; single supplement IR£1

GLENCOLUMBKILLE

Corner House
Cashel, Glencolumbkille, Co. Donegal
Tel: 073 30021

Corner House is situated in the centre of the village and, as the name implies, located on the corner. Mrs Byrne is a pleasant and considerate host who runs the adjoining shop, as well as the bed & breakfast, and her son runs the pub. The house looks quite modest from the outside but it is surprisingly spacious inside. It has an enormous dining room and a small upstairs lounge. The house is well maintained; the bedrooms are average in size, and are immaculate, fresh and bright. The surroundings are beautiful and this is a great spot for hill walking. A lovely old grandfather clock stands in the hallway and there is an interesting doll collection displayed in a cabinet on the landing.

OWNER Mrs J. P. Byrne   OPEN April 1 – September 30   ROOMS 2 double, 2 twin, family; 3 en suite   TERMS B&B IR£15–17; reduction for children; single supplement IR£5

GWEEDORE

Min-a-Locha
Bloody Foreland, Gweedore, Co. Donegal
Tel: 075 32279

This purpose-built modern bungalow, although it does have a second storey, overlooks what is said to be the best views in Ireland, the Bloody Foreland and the Atlantic Ocean. The house was purpose-built for B&B and offers every comfort in a peaceful and tranquil setting. The bedrooms have a medieval décor and are of a good size, as are the bathrooms. The beds have attractive colourful duvets. All of the curtains and bed covers were made by Kathleen Duggan, who extends a warm welcome and prides herself on the personal attention to her guests' needs. The spacious lounge has a Victorian-style fireplace where turf fires burn on cool evenings. Breakfasts are served in the bright and airy dining room, overlooking the view, and include home-baked bread and scones.

Three-course and light dinners, often featuring fresh local seafood, and good home-cooking are also served, if pre-arranged. There are sandy beaches, hill and coastal walks, cycling and day trips to the Islands. This is a perfect place from which to explore this dramatic and rugged area. A baby-sitting service can be arranged. Traditional Irish music can be found at several local venues.

OWNER John & Kathleen Duggan OPEN All year ROOMS 2 double, 2 twin, 1 family w. private bath/shower; all en suite TERMS B&B IR£15; reduction for children; single supplement IR£3 MEALS Dinner

INISHOWEN

Fernbank
Redcastle, Inishowen, Co. Donegal
Tel: 077 83032 Fax: 077 83164

Fernbank, built in 1970, with later additions, is extremely good value and is situated in an elevated position with spectacular views of Lough Foyle. Elizabeth, who is from Buncrannon, has been offering her special brand of hospitality for 28 years; there is a home-away-from-home atmosphere and the house is immaculate. A hot drink is available at just about any time, and Elizabeth is happy to give advice on what to see and do in the area. The bedrooms are all on the ground floor and some have lough views. The sitting room and dining room have pine ceilings and the rooms are bright and cheery. Greencastle, with its maritime museum and award-winning fish restaurant, is 11 km away.

OWNER Elizabeth McLaughlin OPEN All year ROOMS 2 double, 2 family; 2 en suite TERMS B&B IR£15–17; reduction for children; single supplement IR£3

Culdaff House
Culdaff, Innishowen, Co. Donegal
Tel: 074 79103

This large, slightly forbidding grey stucco building is approached by a long driveway on the edge of the village of Culdaff, with views of the hills and sea. The sombre exterior in no way reflects the great hospitality and the bright and fresh interior. This is very much a family home, with large rooms and high ceilings. The spacious drawing room has a real fire and there is a separate dining room. The bedrooms are large and have old-fashioned linen bedspreads. The property has been in the Mills family for over 300 years. Since taking over the house about 10 years ago, the Mills have done a tremendous amount of remodelling and redecorating, taking in bed & breakfast guests as they worked their way through the project. There are no private bathrooms, but there are two bathrooms exclusively for guests' use. The motto of this informal happy house is, "We share our home with our guests." Culdaff House was the proud recipient of the BHS "Farmhouse of the Year award."

OWNER Mrs Frances Mills OPEN March 1 – October 31 ROOMS 3 double, 2 twin TERMS B&B IR£16; reduction for children; single supplement IR£5

INISHOWEN PENINSULA

Barraicin
Malin Head, Innishowen Peninsula, Co. Donegal
Tel: 077 70814 Fax: 077 70814

Barraicin takes its name from the field on which it was built by the Doyles in 1971, and means "the square toecap." It stands in a superb position, Ireland's most northerly point, about 1 km from the sea, and has lovely sea views. The cosy dining room, where guests share two tables, overlooks the pretty garden, which has an old pump. The Doyles are a delightful couple who have a great sense of humour, and guests feel immediately at home in this warm and friendly house. The bedrooms, all on the ground floor, are clean and bright. The large, sunny lounge has an open fire and sea views, and a TV is available on request.

Malin Head is a thriving fishing area and two important government services are located here, the Meteorological Station and the Radio Station, which plays a major role in the safety of local fishermen.

It is within easy reach of Innishowen's five golf links, including the internationally known Ballyliffen Glashedy Golf Links.

OWNER Marie Doyle OPEN Easter – November 30 ROOMS 1 double,
1 twin, 1 family; 1 en suite TERMS B&B IR£16; reduction for children;
single supplement IR£3

INVER

Cloverhill House

Cranny, Inver, Co. Donegal
Tel: 073 36165

Cloverhill House is approached by a private drive bordered with
high yew hedges and is an attractive long, low, modern
whitewashed house in an elevated position which has lovely river
views. The extensive gardens are beautiful and there are fruit trees
and strawberry fields. There is an enormous and very pleasant
sitting/dining room with a turf fire. The bedrooms are spacious
and well furnished; three are on the ground floor. An annex
bedroom with an en suite bathroom has been added, ideal for
guests who prefer more privacy. Evening meals are available if
ordered in advance and can be enjoyed with a glass of wine.
Fishing, golfing and mountain climbing is available locally.

OWNER Terry & June Coyle OPEN April – October ROOMS 3 double,
3 twin; 2 en suite TERMS B&B IR£16–18; reduction for children; single
supplement IR£7

KILLYBEGS

Bannagh House

Fintra Road, Killybegs, Co. Donegal
Tel: 073 31108

This modern house stands in an elevated position in a small front
garden and has wonderful views of the harbour, town and near and
distant hills. Killybegs is a large fishing port, and the harbour
always seems to be full of enormous fishing boats, making this an
ideal place for fresh fish. Melly's café does an excellent fish and
chip meal in vast portions. The lounge and dining room also have
bay views. The bedrooms, all on the ground floor, are well-

appointed and tastefully furnished. Phyllis Melly works hard at creating a comfortable home for guests and is happy to give advice on local activities and recommend local restaurants.

OWNER Phyllis Melly   OPEN Easter – October 31   ROOMS 2 double, 1 twin, 1 family; all en suite   TERMS B&B IR£17.50; single supplement IR£5

Hollycroft Lodge

Donegal Road, Killybegs, Co. Donegal
Tel: 073 31470

Guests continue to enjoy the relaxing atmosphere and warm welcome found here at this attractive Georgian-style house, which sits off the road in a large, well maintained garden. Guests are welcome to make use of the garden, which is a pleasant spot in which to relax on fine days. Anne Keeney is a very personable lady who enjoys meeting people, and nothing is too much trouble to ensure her guests are comfortable. The house is well maintained and decorated and furnished to a high standard. The colour-coordinated bedrooms are on the ground floor and one has a brass bed. There is a guest lounge with TV and a separate dining room where filling breakfasts are served. Evening meals are not served, but there are plenty of eating establishments close by.

OWNER Anne Keeney   OPEN March – November   ROOMS 3 double, 1 twin, 1 single; 3 en suite   TERMS B&B IR£17; reduction for children; single supplement IR£5

LAGHEY

Hillcrest

Ballyshannon Road, Laghey, Co. Donegal
Tel: 073 21837   Fax: 073 21674

Hillcrest is a pleasant place to stay – the welcome is warm and friendly, a hot drink usually greets guests upon arrival and the house is spotlessly clean. It is a modern bungalow and stands on the side of a hill in an attractive garden. All the bedrooms, which are on the small side, have pretty front-facing views and are located on the ground floor. The small TV room has comfortable chairs and a piano, which guests are welcome to play.

OWNER Mrs Sheila Gatins OPEN April – October ROOMS 1 double, 1 twin, 1 double/single; 2 en suite TERMS B&B IR£15–17; reduction for children

LETTERKENNY

Hillcrest House
Lurgybrack, Sligo Road, Letterkenny, Co. Donegal
Tel: 074 22300 / 25137 Fax: 074 25137

Hillcrest is a friendly house, where a warm welcome is extended and guests are greeted with a complimentary hot drink and cakes upon arrival. The house is situated on the main Sligo Road, a kilometre from Letterkenny. The house is potentially noisy, but there are great water, mountain and town views. The Maguires are a friendly and helpful couple who have five children. They take excellent care of their guests, and are helpful in every way. The four rooms, although a little small, are spotlessly clean and comfortable; four of them are on the ground floor. Hillcrest offers good value and a high standard of accommodation. Breakfast only is served at separate tables in the bright dining room, and there is a wide choice for evening meals close by. The Maguires are happy to recommend places to eat and to assist guests with daily activities. Visa, Mastercard, American Express accepted.

OWNER Larry & Margaret Maguire OPEN All year ROOMS 2 double, 2 twin, 2 family; 5 en suite TERMS B&B IR£17–18; reduction for children; single supplement IR£5–10

Rinneen
Woodland, Letterkenny, Co. Donegal
Tel: 074 244591

Rinneen, which means "little plot of land at the top of the hill," is a cheery and bright bungalow, with panoramic views of Lough Swilly, the mountains and green fields, where contented sheep graze. The house has a home-away-from-home ambience and the good-sized bedrooms have modern furniture, and floral and autumn colours. There is a real fire in the cosy lounge, which overlooks the view. An additional bonus is Mary McBride, a congenial and helpful host, almost always on hand to assist with itineraries, and who is particularly interested in literature. Excellent breakfasts are served in the dining room; dinners are not available, but Mary is happy to make suggestions for local pubs and restaurants for evening meals.

OWNER Mary McBride OPEN All year ROOMS 1 double (en suite), 1 family, 1 single TERMS B&B IR£15–17; reduction for children; single supplement IR£3

White Gables

Derry Road, Letterkenny, Co. Donegal
Tel: 074 22583

White Gables is a spacious house in an elevated position overlooking the river and the town. It is situated between a dual carriageway and the former main road, but double-glazed windows keep traffic noise to a minimum. There is a pleasant view from the dining room/lounge, which has a small sitting area and a table for breakfast which faces the window. The small bedrooms are clean and simply furnished; two are on the ground floor. There is a pleasant garden that guests may sit in on fine days.

OWNER Mrs Cabrini & Mr Comwellogue OPEN All year ROOMS 2 double, 2 twin, 2 family; 4 en suite TERMS B&B IR£15; reduction for children; single supplement IR£5

LIFFORD

The Hall Green

Port Hall, Lifford, Co. Donegal
Tel: 074 41318

This traditional farmhouse has undergone several improvements. The exterior has been painted terra-cotta and there are new period-style windows. The bedrooms are decorated with pretty wallpapers and matching fabrics. There is one ground floor bedroom with a toilet and wash basin close by, and an ideal family suite consisting of two self-contained en suite bedrooms. All the beds are orthopedic and have electric blankets. The dining room, which is to the rear of the house, was the original farmhouse kitchen, dating back over 100 years. The house has antique furnishings and there are uninterrupted views over and beyond the River Foyle. The cosy lounge has a TV and a fireplace. Salmon and trout fishing are available in the River Finn, which runs through the farm. Golf, walking, bird-watching and a fully equipped leisure centre are close by. A visit to the Lifford Old Courthouse, Visitor and Clan Centre is worthwhile. This is a friendly house with a home-away-from-home atmosphere. Access, Visa, Eurocheque accepted.

OWNER Mervyn & Jean McKean OPEN January 5 – December 12, and Christmas by arrangement ROOMS 1 double, 2 family, 1 double/single; 2 en suite TERMS B&B IR£15–17.50; reduction for children; single supplement IR£5 (high season) MEALS Dinner

The Haw Lodge
The Haw, Lifford, Co. Donegal
Tel: 074 41397 / 41985 Fax: 074 41985

This traditional farmhouse with its newly restored exterior is easily located on the main road about 2.5 km from Lifford. The original farmhouse kitchen dates back 100 years and is now used as the dining room. The bedrooms are prettily decorated with coordinating colours; one is on the ground floor and has a close by toilet and washbasin. There is also an ideal family suite, consisting of two bedrooms with en suite facilities; all the beds are ortho-pedic, and a cot is available. The cosy TV lounge has a fireplace. Evening meals are no longer served, but there are some excellent local eating places for meals, and Eileen is happy to make recommendations. Salmon and trout fishing are available in the river Finn, which flows through the farm, and golf, walking, bird-watching and a fully equipped leisure centre are close by. Of special interest is the Lifford Old Courthouse, Visitor and Clans Centre. This friendly house with its home-away-from-home atmosphere would be an excellent choice from which to explore this interesting and scenic area. Access, Visa accepted.

OWNER Eileen Patterson OPEN January 1 – December 1 ROOMS 1 double, 1 twin, 1 family, 1 single; 2 en suite TERMS B&B IR£15–18; reduction for children; single supplement IR£5

MOVILLE

Admiralty House
Carrownaffe, Moville, Co. Donegal
Tel: 077 82529 / 82377

Admiralty House, a beautifully restored Georgian house, was in a derelict condition when it was purchased by the McFeelys. The restoration took over two years, and the result is a beautiful country house set in a pleasant wooded garden, with views of Lough Foyle. The entryway is very attractive, and has marble floors as does the lounge. There are rich colours throughout and stained-glass windows depicting various sea scenes. The house is furnished in keeping with its character; most of the pieces were found by the owners at various venues around the country. The bedrooms are individually decorated and are warm and comfortable. The conservatory, with its wicker furniture, is the only new addition to the house. The owners, who have three children, are extremely helpful and provide a portfolio of places to visit in the area. Breakfasts only are served, but there are plenty of places to eat in Moyville, an eight-minute walk away. Of local interest is the Greencastle Maritime Museum, a Norman Castle and Napoleonic fort.

OWNER Suzanne McFeely OPEN May 1 – September 30 ROOMS 2 double, 1 twin, 1 family TERMS B&B IR£15–18; reduction for children; single supplement IR£5

RAMELTON

Ardeen
Ramelton, Co. Donegal
Tel: 074 51243

This splendid country house built in 1845 is situated in its own grounds overlooking Lough Swilly. It stands in a well-tended pleasant lawned front garden in a peaceful and tranquil spot. The spacious bedrooms are individually and elegantly decorated in lemon, blue and buttermilk; all have patchwork quilts made by the owner, Anne Campbell. The drawing and dining room are furnished with antiques and have open fires.

The house at one time belonged to a private nurse of King George V and, more recently, to two doctors. Anne Campbell is an excellent host who knows just how to make her guests feel at home. She formerly ran a village shop, but now concentrates on running her very successful bed & breakfast.

There are several places for an evening meal in Ramelton, which has been designated a National Heritage town, and is a pleasant, short stroll away. The county Genealogical Centre is located in the old Meeting House, which is one of the oldest Presbyterian churches in Ireland. All major credit cards accepted.

OWNER Mrs Anne Campbell OPEN Easter – October 31 ROOMS 2 double, 1 twin, 1 family, 1 single; 3 en suite TERMS B&B IR£20–22; reduction for children; single supplement IR£5

Crammond House
Market Square, Ramelton, Co. Donegal
Tel: 074 51055

Crammon House is easily located in this unspoiled historical village. It has origins from 1760 and was formerly a grocery and hardware shop, as well as a wholesale tea importers. It was home to the same family for four generations, and of special interest are the old photographs of the old shopfront, which the warm and welcoming present owner, Ena Corry, is happy to show guests. The house has undergone a tasteful restoration; the rooms are well furnished and it has all-modern comforts and is spotlessly clean. The bedrooms are bright, decorated mostly with floral wallpapers, and the non–en suite rooms all have sinks. There is a pleasant and friendly atmosphere, and recommendations on places to eat in the village, as well as information on what to see and do in the area, is provided. A hot drink is offered upon arrival, and at other times on request.

OWNER Mrs Ena Corry OPEN All year ROOMS 1 double, 1 twin, 1 en suite family TERMS B&B IR£15–17; reduction for children; single supplement IR£5

Gleann Oir

Ards, Ramelton, Co. Donegal

Tel: 074 51187

This modern house is situated in a hilly area and has spectacular views of farmland and hills. It is a quiet and peaceful, simply furnished family home. Mrs Crawford has seven children, and children are very welcome here; they can wander around the farm if accompanied by an adult. There are 14 hectares and the farm is quite an attraction, with sheep, two milking cows and arable land. There is a comfortable sitting room with TV and open fire, as well as a small dining room where excellent breakfasts and pre-arranged dinners are served, and an additional family room. There is no licence, but guests may bring their own wine. Two of the bedrooms are on the ground floor.

OWNER Rosemary Crawford   OPEN Easter – October 31   ROOMS 2 double, twin, 2 family; all en suite   TERMS B&B IR£17; reduction for children; single supplement IR£3

COUNTY GALWAY

Galway contains the widely renowned area of Connemara, which stretches northward from Galway city up to Killary Harbour and is bordered on the east by beautiful Lough Corrib, which boasts an island for every day of the year.

Galway, the "city of the tribes," and the nearby popular resort of Salthill, which overlooks the famous Galway Bay, have lovely beaches, a promenade for walking and lots of restaurants: an ideal holiday spot.

Wild Connemara has inspired song and poetry. Today, Galway, Connemara and the west of Ireland are a haven for ancient customs and culture. You will hear lilting and evocative Irish music in the pubs and often the Irish language being spoken. Travel offshore and you become immersed even deeper into Ireland's traditional way of life, with trips to Inishbofin, County Clare, Achill and the Aran Islands.

There's plenty to see and do in the west of Ireland: pony trekking, dramatically located golf courses, angling (which is well catered for, with abundant salmon and trout in clean waters).

If you are interested in sixteenth-century castles, visit the ruins of Ardamullivan Castle, 7.5 km south of Gort, an O'Shaughnessy stronghold. Fiddaun Castle, 7.5 km south southwest of Gort, is another of their strongholds.

Clarinbridge is a popular place in September, when it hosts the Oyster Festival. Portumna, a market town, is at the head of Lough Derg.

For the more adventurous, a climb up the Slieve Auchty Mountains is well worth the view.

Two castles worth seeing are Derryhivenny Castle, 4.5 km northeast of Portumna. Built in 1653, it is well preserved, as is Pallas Castle, 9 km from Portumna on the Loughrea Road.

Ballinasloe is well-known for the October Horse Fair, which lasts for eight days and includes carnival events and show-jumping exhibitions.

ANNAGHDOWN

Corrib View Farm
Annaghdown, Co. Galway
Tel: 091 791114 Fax: 093 55356

This 100-year-old, friendly farmhouse, situated in a peaceful area near Lough Corrib, offers good old-fashioned hospitality. It has received the Agri-Tourism Regional Award. The bedrooms are clean and comfortable and have big fluffy towels. The lounge is warm and there is a separate dining room where breakfasts are served at separate tables. For guests who prefer a continental breakfast, there is a reduction in price. Evening meals are no longer available, but Regina's Pub, 3 km away, serves light meals and full dinners. This is a family-run bed & breakfast and guests are made to feel immediately at home.

OWNER Mary Scott Furey and Family   OPEN April 1 – end October
ROOMS 2 double, 2 twin, 1 family, 1 single; 3 en suite   TERMS B&B
IR£20; reduction for children; single supplement IR£8

Cashel House

Cashel, Co. Galway
Tel: 095 31001 Fax: 095 31007

Situated at the head of Cashel Bay, this gracious, nineteenth-century country house is set in 20 hectares of award-winning gardens and woodland walks. It has gained an international reputation for good food and luxurious comfort in a quiet, relaxing atmosphere. Carefully cooked fresh garden and sea produce, such as fresh lobsters, clams, mackerel, salmon and scallops, are its specialities, and there is a carefully chosen wine list. Meals are tastefully presented in the elegant dining room with open turf fires. In 1969 General and Madame de Gaulle spent two weeks of their Irish holiday here. The house is furnished with antiques and other fine treasures, and the bedrooms are beautifully appointed. There are several areas in which to sit, including a conservatory and a patio area. Guests may walk along the seashore, through woods and streams, and drive through the beautiful scenic Connemara. All major credit cards accepted.

OWNER Dermot & Kay McEvilly OPEN Closed January 10–31 ROOMS 32 rooms (mixed); all en suite TERMS B&B from IR£49; reduction for children; single supplement (seasonal) MEALS Full dinner and lighter meals

CLARINBRIDGE

Springlawn
Stradbally, Clarinbridge, Co. Galway
Tel: 091 796045

This attractive house with dormer windows stands in a hectare in the heart of oyster country. There is a wooded area behind the house, and the sea is within walking distance. The good-sized bedrooms maintain a high standard and have modern comfortable furnishings. Maura McNamara, who has been running her successful bed & breakfast for 11 years, takes a personal interest in her guests and is happy to provide information on golf, fishing and pony trekking, all of which are within a 15-minute drive. There is a TV lounge and a separate dining room where breakfasts, pre-arranged dinners and light meals are served at modest prices. As an alternate, there are three restaurants close by. There is no public phone, but guests may use the owners' on request. Visa, Access, Mastercard, Eurocard accepted.

OWNER Maura McNamara OPEN March 1 – November 30 ROOMS 1 double, 1 twin, 1 family, 1 single, triple; 3 en suite TERMS B&B IR£17; reduction for children; single supplement IR£6 MEALS Light teas and dinners

CLIFDEN

Ardmore House
Sky Road, Clifden, Co. Galway
Tel: 095 21221 Fax: 095 21100

This luxurious farmhouse is set in beautiful scenic countryside overlooking the sea. It is warm and inviting and Kathy Mullen is a delightful and pleasant host – guests here are assured of true Irish hospitality. The immaculate bedrooms are well decorated and have comfortable beds. There are two lounges, one with a TV and an open fire, and one quiet lounge for chatting or reading. Seafood is a specialty for evening meals, and light meals are also available. Dinners must be ordered in advance. Lake and deep-sea angling, pony trekking, beautiful walks and golf are all available in the area. Scenic farm walks to the cliff and picnic areas can also be taken.

OWNER Kathy Mullen OPEN April 1 – October 1 ROOMS 2 double, 1 twin, 3 family; all en suite TERMS B&B IR£20; reduction for children; single supplement IR£10 MEALS Dinner

Mallmore House
Clifden, Co. Galway
Tel: 095 21460

This lovingly restored Georgian house (formerly the home of the Darcy family, the founders of Clifden, and his excellency, the Archbishop of Tuam), is set in 14 hectares and is within walking distance of the sea. The house overlooks the bay, and most of the bedrooms have lovely views. All the bedrooms are on the ground floor and are spacious and comfortable. The large lounge has a turf fire and is a peaceful place in which to relax after a busy day. Award-winning breakfasts are served in a separate dining room, and for other meals there are several establishments in Clifden. Kathleen Hardman is a considerate and helpful host and guests are assured of personal attention. The world-famous Connemara ponies are bred at Mallmore and can be seen in the grounds, and the woodland is a haven for a great variety of wildlife.

OWNER Kathleen & Alan Hardman   OPEN March 1 – October 31 ROOMS 3 double, 2 twin, 1 family; all en suite TERMS B&B IR£20; reduction for children

Sunnybank House
Clifden, Co. Galway
Tel: 095 21437

This charming period house in an elevated position sits in well tended, landscaped grounds overlooking Clifden town. The immaculate, well-appointed bedrooms are tastefully decorated and furnished to a high standard. There are two ground floor rooms with their own sitting rooms. There is also a spacious lounge which has some antique pieces, including a grandfather clock and soft, comfortable furnishings, and there is an additional lounge with TV. The house is bright and decorated mostly with pastel shades. There is a heated swimming pool, a sauna, tennis courts and mature gardens for guests' use. Evening meals are not served, but the charming owners, Jackie and Marion O'Grady, have an award-winning seafood restaurant with a bistro bar that is open for lunch and dinner daily. Sunnybank would be an ideal base from which to explore this beautiful area of Ireland. Visa, Access, Mastercard accepted.

OWNER Jackie & Marion O'Grady   OPEN March 1 – November 1
ROOMS 6 double, 4 twin, 1 single; all en suite   TERMS B&B IR£30; reduction for children; single supplement IR£10

CLONBUR

Ballykline House
Clonbur, Co. Galway
Tel: 092 46150 Fax: 092 46150

Ballykline House is situated on the road between the picturesque villages of Cong and Clonbur, the gateway to Connemara. The house continues to maintain its high standard and offers good value accommodation. It overlooks the famous fishing lake of Lough Mask. It has its own private grounds of gardens and lawns, surrounded by beautiful woodlands. The oldest part of the house belonged to the Guinness family; the house and the land were purchased by the family in 1940, with an addition in 1992. Mr and Mrs Lambe are a very congenial couple who have created a warm and inviting atmosphere. There is a cosy sitting room and open fire, and a conservatory to relax in with tea and coffee makers provided. There are wonderful forest walks (guides can be provided) as well as walks to the summit of magnificent Benlevi. The immediate area is a fisherman's paradise. Restaurants are within walking distance of the house.

OWNER Ann Lambe OPEN April 1 – November 1 ROOMS 2 double, 2 twin, 1 family; all en suite TERMS B&B IR£18; reduction for children; single supplement IR£5

Cregg House

Galway Road, Connemara, Co. Galway
Tel: 095 21326

This immaculate dormer bungalow stands in an elevated position on half a hectare of grounds. The house has a spectacular view of Roundstone Bog and the mountains beyond. Mary O'Donnell continues to maintain her high standards and the bedrooms are prettily and individually decorated with soft pastel colours. The O'Donnells have been offering their special brand of hospitality for over 13 years; guests feel very much at home here, and enjoy chatting round the turf fire, which is lit at the first sign of a chill in the air. Excellent breakfasts include fresh fruit, homemade yoghurt and soda bread. An ideal base from which to tour Connemara, there is a fishing river less than five minutes away and golf and horseback riding are also available.

OWNER Mary O'Donnell   OPEN April 1 – October 31   ROOMS 3 double, 2 twin, 1 family; 5 en suite   TERMS B&B IR£17; reduction for children; single supplement IR£5

Lake Side Farm House

Oughterard, Connemara, Co. Galway
Tel: 091 552846

This warm and friendly, immaculately kept house is in a superb position on the shores of Lough Corrib with panoramic views of the lake and its many islands. This is a working farm of sheep and cattle, and there is also a donkey and a Connemara pony. An additional bonus are the delightful and charming owners, Josie and Mary O'Halloran – little wonder guests return here often to enjoy their special brand of Irish hospitality. The bedrooms, all on the ground floor, are of a good size and have patchwork quilts or Country Diary duvets. There is a bog on the property which provides the turf for the fireplace in the sitting room. Breakfasts only are served in the dining room with pine furniture, and there are several options for evening meals close by. Josie can easily be persuaded to take guests up the river, and there is an angling centre almost adjacent to the property. You may arrive here as a guest, but you will leave as a friend. It is a wonderful spot from which to explore this beautiful area.

OWNER Mary O'Halloran OPEN March 1 – November 30 ROOMS 2 double, 1 twin, 1 family; all en suite TERMS B&B IR£17; reduction for children; single supplement IR£6

Waterfall Lodge
Oughterard, Connemara, Co. Galway
Tel: 091 552168

This superb period residence stands in a secluded setting, with beautiful grounds ablaze with colour in spring and summer, and a cascading waterfall. The river Owen Riff runs through the property, and private game fishing is available to guests. The house is furnished with antiques, including a grandfather clock, and the tastefully furnished bedrooms are reached by a pitch pine stairway. Breakfasts only are served in the elegant dining room at separate tables, and the spacious TV lounge has a cast-iron and marble fireplace. Tea and coffee making facilities are in the lounge and guests may help themselves at just about any time. Kathleen Dolly is a delightful lady and is very knowledgeable about the area. The atmosphere is friendly and informal. This is a popular bed & breakfast establishment and early reservations are recommended.

OWNER Kathleen Dolly OPEN Easter – October ROOMS 3 double, 2 twin, 1 family; all en suite TERMS B&B IR£20; reduction for children; single supplement IR£5

CORRONDULA

Cregg Castle
Corrondula, Co. Galway
Tel: 091 791434 Fax: 091 791434

Cregg Castle, the last fortified castle to be built west of the Shannon, sits in a peaceful and tranquil spot on 67 hectares of wildlife preserve. This is a very lived-in, casual, informal property, and there are no strict rules here. Guests may walk in the woods and spot the wildlife, or go farther afoot and take a walk by the river. Breakfasts, which include free-range eggs and home-baked

bread, are served until noon, and dinners are served in the Great Hall with its huge log fire. The emphasis here is on relaxation, and guests are encouraged to get to know each other, enjoying conversation and the occasional musical evening. This is an ideal place for those who want to be involved in Irish music. Owners Pat and Ann Marie are experienced musicians and are delighted to play with or for guests. Most of the bedrooms are of a good size and have comfortable beds. This is a unique property with many original features, such as the huge locks and security bars, the foot scraper with the rampant black cat of the Blake's crest and the shutters on the big windows. The Blake crest is also on the fireplace with its black marble. Outside in the courtyard is a Queen Anne bell tower; in the inner yard is the original forge and the remains of an oven for firing pottery. A spring well provides the castle with water. Cregg Castle's welcome, as described in their brochure, is exactly right – "Hail Guest, we ask not what thou art; if friend we greet thee hand and heart; if stranger, such no longer be, our friendly faith shall conquer thee." Cregg Castle is a place to capture Ireland's history and culture. Visa, Access accepted.

OWNER The Broderick Family   OPEN March – October   ROOMS 2 double, 1 twin, 1 family, 1 single; 4 en suite   TERMS B&B IR£25–35; reduction for children; single supplement IR£10   MEALS Dinner

Carraig Beag

1 Burren Hill Heights, Knocknacarra Road, Galway, Co. Galway
Tel: 091 521696

This luxurious, red brick house is just off the promenade and has excellent views of the bay. The bedrooms are a good size and are furnished with every comfort in mind. There are attractive, rich wood doors and a handsome staircase. Breakfasts are served at separate tables in the elegant dining room, which has a beautiful crystal chandelier and marble fireplace. The owners, Paddy and Catherine Lydon, are an added bonus. They are a very helpful and accommodating couple. Catherine and Paddy often take walks along the promenade in the evening; guests may join them, but beware, you might find it hard to keep up with them! This good value bed & breakfast offers a high standard of accommodation at modest prices, and it is well situated for all of the local amenities. Mastercard accepted.

OWNER Catherine & Paddy Lydon OPEN All year ROOMS 2 double, 2 twin, 1 family; all en suite TERMS B&B IR£17.50–19.50; reduction for children; single supplement IR£7.50–15.50

Dun Roamin

Gratton Road, Galway, Co. Galway
Tel: 091 582570

The Bogan family named their modern, attractive, red brick house after their decision to stay put and enjoy Galway and the beautiful scenic countryside. The house has a warm and welcoming atmosphere and the rooms are clean with comfortable beds and warm duvets. The guest lounge is cosy and breakfasts only are served in a separate dining room, consisting of cereals, fruit and a traditional Irish platter. Dun Roamin is located less than two minutes from the beach, restaurants and other amenities. Jo Bogan is a down-to-earth, friendly lady, and a helpful and considerate host. Guests are welcomed with a hot drink upon arrival.

OWNER Mrs Jo Bogan OPEN All year ROOMS 2 double, 2 twin; all en suite TERMS B&B IR£18; reduction for children; single supplement IR£12

Eureka

Bushy Park, Galway, Co. Galway
Tel: 091 523555 Fax: 091 523229

Eureka is set back off the main road in a quiet position, yet is just five minutes from Galway town on the road to Connemara. This attractive modern house is very well maintained and an added bonus are the accommodating owners, John and Mary Connell. Mary is very knowledgeable about the area and enjoys sharing information with guests. The bedrooms are well maintained and decorated to a high standard. The front rooms have views of the lake, river and golf course. The small sun lounge has a TV and a conservatory has been added for guests' use. A complimentary hot drink and biscuits are offered upon arrival. Breakfast only is served, and guests not wanting the traditional Irish breakfast have a choice of yoghurts and fresh fruit. There is a restaurant close by for evening meals, and bar food is also served. The house is directly opposite the Glenlo Abbey golf course. Visa, Access, Mastercard accepted.

OWNER John & Mary Connell OPEN May 1 – September 30 ROOMS 2 double, 1 double/single; all en suite   TERMS B&B IR£18–20; reduction for children; single supplement IR£6–8

Killeen House

Bushypark, nr. Galway, Co. Galway
Tel: 091 524179 Fax: 091 528065

This charming house, built in 1840, is approached by a tree-lined driveway. It nestles in 10 hectares of beautifully landscaped gardens that extend down to Lake Corrib. Catherine Doyle is a wonderful host with a flair for décor and a passion for antiques. The house has been tastefully refurbished, combining all-modern comforts without detracting from the original ambience. The rooms are enormous and luxuriously appointed. One room reflects the Victorian era, another the Edwardian. The elegant drawing room has the original marble fireplace and an interesting teapot collection. A varied breakfast is tastefully presented in the dining room. For those who enjoy gracious living in a tranquil atmosphere, Killeen Lodge is an excellent choice. A path from the house leads down to the shores of Lough Corrib. All major credit cards accepted.

OWNER Catherine Doyle OPEN All year ROOMS 4 double, 1 twin, 1 family; 5 en suite TERMS B&B IR£40; single supplement IR£15

Mandalay by the Sea
10 Gentian Hill, Galway, Co. Galway
Tel: 091 524177 Fax: 091 529952

This beautiful, new Georgian-style house is in a superb location overlooking the bay and the Aran Islands. Owner Georgianna Darby is from Rhode Island in the USA. Mandalay is furnished and decorated to extremely high standards; there are rich wood furnishings and antiques. The rooms are spacious, two have balconies and all have views. The entry hall and the kitchen have Liscannor stone floors from the Burren. There are two lounges, one with a piano and TV. There are lots of plants and dried flower arrangements throughout the house. Excellent breakfasts are served in the bright dining room. For nature lovers there are some very pleasant walks close by, and a bird sanctuary can be seen in front of the house. Visa, Mastercard accepted.

OWNER Georgianna Darby OPEN All year ROOMS 2 double, 2 twin, 2 double/single; 5 en suite TERMS B&B IR£16–20; reduction for children; single supplement IR£5

Seaview
Beach Court, Gratton Road, Galway, Co. Galway
Tel: 091 582109 Fax: 091 582109

This detached, attractive white house faces the seafront. The front bedrooms overlook the sea; they are all colour-coordinated and are spotlessly clean, and two have orthopedic beds. There is a balcony for guests' use and a small TV lounge. The house is a five-minute walk from the town centre and directly across from the beach. Mrs Bready Tracey is an accommodating host and there is plenty of information provided on what there is to do and see in the area. This is good value accommodation in a central position. All major credit cards accepted.

OWNER Mrs Bready Tracey OPEN All year ROOMS 2 double, 1 twin, 1 family; all en suite TERMS B&B IR£17; reduction for children; single supplement IR£6–8

LEANAUN

Glen Valley Farm and Stables
Leanaun, Co. Galway
Tel: 095 42269 Fax: 095 42365

This friendly, award-winning, modest farmhouse is found down a rather bumpy road in a remote location amidst lovely countryside, nestled in the foothills of Lettershanbally Mountain. The rooms are spacious, clean and simply furnished. The small, cosy lounge has turf fires. This is an ideal base for those who enjoy hill walking. Pony trekking is available on the farm, which is run by Mr O'Neill. Substantial breakfasts, and evening meals if pre-arranged, are served in the farmhouse dining room.

OWNER Josephine & Joseph O'Neill OPEN February 1 – November 30
ROOMS 2 double, 2 twin, 1 family; 3 en suite TERMS B&B IR£16–18; reduction for children; single supplement IR£6 MEALS Dinner

LEENANE

Delphi Lodge
Leenane, Co. Galway
Tel: 095 42222 Fax: 095 42296 E-mail: delfish@iol.ie

This magnificent 1830s house was beautifully restored in 1988, and is now one of the finest sporting lodges in Ireland. Set in 400 hectares with three loughs in a stunning lakeside location, and surrounded by ancient woodlands and towering mountains, it is the ultimate Connemara retreat. The house has antique pine furniture and the bedrooms have lovely views. Originally the sporting estate of the Marquis of Sligo, Delphi is now the home of Jane and Peter Mantle. Jane is a Cordon Bleu cook who specialises in local seafood. The Lodge has a strong emphasis on salmon and trout fishing, and Delphi is one of the finest game fisheries in Ireland. The fishing season runs from spring to September. Outside the fishing season the lodge is popular with shooting parties, ramblers and golfers. Horseback riding and hunting can also be arranged. Superb, safe and uncrowded beaches are within a 20-minute drive, and the Lodge is conveniently placed for visiting

Westport and all the sites of Connemara. A huge snooker room and a magnificent library are open to guests. Evening meals are served at an old oak table and the wine cellar is extensive. Not suitable for children. French spoken. There are four charming country cottages available for self-catering. Access, Visa, American Express accepted.

OWNER Peter & Jane Mantle OPEN All year ROOMS 6 double, 6 twin; all en suite TERMS B&B IR£30–45; single supplement IR£20 MEALS Dinner

MOYCULLEN

Moycullen House
Moycullen, Co. Galway
Tel: 091 555566 Fax: 091 555566

Moycullen House lies on a narrow, quiet road, on one of the highest points in the area overlooking Lough Corrib. It is on the edge of Connemara, making it an ideal location for touring, trips to the Aran Island and Lough Corrib. It was built in the 1930s by Lord Campbell, and has great oak doors with the original iron locks. The servants' bells still exist in the sitting room. During the time of remodelling for the new dining room and restaurant, two stone fireplaces were exposed. The restaurant, which is open to the public, features excellent, freshly prepared meals prepared by the owner's son, who is a trained chef. The house stands in 12 hectares of rhododendrons and azaleas, and a pure spring provides the house with water. The bedrooms are large, tastefully decorated and well furnished, most with period fireplaces. There is an elegant and comfortable sitting room which has an old stone fireplace, and also a conservatory. Philip and Marie are charming hosts who can organise coarse, trout and salmon fishing as well as boats on Lough Corrib. There are four 18-hole golf courses within a half hour's drive. American Express, Visa, Mastercard accepted.

OWNER Marie & Philip Casburn OPEN March – December ROOMS 2 double, 2 twin, 1 family; 2 en suite TERMS B&B IR£40; reduction for children negotiable; single supplement IR£10 MEALS Full à la carte menu

OUGHTERARD

Corrib Wave House
Portacarron, Oughterard, Connemara, Co. Galway
Tel: 091 552147 Fax: 091 552736

Corrib Wave House has been upgraded to a three-star guest house, situated in picturesque surroundings overlooking the lake and Connemara mountains. This is a peaceful and tranquil spot, part of a working sheep farm of 10 hectares. The bedrooms, all of which overlook the view, have been upgraded with sturdy seating, made by owner Michael Healy, and have good-sized bathrooms. The lounge has an open fire and there is a separate dining room where breakfasts and excellent evening meals, if pre-arranged, are served. This is an ideal spot for people who enjoy the outdoors; there are lovely walks close by, and salmon, trout and coarse fishing. There are boats for hire, and ghillies can be arranged. Swimming, canoeing and sailing can be enjoyed on the lake, and there is an 18-hole golf course within a kilometre. The house is conveniently located near Galway and Connemara. Visa, Mastercard, Access accepted.

OWNER Michael & Maria Healy OPEN April 1 – October 15 ROOMS 3 double, 4 twin, 3 family; all en suite TERMS B&B IR£25; reduction for children; single supplement IR£10 MEALS Dinner

ROUNDSTONE

The Anglers Return
Toombeola, Roundstone, Co. Galway
Tel: 095 631091

This house of character, with thick stone walls, dates back to the 1800s, and has an interesting history. It was first built as a single storey cottage known as "The Fishery." At that time, John Robertson, a Scottish gentlemen, leased the building and started a salmon cannery on the island. It was rebuilt and opened as a hotel in 1839, known as the Old Anglers Hotel, and has been a bed & breakfast since 1954. The house stands in 5.5 hectares, including 1.2 hectares of gardens ablaze with colour in the spring and summer. The spacious bedrooms are not en suite but do have sinks, and there are two bathrooms exclusively for guests' use. The ambience here is relaxed and informal, and the lounge, which has a log fireplace and 100-year-old terra-cotta tiles, is a good place to sit after a busy day. This is a TV-free zone, but there are lots of books to read. There are no petty rules here – guests may come and go as they please, and Lynn Hill goes out of her way to ensure guests' needs are met. Breakfasts are excellent and feature free-range eggs, homemade yoghurt and honey, home-baked breads and homemade marmalades and jams. Evening meals are available by prior arrangement, and vegetarians can be catered for with advance notice. The Anglers Return overlooks a fresh tidal water pool and guests may fish for brown trout at no extra charge. This would be an excellent choice of a place to stay when touring this scenic area; Connemara has long been regarded as one of the most unspoiled and beautiful landscapes in Europe.

OWNER Lynn Hill OPEN April 1 – November 30 ROOMS 2 double, 2 twin   TERMS B&B IR£20; single supplement (seasonal)   MEALS Dinner, snacks

SALTHILL

The Connaught
Barna Road, Salthill, Galway, Co. Galway
Tel: 091 525865 Fax: 091 525865

This pleasant, friendly residence is set back off the road in a quiet position. It is a well maintained house, decorated to a high standard. The well-appointed bedrooms are nicely furnished, and have comfortable beds with electric blankets. The lounge has rich red carpeting and there is a bright dining room where substantial, freshly prepared breakfasts are served. An extremely cordial and helpful couple, the Keaveneys do everything to ensure their guests are comfortable and well taken care of. There is a warm and friendly atmosphere and guests feel relaxed and very much at home here. The Connaught offers good value bed & breakfast and this would be an ideal place from which to explore this diversified and beautiful area.

OWNER Colette & Tom Keaveney OPEN April 1 – October 31 ROOMS 3 double, 1 twin, 2 family; 5 en suite TERMS B&B IR£17; reduction for children; single supplement IR£5 (high season)

SPIDDAL

Ard Mhuirbhi

Aille, Inverin, Spiddal, Co. Galway
Tel: 091 593215

Ard Mhuirbhi, which means "seashore height," offers quality accommodation. The house is located on the sea side of the coast road on a small, peaceful road, and is set in mature, landscaped gardens. The entrance to the house is through a small porch full of colourful potted plants and flowers. The bedrooms, all of which are on the ground floor, are large and well furnished. They have large wardrobes, soft pastel colours and coordinated fabrics, and two have excellent views of the Burren and the bay. The lounge is well furnished and breakfast is served on the patio on fine days. The house is immaculately maintained and is delightful in every way. Owner Rita Feeney has thought of just about everything for her guests' comfort and is an attentive, courteous host. There are no TVs in the room, but one is available on request. This is a tranquil place to return to after a busy day and guests can enjoy walks on the beach three minutes from the house, or the moors and bog, which are just a five-minute drive away.

OWNER Rita Feeney OPEN All year ROOMS 2 double, 1 twin, 2 family; 4 en suite TERMS B&B IR£17; reduction for children; single supplement IR£5

Cala 'n Uisce

Greenhill, Spiddal, Co. Galway
Tel: 091 553324

Cala 'n Uisce means "little harbour," which is apt, as the house is in a picturesque setting facing the bay. The house was designed by owner Pádraig Feeney and has leaded windows and a red brick exterior. High standards are found here, and the house continues to be exceptionally well maintained. There are three ground floor bedrooms, attractively decorated with coordinated fabrics. Many interesting paintings of local scenes, by Mrs Feeney and other family members, are on display throughout the house. The lounge, which has a turf fire, leads out onto a patio. The dining room, where a tasty breakfast is served on linen table-cloths and pretty china, overlooks the bay. Pádraig Feeney's father was a cousin of John Ford, who directed *The Quiet Man*. This is an Irish-speaking area, and the Feeney family speaks Irish. Cala 'n Uisce is a most comfortable and peaceful place; the house stands in half a hectare of landscaped gardens, and there are beautiful bog areas and sea walks close by. No smoking in the bedrooms. No pets. Situated 2.5 km west of Spiddal village.

OWNER Moya Feeney   OPEN March 1 – November 1   ROOMS 3 double, 1 twin, 2 family; all en suite   TERMS B&B IR£18; reduction for children; single supplement IR£5

Cloch na Scith – Thatched Cottage
Kellough, Spiddal, Co. Galway
Tel: 091 553364

This cosy, 130-year-old, traditional thatched cottage, part of a working farm, has played host to actress Julie Christie and the Swedish ambassador. There are thick stone walls, uneven floors, plenty of history and an old-world charm. Owner Nancy Hopkins-Naughton offers one of the warmest welcomes in Ireland. She is a delightful, down-to-earth host and guests are greeted with a hot drink on arrival, often with homemade cake. The family are Irish speaking and into Irish music. The lounge/dining room has turf fires, and a Galway wedding shawl which belonged to Nancy's grandmother hangs on the wall. Breakfast, and four-course home-cooked dinners if ordered in advance, are served on old pine tables and blue willow china. Guests may bring their own wine to dinner. Nancy is an absolutely delightful lady; there are no petty rules here and guests are treated as friends, so it is little wonder that many of her guests are repeat visitors. The bedrooms are comfortable with firm beds; two are on a lower floor and one room is quite large with its own bathroom. The beach is two minutes away and there are maps provided for folks interested in walking. Cloch na Scith has been featured on TV's *Holiday*. A one-bedroom, self-catering cottage is available.

OWNER Nancy Hopkins-Naughton   OPEN March 1 – September 30
ROOMS 1 double, 1 twin, 1 family; 2 en suite   TERMS B&B IR£17.50;
reduction for children; single supplement IR£11   MEALS Dinner

TUAM

Gardenfield House
Tuam, Co. Galway
Tel: 093 24865

This rambling, comfortable period house dates from 1860 and is
part of a 26-hectare working farm of sheep and cattle. The
atmosphere is casual, friendly and welcoming. The house is in a
tranquil setting and is approached up a gravel drive through fields
dotted with sheep. The rooms are all good-sized, and are
individually decorated in burgundy and gold, and a mixture of soft
pastel shades. There are tall ceilings, and the dining and sitting
rooms have the original casement shutters. Free-range chickens
provide the eggs for breakfast and Esther, who is a good cook,
prepares excellent evening meals, with plenty of organic
vegetables; lamb from the farm is often on the menu. Vegetarians
can be catered for with advance notice. Both the small, snug sitting
room and the lounge have coal fires. There are two self-catering
units available.

OWNER Mrs Esther Mannion   OPEN All year   ROOMS 1 double, 1
twin, 1 family; 2 en suite   TERMS B&B IR£17; reduction for children;
single supplement IR£5   MEALS Dinner

COUNTY LIMERICK

Bordered on the north by the expanses of the Shannon, Limerick is
a peaceful farming county with its fair share of relics from the past.
   The origins of the city of Limerick go back to the days of the
Vikings. Always a principal fording point for the Shannon River,
it has played an important part in Irish history, particularly during
the 1690s. Old English Town and the old Irish part of the city
across the river are the most interesting parts of the city to explore,

particularly around St John's Square with its Georgian architecture. The most noteworthy sight to visit is the Granary, a restored eighteenth-century warehouse, which houses the tourist office as well as restaurants, shops and an exhibition gallery. King John's Castle with its massive rounded tower, St Mary's Cathedral, dating from 1172, and the Hunt Collection at the National Institute for Higher Education can also be visited.

Adare has some splendid ruins to see, the finest one being the Franciscan Friary. Others include the Trinitarian Abbey, the Augustian Abbey and St Nicholas Church. It is a most attractive town, with pretty thatched cottages and lovely views of Desmond Castle and Adare Manor on the river.

It is thought the "limerick" may well have come from Croom, which was the meeting place of eighteenth-century Gaelic poets, who wrote extremely witty verse.

ADARE

Adare Lodge
Kildimo Road, Adare, Co. Limerick
Tel: 061 396629

Agnes Fitzpatrick is a charming lady who has created an informal and welcoming atmosphere at this luxurious mock-Tudor house on a quiet side street, surrounded by an award-winning garden. The picturesque centre of Adare village, with its thatched cottages, is just a two-minute walk away. The house is tastefully appointed and the bedrooms are exquisitely decorated, and provide Ballygowan water and sweets. Guests are well looked after here and can enjoy high standards with a taste of luxury at affordable prices. Excellent breakfasts are served in the bright, attractive dining room, and there is a conservatory lounge and an additional lounge with plenty of literature on the area and a good supply of books for browsing. Evening meals are not available here, but Agnes Fitzpatrick has menus of local restaurants available and is happy to suggest venues for evening meals. All the bedrooms are on the ground floor, and are suitable for the slightly less mobile. On pleasant days guests can enjoy a cup of tea on the patio.

OWNER Agnes Fitzpatrick ROOMS 2 double, 2 twin, 2 family; all en suite TERMS B&B IR£22.50; reduction for children; single supplement IR£12.50

ARDAGH

Reems House
Ardagh, Co. Limerick
Tel: 069 64276

This wonderful, elegant but cosy 400-year-old stone and brick house, with a large conservatory to the front of the house, is part of a working dairy farm. It is approached via a private drive, bordered by fields and mature trees, and has been in the family for four generations. The present owner, Tilly Curtin, is a delightful lady, who loves meeting people and always has a cheery smile for her guests. There is a large entrance hall, and a wide staircase leads to the bedrooms, which are furnished with antiques. The rose room is very large, and there are two other good-sized rooms; one has a bright cream décor, the other is blue and white. This is a superb place to stay; there are plenty of items of interest to pique guests' interest and there are rich carpets and drapes throughout the house. The lounge, where guests are greeted with a hot drink and sometimes homemade cakes on arrival, has a marble fireplace with a log fire and a piano. Breakfasts only are served, but there is a good choice of pubs and restaurants in Adare. A conservatory is also available. French and Irish are spoken.

OWNER Tilly Curtin OPEN April 1 – October 1 ROOMS 1 double, 1 twin, 1 family; 2 en suite TERMS B&B IR£20; reduction for children; single supplement IR£6.50

Clonunion House
Limerick Road, Adare, Co. Limerick
Tel: 061 396657

This traditional eighteenth-century farmhouse is 100 m off the main road in tranquil surroundings, and is part of a working sheep, deer, beef and tillage farm. At one time it was the stud farm belonging to Lord Dunraven, and interested guests can see the

Horse Cemetery, with its horseshoe-shaped headstones, where several famous stallions were buried. The house is furnished in keeping with its character; three bedrooms have the original fireplaces, and one a high bed. They are clean and comfortable. Deer now inhabit the paddocks and there is a viewing stone where interested guests can watch the fallow deer. Breakfast only is served, but there are plenty of venues for evening meals and Irish music in Adare, Ireland's prettiest village, which is just 2 km away. Visa, Access, American Express accepted.

OWNER Mary & Michael Fitzgerald OPEN April 1 – November 1 ROOMS 1 double, 1 twin, 1 family; all en suite TERMS B&B IR£18; reduction for children; no single supplement in single room

LIMERICK

Clonmacken House
Off Ennis Road, Limerick, Co. Limerick
Tel: 061 372007 Fax: 061 327785 E-mail: clonmack@indigo.ie

This large, purpose-built, attractive yellow-and-green-trim guest house stands in its own grounds in a quiet setting, yet is just five minutes' drive from Limerick City. Brid McDonald thoroughly enjoys her bed & breakfast business; guests receive a warm welcome in this friendly and hospitable house. Excellent standards of décor prevail and the house is comfortably furnished. The bedrooms are standardised and have attractive rose-patterned duvets, and multichannel TV. The comfortable lounge has soft furnishings and dainty wallpapers. Bunratty Castle is a 10-minute drive and Shannon Airport is a 15-minute drive. Breakfast only is served, but a pub serving evening meals is just 200 m away. Visa, Mastercard accepted.

OWNER Brid & Gerald McDonald OPEN All year ROOMS 3 double, 3 twin, 2 family, 2 double/single; all en suite TERMS B&B IR£18–22.50; reduction for children; single supplement from IR£6

Trebor

Ennis Road, Limerick, Co. Limerick
Tel: 061 454632 Fax: 061 454632

Trebor, which is the name of the owner's son spelt backward, is a well maintained, comfortable turn-of-the-century townhouse. The bedrooms are spotless and tastefully decorated with colour-coordinated wallpapers and fabrics. Breakfast includes fresh-squeezed orange juice, muesli or porridge and homemade breads, followed by a cooked breakfast. Mrs Joan McSweeney takes excellent care of her guests and is happy to give advice on what to see and do in the area. Trebor is popular with cyclists. Drying facilities are available. Evening meals are available (vegetarian and special diets catered for) if arranged in advance. Access, Visa, Mastercard accepted.

OWNER Mrs Joan McSweeney OPEN April 1 – November 1 ROOMS 2 twin, 2 family; all en suite TERMS B&B IR£18; reduction for children; single supplement IR£5 MEALS Dinner

LISNAGRY

Willowbank

Lisnagry, Co. Limerick
Tel: 061 336553

Willowbank is a spacious dormer bungalow, standing in a quiet position on 18.5 hectares of land, which includes a private lake inhabited by swans. The large bedrooms are elegantly furnished, with fitted wardrobes and cheval mirrors. Excellent breakfasts are served in the tasteful dining room which overlooks the well-kept garden. Sean and Gertie Leonard have exacting standards and offer a touch of luxury in their bright and friendly home. Guests can enjoy walks around the lake, as well as other areas on the property, and there is fishing, boating, golfing and horseback riding close by. Plans have been applied for to build 10 additional en suite rooms. Self-catering apartments are available.

OWNER Gertie Leonard OPEN April 1 – October 1 ROOMS 2 double, 2 twin, single; 2 en suite TERMS B&B IR£20; reduction for children; single supplement IR£5

Ballingowan House
Newcastle West, Co. Limerick
Tel: 069 62341

This light and airy Georgian house, known to locals as the "pink house," stands back a good distance from the road behind a well-landscaped front garden. The bedrooms are quite spacious, are colourfully coordinated, and have multichannel TV. Two have a bath and shower and the rear rooms overlook peaceful countryside. One bedroom is on the ground floor. The lounge is bright with a blue and terra-cotta décor, interesting coving, and a marble fireplace. The conservatory area, which is full of colourful potted plants in summer, is a good spot in which to relax with a book and a cup of tea. Breakfast only is served at a large table, and tea is offered upon arrival and by request at other times. The owners are most accommodating and guests receive lots of personal attention; there is plenty of information on what to see and do in the area. Self-catering units are also available.

OWNER Carmel O'Brien OPEN All year, including Christmas ROOMS 2 double, 1 twin, 1 triple, 1 double/single; all en suite TERMS B&B IR£17; reduction for children; single supplement IR£3

COUNTY MAYO

County Mayo is a maritime county, with the Atlantic Ocean making deep inroads into its coastline on the west and on the north. The sea influences the shape of its beauty, from the long, narrow fjord of Killary Harbour to the island-studded Clew Bay. Castlebar is the country town of Mayo and a good centre for touring. The most interesting building in the town is that occupied by the art centre and the education centre. It was formerly a chapel, the cornerstone of which was laid by John Wesley in 1785.

Westport is a gem of a town. The architect is not known, although some locals believe him to be a French architect left behind from Humbert's expedition in 1798. The main feature is the Octagon, a fine piece of planning. In the centre stands a Doric pillar, mounted on an octagonal granite base, on which the statue of George Glendenning once stood.

Innisturk Island can be visited from Roonah Point. It is an exceptionally attractive island with a lovely harbour; there is a glorious beach on the south side.

Killary Harbour is a striking example of a fjord. Its 8 km cut deep into the surrounding mountains.

At Knock there is the Knock Fold Museum, which pays tribute to the area's forefathers. The collections and exhibitions on show help us to understand what life was like for our ancestors.

ACHILL ISLAND

Aquila
Saheens, Achill Sound, Achill Island, Co. Mayo
Tel: 098 45163

This cosy, clean, modern bungalow is situated in an elevated position, with magnificent views of Achill Sound and the Corraun Mountains. The bedrooms are well-appointed, prettily decorated and have comfortable beds. One very popular room is the converted attic room, but it is not for everyone, as the approach is via a very narrow staircase. There are four rooms on the ground floor. There is a comfortable sitting room and lounge with TV/VCR and an open turf fire. Cots are available. The house is located near three "Blue Flag" beaches. Self-catering is available.

OWNER Mrs Kay Sweeney OPEN March 1 – October 31 ROOMS 2 double, 1 twin, 1 family, 1 single; 4 en suite TERMS B&B IR£17; reduction for children; single supplement IR£6 MEALS Tea and scones

BALLINA

Ashley House
Ardoughan, Crossmolina Road, Ballina, Co. Mayo
Tel: 096 22799 Mobile: 088 2141889

Ashley House is an attractive, Georgian-style dormer bungalow situated off the main road and set in a beautifully landscaped garden, where guests are welcome to sit on fine days. It was established as a bed & breakfast over 11 years ago and has built a good reputation for offering a high standard of accommodation. The bedrooms are well-appointed and are all on the ground floor. Carmel Murray is a friendly lady with a good sense of humour. The dormer was converted several years ago into private quarters for the family. The owner's son is an enthusiastic fisherman and can advise guests on the best spots. Carmel is into dancing and could easily be persuaded to give guests a lesson and/or a demonstration. A self-catering unit is available. Visa, Mastercard, Access accepted.

OWNER Carmel Murray   OPEN March 1 – October 31   ROOMS 2 double, 1 twin, 1 family; all en suite   TERMS B&B IR£17; reduction for children; single supplement IR£5

Belvedere House
Foxford Road, Ballina, Co. Mayo
Tel: 096 22004

This spacious, modern two-storey house stands in its own grounds, a 10-minute walk from the town centre. The bedrooms are of a good size, are attractively decorated and clean and have orthopedic beds. There is a very large dining room and lounge with a TV and fireplaces. The owners are attentive and work hard to maintain the high standards. Breakfast only is served, but there are many fine eating places in the area. Ballina is situated on the lower reaches of the River Moy, directly between Lough Conn/Cullen and Killala Bay. Bicycles are available for hire locally. For guests who would like a day trip to Dublin, there is a good local bus service. Ballina is a bustling town and there are several venues where traditional Irish music can be heard.

OWNER Mary Reilly OPEN All year ROOMS 2 double, 2 twin, 2 family; 5 en suite TERMS B&B IR£17; reduction for children

The Hawthorns
Belderigg, Ballina, Co. Mayo
Tel: 096 43148

This clean and cosy bungalow stands in an open area with wonderful views of Ben Head and the Twang Mountains. There are cliff walks close by and the sea is a five-minute walk. Owner Carmel Hawthorn is a local lady who enjoys sharing her knowledge of the area with interested guests. The bedrooms, all on the ground floor, are spotlessly clean. The lounge has a turf fire, which is lit on cool days, and breakfasts, dinners and light meals are served in the bright dining room. Vegetarians can be catered for; all meals must be ordered in advance. This is a pleasant family home – the Hawthorns have three children. Self-catering is available. Baby-sitting can be arranged.

OWNER Carmel Hawthorn OPEN All year, including Christmas ROOMS 2 double, 1 twin; 2 en suite TERMS B&B IR£15; reduction for children; single supplement IR£5 MEALS Dinner, light meals

The Yellow Rose
Belderigg, Ballina, Co. Mayo
Tel: 096 43125

This bright, modest bungalow is in a remote spot with such spectacular views of the surrounding countryside, it is hard not to imagine you are sitting on top of the world. There is a prehistoric farm site within walking distance. The rooms are clean and comfortable – all are now en suite – and as the congenial and welcoming owners now have their own private quarters, the large dining room and TV lounge are exclusively for guests' use. Two of the bedrooms have views and look out on an impressive ruin in the distance. Excellent evening meals are served here and include home-baked breads, spring lamb and fresh wild salmon, courtesy of Stephen McHale, who is a fisherman. Situated 8 km from the Ceidi Fields Interpretative Centre, this is extremely good value accommodation. During the tourist season they are very busy; advance reservations recommended.

OWNER Mrs Eileen McHale OPEN All year ROOMS 1 double, 1 twin, 1 family; 2 en suite TERMS B&B IR£14; reduction for children; single supplement IR£4 MEALS Dinner

BALLINAMORE

Kingfisher Lodge

Mount Falcon, Foxford Road, Ballinamore, Co. Mayo
Tel: 096 22718 Fax: 096 22718

This family-owned charming country house stands in extensive grounds 6.5 km from Ballina. It is nestled between two mountain ranges and surrounded by unspoiled beaches. It opened in 1990 and has been successful since the beginning; many guests are repeat visitors. Kingfisher Lodge has fast become known as one of the premier guest houses in the area. There is a sitting room and reading room with a real fire. The bedrooms are beautifully decorated; one has a four-poster bed with a floral and lace canopy. This is exceptionally good value, the perfect combination of superb hosts, pleasant surroundings and comfortable accommodation. Kingfisher Lodge is an ideal base for anglers; Kevin Gallagher, a keen angler himself, will assist with all the arrangements for a fishing holiday and secure the correct permits. Ghillie service is available upon request. Freshly prepared, home-cooked modestly priced evening meals are available if arranged in advance. There are five golf courses in the area and Ballina is a lively town where traditional Irish music can be found most nights. Early reservations are recommended at this popular establishment.

OWNER Kevin & Bernadette Gallagher OPEN March 1 – September 30
ROOMS 2 double, 2 twin, 2 family; all en suite TERMS B&B IR£16; reduction for children; single supplement IR£9 MEALS Dinner

BALLYCASTLE

Ballyglass B&B

Ballycastle, Co. Mayo
Tel: 096 43343

This old stone house was totally gutted for the purpose of building a holiday home for the down-to-earth owners, Jim Hennelly and Carmel Kelleher, but with more tourists visiting this beautiful and interesting region, they opened the house as a bed & breakfast instead. This is good-value, clean, no fancy frills accommodation; the bedrooms are simply furnished. Jim cooks breakfast and takes care of guests, Carmel works outside the home, but helps out when she can. The dining room is adjacent to the cosy lounge with its turf fires. Jim also makes clocks from pine, yew and oak, which are on display, and are available for purchase. There are archeological digs going on and Jim will take interested people along to see them, and to the second tallest stone in Ireland, which is close by. An ideal spot from which to visit the Ceide Fields, Belderrig prehistoric farm, fifteenth-century Moyne abbey, or take a walk on the Western Way.

OWNER Jim Hennelly & Carmel Kelleher OPEN May 4 – October 1
ROOMS 2 double, 1 twin, 1 family; 2 en suite TERMS B&B IR£15;
reduction for children; single supplement IR£10

Keadyville
Carrowcubbic, Ballycastle, Co. Mayo
Tel: 096 43288

Keadyville is in a beautiful location overlooking Downpatrick Head and the sea. Mrs Kelly went into business as more tourists came to the area to visit the interpretative centre of the fascinating Ceide Fields, which are older than the pyramids. The top floor, all in pine, was added to the property in 1992 and a conservatory was added in 1997. The rooms are average in size and are clean and comfortable, and all offer scenic views. One bedroom is on the ground floor. The friendly owners are local people and greet guests with a cup of tea, and are happy to provide information on the area. There is a cosy lounge/dining room where a fire is lit on chilly days. Evening meals are available if pre-booked. There are self-catering units available.

OWNER Michael & Barbara Kelly OPEN All year ROOMS 2 double, 2
twin; all en suite TERMS B&B IR£20; reduction for children; single
supplement IR£5 MEALS Dinner

BANGOR

Hillcrest House
Main Street, Bangor, Co. Mayo
Tel: 097 83494

This is a modern, cosy bungalow, located in the centre of the village, very close to the Owenmore River. Mr and Mrs Cosgrove are a very congenial couple, and Mr Cosgrove was born in the village. The restaurant, which is part of the house, is very popular with the locals. Mrs Cosgrove, who does all the cooking, has built up an excellent reputation for providing good food. The bedrooms are comfortable and hot water bottles are provided. This is a popular spot with fishermen, with river and lake fishing close by.

OWNER Evelyn Cosgrove OPEN All year ROOMS 2 double, 2 twin
TERMS B&B IR£17; reduction for children; single supplement IR£5
MEALS Dinner, high tea

CASTLEBAR

Fort Villa House
Moneen, Castlebar, Co. Mayo
Tel: 094 21002 Fax: 094 24395

This Georgian house, although just off a roundabout, stands in $1/2$ hectare of grounds. The bedrooms are individually decorated, and have solid old-fashioned furniture; one has a high-back mahogany bed, which is of special interest. The house was built by the present owners' great grandmother and has always been in the family. There is a cosy guest lounge warmed by a gas fire and lots of china displayed on ceiling racks. There is a good choice for breakfast, which is served in the dining room, which has a beautifully carved, antique sideboard. The friendly owners, Patrick and Breeda Flannelly, enjoy chatting with their guests and are happy to provide information on what to see and do in the area. Visa, Access accepted.

OWNER Breeda Flannelly OPEN All year ROOMS 1 double, 2 twin, 2
family; all en suite TERMS B&B IR£17; reduction for children; single
supplement IR£5–7

CHARLESTOWN

Ashfort
Airport/Knock Road, Charlestown, Co. Mayo
Tel: 094 54706

Ashfort is an impressive two-storey Tudor-style house set off the road in spacious grounds. The bedrooms are well-appointed, and have rich wood furnishings. The house is decorated to a high standard throughout; there are plush carpets and a luxurious lounge for guests to relax in. This is an ideal base from which to explore the unspoiled area of the west of Ireland, and there are lots of things to see and do in the area. Owners Carol and Philip O'Gorman are a delightful couple who are always happy to assist guests with itinerary planning, and to make recommendations for evening meals. Guests are greeted with a hot drink upon arrival. The bedrooms are roomy and comfortable. Ashfort is modestly priced for the comfort and high standards found here; guests would be well advised to book in for several nights and use this as a base. Knock Airport is 3 km away and Knock Shrine is a 20-minute drive.

OWNER Carol & Philip O'Gorman   OPEN March 17 – October 31
ROOMS 2 family, 3 double/single; all en suite   TERMS B&B IR£17.50; reduction for children; single supplement IR£6.50

CROSSMOLINA

Kilmurray House
Crossmolina, Co. Mayo
Tel: 096 31227

Kilmurray House is a large, attractive, welcoming farmhouse on 22 hectares of dry stock farmland, beautifully situated under Nephin Mountain. It is hard to believe that the house was a ruin before Joe and Madge lovingly restored the interior, cleverly combining modern conveniences and a traditional setting. The original oak staircase and wooden doors have been retained, as has the fireplace in the lounge, made by a local craftsman. The house is the recipient of two awards: the "Farmhouse of the Year" and the

"BHS and Bord Fáilte Award." The bedrooms are large, tastefully decorated with matching fabrics and comfortably furnished. A turf fire burns brightly in the lounge on chilly days. It's an ideal base from which to explore this scenic area, and a fisherman's delight – the farm has its own boats for guests' use on Lough Conn. Breakfast only is served, but there are several restaurants and pubs in the area for evening meals. Very enjoyable Irish musical evenings are less than half a km away. The Heritage Museum for tracing ancestry is 2.5 km away. Baby-sitting is available.

OWNER Madge & Joe Moffat OPEN April 1 – October 30 ROOMS 2 double, 2 twin, 2 family, 2 single; 4 en suite TERMS B&B IR£17; reduction for children; single supplement IR£3

KILLALA

Gardenhill Farmhouse
Crossmolina Road, Killala, Co. Mayo
Tel: 096 32331 Fax: 096 32331

This is a large, modern farmhouse, set in 20 hectares of mixed farming, standing back off the road in a peaceful location. The spacious bedrooms are colour-coordinated and have tasteful furniture; one bedroom is on the ground floor. Owner Mary Nunnelly is a registered nurse, and an alternative medicine practitioner skilled in reflexology. The cosy lounge has an open fire and hearty breakfasts are served in the dining room, which overlooks the distant hills. Evening meals can be served, if pre-arranged, and feature tasty home cooking, with local salmon often on the menu. Tea making facilities are provided in the hallway. The Interpretative Centre for the Ceidi Fields is within an easy drive and there is golf, deep-sea and shore fishing and miles of sandy dunes and beaches at Killala Harbour.

OWNER Kevin & Mary Nunnelly OPEN May 1 – September 30 ROOMS 2 double, twin, 2 family, 1 single; all en suite TERMS B&B IR£17; reduction for children; single supplement IR£5 (high season only) MEALS Dinner

Ashford Manor
Claremorris Road, Knock, Co. Mayo
Tel: 094 88514

Ashford Manor is a large, attractive house with hanging baskets, potted plants, and leaded windows. The congenial owners, James and Mary Flatley, are a friendly couple who formerly ran an adjacent hotel prior to its conversion to a convent, and have been successfully running this establishment for seven years. The house is beautifully maintained and immaculately kept. The entryway has rich carpets, and the relaxing sitting room has tasteful furniture and rich red carpet. The bedrooms are of a good size and are well furnished. Breakfasts are excellent and are cooked on the Aga. On fine days guests can enjoy a cup of tea outside where seating is provided.

OWNER James & Mary Flatley OPEN March 1 – October ROOMS 2 double, 2 twin, 2 family; all en suite TERMS B&B from IR£15; reduction for children; single supplement IR£5

Drumeagles
Ballyhaunis, Knock, Co. Mayo
Tel: 094 88393

This large, spacious modern house is set back off the road in its own grounds. The house was built in 1990, but has some traditional features, such as interesting coving and ceiling roses. Kathleen Henry, who had a bed & breakfast in another residence, had this house specifically designed to ensure her guests had the finest accommodation in a comfortable and pleasant ambience. A mahogany staircase leads to the bright, colour-coordinated bedrooms, where there are rich fabrics, curtains and light pastel colours of peach, green and pink. Kathleen, a local lady, is happy to assist guests with itineraries and to make suggestions for evening meals. Guests are greeted with a hot drink upon arrival. The sitting room is pleasantly furnished and the house offers excellent value accommodation. It is just a pleasant seven minutes' walk to Knock Shrine and a 20-minute drive to the airport.

OWNER Kathleen Henry OPEN Easter – October 1 ROOMS 2 double, 3 twin, 1 family; all en suite TERMS B&B IR£17.50; reduction for children; single supplement IR£4.50

LISCARNEY

Moher House
Liscarney, Co. Mayo
Tel: 098 21360

Marion O'Malley is a delightful lady who knows just how to make her guests feel at home, offering a cup of tea and some of her delicious home-baked scones upon arrival. The bedrooms are clean with pretty duvets; there are electric blankets, hot water bottles, and the house has been freshly redecorated. Excellent breakfasts and dinners are served, using the best cuts of meat provided by Mr O'Malley, who is a local butcher. Vegetarian meals are served by request, dinners must be ordered in advance. There is a pleasant sitting room with an open fire where guests receive a complimentary Irish coffee after dinner. This is an ideal area for walking and there are four designated walks. The more adventurous can climb Croagh Patrick Mountain, with its magnificent view of 365 islands. Fishing is available in Moher Lake across the road from the house. Visa accepted.

OWNER Marion O'Malley OPEN March 1 – October 31 ROOMS 1 double, 2 twin, 1 family; 3 en suite TERMS B&B IR£17; reduction for children; single supplement IR£5 MEALS Dinner

LOUISBURGH

Rivervilla
Shraugh, Louisburgh, Co. Mayo
Tel: 098 66246 Fax: 098 66246

Rivervilla is a bungalow situated in a peaceful and secluded spot along the banks of the Runrowen River, on a 10-hectare sheep farm. Salmon and trout fishing are available as well as lovely riverside walks. A real home-away-from-home atmosphere pervades here, and home-baked breads are a feature. Modestly priced light meals and snacks are available, and guests are welcome to bring their own wine. The bedrooms are tastefully decorated; some have glorious views of Shreffy Mountain and Croagh Patrick. Of special interest is the Great Famine and Granville interpretive centre. There are some excellent places for evening meals in Louisburgh. Eurocard accepted.

OWNER Mary O'Malley OPEN April 1 – October 31, Christmas by arrangement ROOMS 1 double, twin, 1 family, 1 single; 2 en suite TERMS B&B IR£23; reduction for children; single supplement IR£5 MEALS Light snacks

NEWPORT

Loch Morchan
Kilbride, Newport, Co. Mayo
Tel: 098 41221

This old-style farmhouse is part of a working sheep and cattle farm situated in a quiet location with good views all round, just 10 minutes from Clew Bay. The house is fresh and bright, the bedrooms average in size with comfortable beds. One of the nicest things about Loch Morchan Farm is Mrs Chambers herself, a delightful lady who is a most caring and attentive host; the bed & breakfast was established over 19 years ago, with many guests returning for the special hospitality found here. There are several good eating establishments close by. The area is excellent for sea, river and lake fishing, with special rates for fishing groups. An 18-hole golf course is close by.

OWNER Celena Chambers OPEN May 1 – October 31 ROOMS 1 double, 1 twin, 2 family; 1 en suite TERMS B&B IR£15; reduction for children; single supplement IR£2

Altamont House

Ballinrobe Road, Westport, Co. Mayo
Tel: 098 25226

Altamont House is a pre-Famine wistaria-covered farmhouse situated within a five-minute walk of the town centre. The standards continue to improve at this pleasant, welcoming house; established as the first guest house in the area, it has built up an excellent reputation for offering good service at reasonable prices. The spotless bedrooms are prettily decorated, and the rooms to the rear of the house overlook the lovely garden, as does the lounge, which has an open fire. The prize-winning gardens are a popular spot with guests. A sun-lounge and patio has been added. Breakfasts are served in the attractive dining room, where a silver service is employed, and when possible there are fresh flowers on the table. Evening meals can be had at several good pubs and restaurants close by.

OWNER Mrs Rita Sheridan OPEN March 16 – November 16 ROOMS 2 double, 3 twin, 1 family, 2 double/single; 5 en suite TERMS B&B IR£17; reduction for children; single supplement IR£5

Brooklodge B&B

Deerpark East, Newport Road, Westport, Co. Mayo
Tel: 098 26654

This spacious house is situated in a quiet residential area 2.5 km from the town centre. This is a relaxed and friendly house, and guests are encouraged to make themselves at home. Owners Michael and Noreen Reddington are extremely pleasant, and early breakfast can be provided if required, or if you prefer, a cooked breakfast is available until 10 a.m. The lounge has a turf and coal fire in the restored Victorian fireplace, a pleasant spot in which to unwind after a busy day. The bedrooms are good-sized, have a soft pastel décor and are tastefully furnished. There is a good choice of pubs and restaurants in town, a five-minute walk away. Access, Visa, Mastercard accepted.

OWNER Michael & Noreen Reddington OPEN March 1 – October 30 ROOMS 4 twin; 2 en suite TERMS B&B IR£15–17; reduction for children; single supplement IR£5

Coral Reef

Lecanvey, Westport, Co. Mayo
Tel: 098 64814

Coral Reef is an attractive house standing in its own grounds. Located across from the beach, it has magnificent views of Clew Bay and is in the shadow of Croagh Patrick, where a pilgrimage climb takes place in July. This is a superb location with lovely walks close by. An added bonus is the wonderful, welcoming atmosphere created by the friendly owners. The house is well-furnished; three of the bedrooms are on the ground floor, while a further two are reached by a spiral staircase. Anne Colgan is a good cook and four-course evening meals are available if prearranged. All breads, cakes and desserts are homemade. There is an extensive breakfast menu, and a specialty of the house is the homemade health bread, the recipe of which has been taken to many parts of the world by satisfied guests. There is a cosy guest lounge. An Adventure Centre is within a three-minute walk and there is golf close by. Irish music can be heard most nights during the season and more restaurants have opened up in Lecanvey.

OWNER Anne Colgan   OPEN March 17 – October 15   ROOMS 4 double, 1 twin; 2 en suite   TERMS B&B IR£19; reduction for children; single supplement IR£3   MEALS Dinner

Riverbank House

Rosbeg, Westport Harbour, Westport, Co. Mayo
Tel: 098 25719

An inviting, spacious house with attractive black shutters, flower baskets and window boxes, situated in a peaceful spot adjacent to a river. The rooms are a good size and are clean and comfortable with modern furnishings. There is a relaxing guest lounge with an open fire. Kay O'Malley is pleased to help guests plan activities or day trips. Freshly prepared tasty breakfasts are served in the sunny dining room; evening meals are not available, but there are several choices for evening meals close by. Local amenities include shooting at the Tirawley Game Reserve, bathing, boating, trout and salmon fishing and golf. Visa, Mastercard accepted.

OWNER Kay O'Malley OPEN April 1 – October 30 ROOMS 4 double, 2 twin, 2 family; 6 en suite TERMS B&B IR£17; reduction for children; single supplement IR£5

Rosbeg Country House

Rosbeg, Westport, Co. Mayo
Tel: 098 25879 Fax: 098 25879

This eighteenth-century house with its friendly old-fashioned ambience is situated in a wonderful location on Clew Bay. Several original features remain, such as ceiling roses and casement shutters. Furnished with antiques, the spacious bedrooms are individually decorated with rich, warm, coordinated fabrics and wallpapers. The parlour-like lounge has sea views, as do some of the bedrooms. Kay O'Briain is a gracious host who has been welcoming guests into her inviting home for over 20 years. Breakfasts are served to the soft sounds of classical music. This is a wonderful place to relax and unwind; it is quiet and tranquil, and the only sound to be heard in the morning are the birds singing. Activities in the area include walks along the award-winning beaches, swimming, hill climbing and fishing. Venues for evening meals are within walking distance.

OWNER Kay O'Briain OPEN Easter – September ROOMS 3 double, 2 twin; all en suite TERMS B&B IR£20–25; single supplement IR£10

Seapoint House

Kilmeena, Westport, Co. Mayo
Tel: 098 41254 Fax: 098 41254

Seapoint House is situated in a beautiful, unspoiled setting overlooking an inlet of Clew Bay. Most of the rooms have views of the sea and mountains. There is a very large lounge and a fireplace, a reading room, and a tastefully decorated dining room, which leads out onto a sun porch. The bedrooms are functional and spotlessly clean and self-catering is available. Fishing, sailing, walking and an 18-hole golf course are available nearby and there is a pony for children to ride. Baby-sitting can usually be arranged. Visa, Mastercard accepted.

OWNER The O'Malley Family OPEN April 15 – October 15 ROOMS 2 double, 2 twin, 2 family; all en suite TERMS B&B IR£18; reduction for children; single supplement IR£5

COUNTY SLIGO

County Sligo is located in one of the most beautiful and least explored regions of Ireland, surrounded by rugged mountains and rolling hills. The landscape is a patchwork of picturesque lakes, lush forests and sparkling rivers, its coastline dotted with peaceful coves.

Sligo's seaside resorts stretch along the coast from Innishcrone to Mullaghmore, with sandy beaches, fishing, golfing, beautiful walks and horseback riding – there is so much to do in this uncrowded corner of Ireland.

Explore the Glenriff Horseshoe, the Ladies Brae, visit Lissadell House, and for the more adventurous, climb to the summit of Queen Maeve's Cairn.

Tour the loughs – Arrow, Gill, Easky, Gara, Glencar, Templehouse and Talt – and feast your eyes on Sligo's beauty.

W. B. Yeats, the poet, is buried at Drumcliffe. He called Sligo "The Land of Heart's Desire," and after you have visited, you will too.

BALLYMOTE

Temple House
Ballymote, Co. Sligo
Tel: 071 83329 Fax: 071 83808

Temple House is approached through an impressive gateway bordered by white iron railings. The drive meanders through parkland to this large Georgian mansion. It is set in 400 hectares of farmland and woodland, and there is a large garden where organic vegetables are grown for the evening meal. The estate has been in the Perceval family since 1665, the present house having been redesigned and refurnished in 1864. The entrance through a portico leads to a large entry hall with tiled floor and shooting gear. This in turn leads to a second, larger hall, off which is an enormous dining room and three sitting rooms, all with open fires. The larger room has lovely views over the garden to the lake and ruins of a castle built by the Knights Templar in 1200. The enormous bedrooms are furnished with antiques and family

portraits. Some have original bathroom fittings, curtains and carpets, etc., which consequently are faded and worn, but this all lends charm and atmosphere to the house. The Percevals are very friendly people. Mrs Perceval does all the cooking and Mr Perceval runs the farm, which is stocked with sheep, Kerry cattle and poultry, providing the kitchen with fresh meat, bacon, eggs, vegetables and fruit. Almost everything is home-grown and home-made, including yoghurt, jams and cream cheese. Evening meals, if pre-arranged, are served at 7:30 p.m. Please note Mr Perceval is chemically sensitive, so guests are asked to avoid all perfumed products. All credit cards except Diners.

OWNER Mrs D. Perceval OPEN April 1 – November 30 ROOMS 3 double, 1 twin, 1 single; 4 en suite TERMS B&B IR£40; reduction for children negotiable if sharing; single supplement IR£7 MEALS Dinner

CLIFFONEY

Villa Rosa
Bunduff, Cliffoney, Co. Sligo
Tel: 071 66173 Fax: 071 66173

This friendly family home has wonderful views of the Donegal Mountains and Bundoff Beach, and overlooks a bird sanctuary and megalithic tombs. The property is well maintained and is decorated to a high standard. It offers clean and comfortable accommodation. There is a TV lounge and an en suite bedroom on the ground floor. John McLoughlin is a qualified chef and has built up an excellent reputation for providing good food. Cookery and lace-making demonstrations are available for groups of six or more, and there are several sea and hill walks locally, as well as a nearby golf course and diving facilities. John and Beatrice pride themselves on the personal touch, doing everything possible to ensure guests enjoy their stay. Guests feel very much at home here. The house is nestled in its own grounds and the ever-changing scenery and views are superb. This is an excellent choice for folks looking for a peaceful and tranquil holiday. American Express, Visa, Eurocheque accepted.

OWNER Beatrice McLoughlin OPEN March 1 – October 31 ROOMS 2 double, 2 twin, 2 family; 4 en suite TERMS B&B IR£18; single supplement IR£7 MEALS Dinner

COOLLOONEY

Union Farm
Coollooney, Co. Sligo
Tel: 071 67136

This 300-year-old house, painted pale blue, stands in a very neat front garden in quiet, peaceful countryside and has lovely views. The house is part of a 20-hectare cattle farm and is well kept, with an old-fashioned parlour-like lounge, which has a piano and TV. There is a separate dining room where freshly prepared, tasty breakfasts are served. Low doorways and thick walls abound, and the small, spotlessly clean bedrooms are modestly furnished. Evening meals or high tea are served at 7 p.m. if arranged in advance. Union Farm offers good value accommodation and fishing is available on the property, which is inhabited by sheep and swans.

OWNER Des & Tess Lang OPEN March 1 – October 15 ROOMS 1 double, 2 twin, 1 single, 1 triple; 2 en suite TERMS B&B IR£16; reduction for children 20%; single supplement IR£2 MEALS Dinner

Benbulben Farm

Drumcliffe, Co. Sligo
Tel: 071 63211 Fax: 071 73009

This large, modern house nestles in the foothills of Benbulben Mountain in a well tended landscaped garden, surrounded by a 36-hectare sheep farm. There are unparalleled views and 250 square kilometres of beautiful Yeats country – his last resting place is Drumcliffe churchyard, which is within view of the farm. This is very much a family home, and the Hennigans are very congenial people, offering a hospitality tray upon arrival. The rooms are spotlessly clean and simply furnished with fitted wardrobes and firm beds, and most have views. This is perfect walking country (there is a nature walk on the farm), and there are 30 mapped hill walks in the vicinity. Transport can be arranged to take visitors to starting points and back to base in the evening. If you're looking for a tranquil holiday, you may wander round the farm, visit the small museum on the property and enjoy some local lane walks. There is a TV lounge and a bright dining room where breakfasts, light meals and pre-arranged dinners are served. There is no licence but guests are welcome to bring their own wine. Sligo also has some fine examples of early megalithic tombs. Benbulben Farm would be a good choice from which to explore this scenic area. Visa, Mastercard, Eurocheque accepted.

OWNER The Hennigan Family   OPEN All year   ROOMS 2 double, 2 twin, 2 family; 5 en suite   TERMS B&B IR£17.50; single supplement IR£7.50   MEALS Dinner, light meals

Urlar House

Drumcliffe, Co. Sligo
Tel: 071 63110

This Georgian house is approached up a private drive in a peaceful location. The house is spacious and well maintained. The TV lounge has an original marble fireplace and two archways with the original Wedgwood figure design. The bedrooms vary in size; there is a family suite, consisting of double and twin rooms with en suite facilities, that is ideal for friends or family travelling together. Mrs

Healy is the proud recipient of the northwest Agri-Tourism Award and a Galtee Breakfast Award. Excellent breakfasts are served family-style on a large antique table, and consist of yoghurts, stuffed pancakes, omelettes, or a traditional Irish breakfast. There is an enclosed sun porch for the children to play in, which leads out onto the garden.

OWNER Mrs Healy OPEN April – October ROOMS 2 double, 2 twin, 1 family, 1 single; 2 en suite TERMS B&B IR£19; reduction for children 25%; single supplement IR£6

RIVERSTOWN

Coopershill
Riverstown, Co. Sligo
Tel: 071 65108 Fax: 071 65108 E-mail: ohara@coopershill.com

Approached through parks and woodland, a long drive winds its way to this Georgian mansion, which has been home to the O'Hara family for seven generations since it was built in 1774. Peacocks strut on the front lawn and there are splendid views over woods, hills and the River Arrow, which runs through the property. The house has been restored by the present owners to an extremely high standard, without in any way detracting from its ambience. Much of the furniture is original, family portraits adorn the walls and the rooms are extremely large and luxurious. Candlelit dinners are served in the elegant dining room, which has enormous sideboards with gleaming family silver. There is a lounge and a spacious drawing room with a log fire. Five of the bedrooms have four-poster or canopy beds. Walks can be taken on the 200-hectare estate, where there is an abundance of wildlife. Coarse fishing is available on the River Arrow, and a boat is available for trout fishing on nearby Lough Arrow. There is a championship golf course nearby, beautiful uncrowded beaches and megalithic monuments. If you are looking for somewhere to stay for a special occasion, Coopershill would be an excellent choice.

OWNER Brian & Lindy O'Hara OPEN April 1 – October 31 ROOMS 7 double, 5 twin; 7 en suite TERMS B&B IR£46–53; reduction for children negotiable; single supplement IR£10 MEALS Dinner, afternoon teas

Ross House

Riverstown, Co. Sligo
Tel: 071 65140 / 65787 Fax: 071 65140

This 100-year-old country house in peaceful surroundings is approached down a quiet country lane. Mrs Hill-Wilkinson is a friendly woman who enjoys baking and welcomes guests into her kitchen. Home cooked meals are available on request from 7.30 pm and a cup of tea is available later in the evening. It is a simple, comfortable family home. Guests have use of a TV lounge with a turf fire. One of the bedrooms is small; the other three are average in size, clean and comfortable. There are two large en-suite bedrooms on the ground floor, suitable for guests with disabilities. There is a tennis court for guests' use. This is a wonderful place for children; there is a donkey, hay-making and cattle on this mixed 48-hectare farm. Many visitors come to Lough Arrow for the fishing. Fishermen can hire boats, tackle and engines at the farm. There are beautiful beaches close by and many ancient monuments to visit throughout County Sligo: in Carrowmore, Carrowkeel, Creevykeel and Deerpark.

OWNER Nicholas & Oriel Hill-Wilkinson   OPEN March – November
ROOMS 1 double, 2 twin, 2 family, 1 single; 2 en suite   TERMS B&B
IR£22; reduction for children 20%; single supplement IR£5   MEALS
Dinner

SLIGO

Aisling

Cairns Hill, Sligo, Co. Sligo
Tel: 071 60704

This immaculate bungalow, whose name means "Irish Dream," stands in its own grounds in an elevated location on the south side of Sligo. The bedrooms are average in size and are comfortably furnished. They are all on the ground floor and now have TVs and dressing gowns. Des and Nan are a very congenial and accommodating couple who work together as a team. Nan cooks breakfast while Des enjoys chatting with guests and helping them plan daily activities. Breakfast only is served, but there are plenty of eating establishments in Sligo. There is a comfortable lounge with a coal fire.

OWNER Des & Nan Faul OPEN All year ROOMS 2 double, 2 twin, 1 family; 3 en suite TERMS B&B IR£16–17.50; single supplement IR£5

Lissadell
Mail Coach Road, Sligo, Co. Sligo
Tel: 071 61937

This purpose-built, new home is within walking distance of the town centre and offers a high standard of accommodation. The rooms are of a good size, well furnished and tastefully decorated. Mary formerly ran a bed & breakfast establishment by the same name in the area for several years and brings her expertise to this new property. Mary is friendly and accommodating and is willing to help her guests in every way to ensure they have a comfortable stay. Freshly prepared breakfasts only are served, but there are several establishments within walking distance for evening meals. Lissadell is a good base from which to explore Yeats' country.

OWNER Mary Cadden OPEN All year ROOMS 2 double, 1 twin; all en suite TERMS B&B IR£17.50; reduction for children

Tree Tops
Cleveragh Road, Sligo, Co. Sligo
Tel: 071 60160 Fax: 071 62301

This well maintained, spacious, modern, attractive house stands in a secluded location with a pretty garden and fishpond just eight minutes' walk from the town centre. The immaculate bedrooms are large, tastefully decorated, well furnished and have orthopedic beds. There is a collection of prints and paintings on display. Wholesome breakfasts are served in the dining room/lounge, which has period furniture. There are some lovely walks and views close by. Tree Tops would be a good choice as a base from which to explore this interesting area.

OWNER Ronan & Doreen MacEvilly OPEN January 15 – December 15 ROOMS 2 double, 3 family; all en suite TERMS B&B IR£18; reduction for children 20%; single supplement IR£6.50

TOBERCURRY

Cruckawn House

Ballymote Road, Tobercurry, Co. Sligo
Tel: 071 85188 Fax: 071 85188

This friendly, welcoming home is set back off the road and stands in its own grounds overlooking a golf course; there are clubs and caddies for hire, and the green fees are moderate. Maeve Walsh is a friendly, outgoing lady who knows how to make her guests feel at home, and greets them with a complimentary hospitality tray. Maeve is also director of the North West Tourism Organisation and an expert on local attractions. The rooms are a little small, but are spotlessly clean and comfortable. There is a pleasant TV lounge and a separate dining room where freshly prepared, substantial breakfasts are served. Evening meals are no longer served, but there are several establishments close by for evening meals. Separating the dining room from a small sun lounge are sliding glass doors with the family crests of the owners' families engraved in the middle of each door. Laundry facilities are provided. Local amenities include salmon and trout fishing, game shooting, mountain climbing, horseback riding and pony trekking. Tubbercurry is quite a lively place, where traditional Irish music and dance can be enjoyed Tuesday and Thursday and on weekends from May to September. Visa, Access, Mastercard accepted.

OWNER Joe & Maeve Walsh OPEN March – October ROOMS 2 double, 2 twin, 1 family; all en suite TERMS B&B IR£17.50; reduction for children 33%; single supplement IR£7.50

Pine Grove

Ballina Road, Tobercurry, Co. Sligo
Tel: 071 85235

This attractive, large house has been repainted white and green and has had Georgian-style windows installed. It stands in a pretty front garden on the edge of town on the Ballina Road. Mrs Kelly is a good cook and caters for nonresidents for lunch as well as evening meals, served in a large dining room overlooking a patio. Breakfasts are substantial and will set you up for the day. The house is simply furnished with old-fashioned furniture. There is a

TV lounge with an open fire. There is no licence, but guests are welcome to bring their own wine. This is a popular venue and early reservations are recommended. On pleasant days guests are welcome to make use of the garden.

OWNER Teresa Kelly OPEN All year ROOMS 1 double, 2 twin, 2 family; all en suite TERMS B&B IR£17.50; reduction for children 33%; single supplement IR£7 MEALS Dinner

The Midlands

COUNTY CARLOW

One of the smallest counties in Ireland, Carlow lies just below Wicklow and is in an area of rich farmland.

The county town, Carlow, has had an eventful history, which includes being captured by Cromwell in 1650. Now the town manufactures beet sugar and has quite a few noteworthy sights, including the ruin of a Norman castle, a Gothic Revival Catholic church, the Carlow Museum and the fine courthouse with a Doric portico fashioned after the Parthenon.

There is a ruined twelfth-century church at Killeshin, with a fine Romanesque doorway, and fourteenth-century Ballymoon Castle, which has apparently never been occupied.

BAGENALSTOWN

Lorum Old Rectory
Kilgreaney, Bagenalstown, Co. Carlow
Tel: 0503 75282

Dating from the eighteenth century, Lorum Old Rectory is set in 7.5 hectares nestling beneath the Blackstairs Mountains. It is surrounded by open countryside, with views as far as Tipperary.

There are plenty of animals about, including goats, horses, dogs, a peacock and Jacob sheep. The bedrooms are spacious, furnished with antiques, and all have their original fireplaces, hairdryers, telephones and tea and coffee making facilities. Five-course imaginative dinners are available, by prior arrangement, with home-grown organic vegetables. The tiny smoking room with a fireplace is the only room where smoking is allowed. There is a comfortable, informal atmosphere, and Don and Bobbie Smith are a friendly couple. Don likes to organise cycling holidays, which include cycle hire, airport pickup and daily baggage transportation. Work has been carried out on the garden recently and guests have use of a croquet lawn. No pets. The Old Rectory is 6.5 km from Bagenalstown on the Borris Road, the R705. Access, Mastercard, Visa, American Express accepted.

OWNER Bobbie & Don Smith   OPEN January 1 – December 20
ROOMS 4 double, 1 twin; all en suite   TERMS B&B IR£30; reduction for children; single supplement IR£10   MEALS Dinner IR£20

BALLON

Sherwood Park House
Kilbride, Ballon, Co. Carlow
Tel: 0503 59117 Fax: 0503 59355   E-mail: sherwoodpark@indigo.ie

This lovely Georgian house is set in peaceful countryside. It has a large garden and pleasant views. Patrick and Maureen Owens are a most welcoming, gentle couple and have friendly dogs. Sherwood Park has an especially beautiful winding staircase, and an unusual raised hallway features an old, flat-topped piano. The drawing room also has a piano, and excellent five-course dinners, by arrangement, are elegantly served by candlelight in the very large dining room. The bedrooms are spacious and comfortable and have some lovely furniture, including several four-poster beds. Families are well catered for, and most of the rooms have private bathrooms with both showers and baths. They each have hairdryer, trouser press and tea and coffee making facilities. Altamont Gardens are nearby, and golf, fishing and riding can be enjoyed locally. No pets. The house is just off the N80.

OWNER Patrick & Maureen Owens OPEN All year ROOMS 2 double, 3 family; 2 en suite TERMS B&B IR£25; reduction for children; single supplement IR£5 MEALS Dinner IR£20

BORRIS

Step House
Main Street, Borris, Co. Carlow
Tel: 0503 73209 Fax: 0503 73395

This early Georgian town house stands right in the centre of Borris. It was originally the dower house to the castle, the entrance gates to which are on the opposite side of the street. It is heavily decorated and furnished with a lot of pieces, some of which are antiques. Both the drawing room and the dining room, which leads from it, have ornate fireplaces. Most of the bedrooms, all with TVs, lie at the back of the house, some with nice views, and one has a four-poster bed. Borris is close to the Leinster Way and there are great walks along the River Barrow. No pets and no smoking in the bedrooms. Not suitable for children. Visa, Mastercard accepted.

OWNER Cait & James Coady OPEN Closed January ROOMS 2 double, 2 twin, 1 four-poster; all en suite TERMS B&B IR£25–35; single supplement

CARLOW

Barrowville Town House
Kilkenny Road, Carlow, Co. Carlow
Tel: 0503 43324 Fax: 0503 41953

A friendly welcome, professional service and comfort in a lovely in-town setting are what visitors can expect at this attractive, eighteenth-century town house. The Dempseys, experienced in hotel ownership, did the whole house up (which was a major undertaking), and created a place of elegance and comfort. The en suite bedrooms have hairdryers, telephones, TVs, shoe shine and tea and coffee making facilities. Exquisitely presented, sumptuous breakfasts are served in the attractive conservatory overlooking the lovely, private back garden. There is also a small TV lounge. Barrowville is on the main Kilkenny road, just a three-minute walk from the centre of town. Pets outside only. Smoking is permitted in the TV lounge. Visa, Mastercard, Access, American Express accepted.

OWNER Randal & Marie Dempsey OPEN All year ROOMS 2 double, 2 twin, 2 family, 1 single; 5 with bath or shower, 2 with shower en suite TERMS B&B IR£20–23; single supplement IR£4.50–5.50

COUNTY CAVAN

Cavan is an undiscovered county, an angler's delight with its unlimited opportunities for coarse and game fishing. Large areas of Cavan seem to have more water than land. The undulating landscape and picturesque settings are dotted with wooded islands providing much of the county's delightful scenery. There is plenty to see and do, including a museum in Virginia, which has 3,000 items dating back to 1700. Saint Killian's Heritage Centre and Fore Abbey are other sites of interest. Cavan Crystal can be bought in the factory shop on the outskirts of Cavan town. Derragara Museum is situated on the Annalee River, and exhibits a full-size mud and wattle homestead.

MOUNTNUGENT

Ross Castle
Mountnugent, Co. Cavan
Tel: 049 40237

This fascinating castle is situated amidst majestic trees and has magnificent views of Lough Sheelin, a lake famous for its brown trout. The castle was built in the sixteenth century, and later fell into a derelict condition. It was restored in 1864 by Anna Maria O'Reilly, a lineal descendant of Myles O'Reilly (known as "The Slasher"), who used the tower in the castle the night before being killed by Oliver Cromwell's troops.

It has a fascinating history and offers unique and interesting accommodation. It is entered through a gateway to an inner courtyard and surrounded by a stone wall. On the ground floor is a large entrance hall connecting the tower and the sitting room. There is an open fireplace, and French windows offer a beautiful view across the lake. One double bedroom has access to its own terrace. The tower is ideal for friends or family travelling together; there are two double en suite bedrooms, plus an additional toilet, and a sitting room – access is by 65 winding stone steps. The rooms are furnished with antiques and the ambience is peaceful. Teamakers are available in the sitting room and evening meals can be taken at nearby Ross House. In addition, guests are able to make use of the rest of the facilities such as boat hire, tennis court, sauna and jacuzzi for a modest charge. A self-catering cottage is also available. This is exceptionally good value accommodation and early reservations are highly recommended. Visa, Mastercard, Eurocheque accepted.

OWNER Viola Harkort OPEN All year ROOMS 1 double, 2 twin, 1 family; 4 en suite TERMS B&B IR£20; children under 3 free, under 12, 30% reduction; single supplement IR£10

Ross House
Mountnugent, Co. Cavan
Tel: 049 40218 Fax: 049 40218

This charming, Virginia creeper–covered old manor house dates from the 1600s and stands in beautiful grounds on the shores of Lough Sheelin. It was built as a dormer House and belonged to the Nugent family, who were the Lords of Delvin. Guests have access to a sandy beach and a private pier with boats for hire. In addition, this 145-hectare farm offers pony trekking, a horseback riding arena and a tennis court. The spacious bedrooms, centred around the courtyard, are in the tastefully restored carriage houses. They have antique furniture, and three rooms have a conservatory and four have their own fireplace. After a busy day sightseeing, guests may, for a modest charge, enjoy the sauna and/or jacuzzi. This is a wonderful place and must be one of the best value bed & breakfast properties in Ireland. A Christmas package is available, but very early reservations are essential. Ulla Harkort is a very congenial and accommodating host. Delicious four-course dinners are prepared, if ordered in advance, using fresh produce and local meats; vegetarian and light dinners are also available. If you are looking for high standards, good food and a tranquil setting with lots of old-world charm, then Ross House should be your first choice. Visa, Mastercard, Eurocheque accepted.

OWNER Petger & Ulla Harkort OPEN All year, including Christmas ROOMS 1 double, 2 single, 5 double/single; all en suite TERMS B&B IR£20; reduction for children – free up to 2 years, 30% thereafter; single supplement IR£5 MEALS Dinner, lighter meal

VIRGINIA

The White House
Oldcastle Road, Virginia, Co. Cavan
Tel: 049 47515

This warm, traditional-style house is in a lovely situation adjacent to the beautiful Deerpark Lakeland Forest, a well-known spot for hiking, horseback riding, golfing, fishing and water sports. It stands in a large garden where there is a display of old farming implements from Mr McHugo's father's farm in Galway. The bedrooms are clean and tidy with bright wallpapers and comfortable beds. There is a conservatory and lounge for guests' use. Breakfasts are excellent and feature smoked salmon and scrambled eggs, fresh fruits and yoghurts or a full Irish breakfast. Emily pampers her guests, with nothing being too much trouble to ensure their stay is comfortable. This is a popular venue for fishermen and tourists. Cavan has 365 lakes, one for every day of the year, so if fishing is your interest you have come to the right place! A visit to Cavan Crystal is worthwhile and the local museum has 3,000 items dating back to 1700.

OWNER Emily McHugo OPEN All year ROOMS 2 double, 1 twin, 1 family; all en suite TERMS B&B IR£18; reduction for children 50%; single supplement IR£3–5

COUNTY KILDARE

County Kildare is famous for horse breeding and training, which takes place on the Curragh, a great plain leading into a boggy area, the Bog of Allen. Many horse-race meetings are held here, including the Irish Sweep Derby, the Irish 2000 Guineas, the Irish Oaks and the Irish St Leger. The town of Kildare is the centre for horse breeding and has a well-preserved Church of Ireland cathedral and round tower.

At Robertstown, the eighteenth-century buildings along the Grand Canal have been restored to look as they did when this was a great water thoroughfare. Here is it possible to visit Europe's largest falconry. Two of Ireland's greatest Georgian houses, Carton and Castletown, are located at Cellbridge. A music festival takes place in June at Castletown, as does one of the hunt balls held during the Dublin Horse Show week.

The very pretty village of Leixlip has many associations with the Guinness family; the twelfth-century Norman castle belongs to Desmond Guinness.

Remains of a Franciscan Abbey can be seen at Castledermot, and Athy has many historic sights worth exploring, including the sixteenth-century Woodstock Castle, just out of town. Moone High Cross, one of Ireland's most beautiful high crosses, is at Moone Abbey, 12 km from Athy.

ATHY

Ballindrum Farm
Athy, Co. Kildare
Tel: 0507 26294 Fax: 0507 26294 E-mail: ballindrumfarm@tinet.ie

In a truly rural setting, Ballindrum Farm, a small modern house, is set in pleasant farming countryside, and reached down a series of country lanes. Luckily the house is well signposted from whichever direction travellers come! Mary Gorman is a cheerful, hardworking young mother, and keeps an immaculate house. The bedrooms are on the small side and all have showers, except one that has the original bathroom of the house. The sitting room opens up into the conservatory, which has table tennis and snooker. There are swings in the garden. Breakfast and high tea, or dinner, by arrangement, are served in the dining room, and the enormous kitchen is set up with big tables for coach parties, who call here for morning/afternoon tea and scones. Tea and coffee making facilities are available on the landing for use at any time. Ballindrum is part of a working dairy farm, and guests are more than welcome to watch the cows being milked. No pets and no smoking in the bedrooms. Visa, Mastercard accepted.

OWNER Mary & Vincent Gorman OPEN April 1 – October 31 ROOMS 1 double, 2 twin, 1 family, 1 single; 4 en suite TERMS B&B IR£17; reduction for children; single supplement IR£6.50 MEALS Dinner IR£12, high tea £IR8

Tonlegee House & Restaurant
Athy, Co. Kildare
Tel: 0507 31473 Fax: 0507 31473

Set in a quiet country position, Tonlegee House was built around 1790 and stands in 2 hectares of grounds, which are currently being landscaped. Mark and Marjorie did a great job restoring the house, which previously had been flatlets, into a place of character and comfort. The drawing room is especially large and pleasant, and the bar has nice old furniture and prints. The nine en suite bedrooms are comfortable and attractively decorated and have TVs, telephones and mineral water. Tea or coffee is served upon arrival. However, it is the food that draws people here. Mark does the cooking, almost single-handedly, which is quite a task as he makes everything possible himself, including pastas, breads and pastries. Organic vegetables and salads come from the walled garden, and fresh fish and game are specialities. Tonlegee is signposted off the Castlecomer to Kilkenny road. Visa, Access, American Express accepted.

OWNER Mark & Marjorie Molloy OPEN Closed first 2 weeks of November, Christmas ROOMS 6 double, 3 twin; all en suite TERMS B&B from IR£32.50; reduction for children; single supplement IR£12.50 MEALS Dinner

Griesemount
Ballitore, Co. Kildare
Tel: 0507 23158

This small Georgian house lies just off the N9 and has lovely views to the ruined mill on the river Griese, which is a well-known trout stream. Griesemount is a comfortable, informal house full of pictures, books and flowers. The rooms are large and the principal guest room has a four-poster bed. They all have hairdryer and tea making facilities. The attractive whitewashed building at the back of the house is the workshop where Carolyn decorates pots and watering cans, etc. – a great idea for presents. The house is just outside the historic Quaker village of Ballitore, and is an ideal centre for racing and golf.

OWNER Robert & Carolyn Ashe OPEN mid-February – mid-November
ROOMS 2 double, 1 twin; 1 en suite TERMS B&B IR£20–25; reduction for children; single supplement IR£5

CASTLEDERMOT

Kilkea Lodge Farm

Castledermot, Co. Kildare

Tel: 0503 45112 Fax: 0503 45112

Kilkea Lodge, which has belonged to the Greene family since 1740, is approached down a long driveway and is set in rolling parkland with a pleasant, rural aspect. Marion runs the riding centre, offering a variety of instructional and fun holidays, and Godfrey runs the 105-hectare farm. It is very much a family home, a typical old country house with guests sharing some of the facilities with family members, and it has a relaxed, informal atmosphere. The comfortable drawing room has a piano and fireplace, and traditional food is served in the dining room. The family room is an enormous studio, converted from an old barn, with its own entrance, four beds, a small loft and a sitting area in the middle – ideal for families or small groups. Kilkea Lodge is suited to those who enjoy country life. Pets outside only, and no smoking in the bedrooms. American Express accepted.

OWNER Marion & Godfrey Greene   OPEN February – December
ROOMS 3 double, 1 twin, 1 family, 1 single; 2 en suite   TERMS B&B
IR£30; reduction for children; single supplement IR£10 MEALS Dinner
IR£15–20

CELBRIDGE

Springfield

Celbridge, Co. Kildare

Tel: 01 627 3248 / 628 8254 Fax: 01 627 3123

This substantial Georgian house with Victorian flavours is set in 5 hectares of fields and gardens with horses, dogs and cats. It was the childhood home of Aidan Higgins and is referred to in his book *Langrish, Go Down,* and was at one time gutted by fire and rebuilt following the original plans. The house is luxuriously decorated with six large en suite bedrooms. There is one family room up a narrow spiral staircase, and another has four bunk beds. The master bedroom has a stereo system, jacuzzi for two, a shower with two jets, and an extra large four-poster bed. All rooms have TVs, video, telephone, hairdryers and tea and coffee making facilities. Libby has six children, and welcomes families. Visiting children muck in with the family and are fed all together in the enormous kitchen, which was originally the old milking rooms and is also available to guests for take-out food, etc. Breakfast is served in the traditional dining room at one large table, or after 12 in the kitchen. There is a selection of 150 videos, a 1 km track in front of the house for runners, and exercise machines. No pets. For directions from Celbridge, cross the Liffey bridge, keep left and follow the main road south for about 2 km. The house is on the right behind electronically controlled gates. Access, Visa, American Express accepted.

OWNER Libby Sheehy OPEN All year ROOMS 4 double, 3 family; 6 en suite TERMS B&B IR£35–125; reduction for children; single supplement

KILDARE

Fremont
Tully Road, Kildare, Co. Kildare
Tel: 045 521604

Fremont is a modern bungalow in a private setting, three minutes' walk to the town centre and the twelfth-century cathedral. The house is in good decorative order, and the ground floor bedrooms are spotlessly clean, with modern furnishings and shower units. The comfortable TV lounge has a Leitrim stone fireplace and there is a display of Waterford, Galway and Cavan crystal in the bright dining room. Mrs O'Connell is a considerate host who enjoys meeting people, and she extends a warm welcome to everyone. The Irish Stud and Japanese Gardens can be reached in 15 minutes on foot. Fremont is signposted from the centre of town. Pets outside only and smoking is allowed in the TV lounge.

OWNER Mrs Frieda O'Connell OPEN March 17 – October 30 ROOMS 2 double, 1 twin TERMS B&B IR£17; reduction for children; single supplement IR£5

Mount Ruadhan

Old Road, Kildare, Co. Kildare
Tel: 045 521637

Mount Ruadhan, signposted at the only set of traffic lights in central Kildare, is a bungalow surrounded by landscaped gardens. The house has a lot of decoration and is a bit dark with a tiled floor. The bedrooms are all on the ground floor and have hairdryers and tea making facilities. The owners are always on hand to answer questions or make a pot of tea. Mount Ruadhan is only 2 km from the centre of town, and is close to the Japanese Gardens and the Irish National Stud. Pets outside only, and no smoking.

OWNER Eileen Corcoran OPEN March 1 – November 30 ROOMS 1 double, 1 twin, 1 triple; 2 en suite TERMS B&B IR£23–31.50; reduction for children; single supplement IR£5

MAYNOOTH

Moyglare Manor

Maynooth, Co. Kildare
Tel: 01 628 6351 Fax: 01 628 5405 E-mail: moyglare@iol.ie

A lovely long driveway flanked by majestic trees, with horses and sheep grazing in fenced fields to each side, leads to this impressive eighteenth-century stone-built mansion. Inside there are a series of small reception rooms and hallways stuffed with antique furniture, ornaments and flowers, giving it a rather dark and sombre air. The bedrooms are spacious, comfortable and well-equipped with hairdryers, telephones and mineral water. The cuisine at Moyglare attracts many visitors. Beautifully presented food is served in the two elegant dining rooms by candlelight, and there is an extensive wine list. Small conferences can be catered for. There are several golf courses in the vicinity, and riding and hunting can be arranged. Moyglare is the nearest country house hotel to the airport. All major credit cards accepted.

OWNER Norah Devlin OPEN Closed at Christmas ROOMS 16 twin or double, 1 suite; all en suite TERMS B&B from IR£75; single supplement IR£20 MEALS Dinner from IR£27.50

Windgate Lodge
Barberstown, Straffan, Maynooth, Co. Kildare
Tel: 01 627 3415

This attractive, modern, red brick house is set back off the road in half a hectare of landscaped gardens. The house is in good decorative order, and there are two bedrooms on the ground floor. Pat Ryan is a friendly lady and is always eager to offer assistance to guests. Good home-cooked breakfasts are served in the dining room, and there is a TV lounge. A self-catering unit is also available. With the new motorway all the way to the centre of Dublin, this is a good location for either Dublin or the airport. Cars can be left at the railway station 3 km away at Maynooth, from which there is a good train service into town, and buses also run frequently. Close by there are country walks, golf, riding, and a butterfly farm and steam museum. Smoking downstairs only. To reach Windgate Lodge from the N4 westbound take the Maynooth exit, turn left and the house is 5 km on the left.

OWNER Pat Ryan OPEN All year ROOMS 1 double, 2 twin, 1 family; 3 en suite TERMS B&B IR£24; reduction for children; single supplement IR£3 MEALS Dinner IR£12

MONASTEREVIN

Cloncarlin Farm House
Nurney Road, Monasterevin, Co. Kildare
Tel: 045 525722

This 200-year-old attractive house was built by Lord Drogheda to entertain his guests, and is reached up a long tree-lined driveway. It is set in pretty countryside in an elevated position, and is part of a 68-hectare, mixed farm. When the McGuinnesses bought it seven years ago it was pretty derelict. The comfortable bedrooms have pleasant views, and there is a lounge and dining room. Fishing is available on the Barrow River, and there are riding stables close by. The Japanese Gardens and National Stud are a 15-minute drive away. The house is signposted off the Dublin/Cork road.

OWNER Marie McGuinness OPEN February 1 – December 1 ROOMS 1 single, 5 double or twin; 2 en suite TERMS B&B IR£15–20; reduction for children; single supplement MEALS Dinner IR£11

NAAS

Setanta Farmhouse
Castlekeely, Caragh, Naas, Co. Kildare
Tel: 045 876481

Joan McLoughlin was born and reared on this 28-hectare beef farm. Her sister lives in the old original house which adjoins Setanta, and Joan built her own house in 1972. It is a small, modern bungalow, standing in pleasant farmland some 6 km from Naas. Joan is a very friendly, talkative lady and enjoys her guests. The accommodation is simple and basic and the lounge has a small open fire. Breakfast, which incudes free-range eggs, is a very flexible meal and can be served at any time to suit individual needs. No pets and smoking only in the lounge. Setanta is signposted from Naas, and can be found on the R409 going towards Galway.

OWNER Joan McLoughlin   OPEN March 1 – October 31   ROOMS 2 double, 1 family, 2 single; 3 shower en suite   TERMS B&B IR£17; reduction for children

STRAFFAN

Barberstown Castle
Straffan, Co. Kildare
Tel: 01 628 8157   Fax: 01 627 7027   E-mail: castleir@iol.ie

Dating from the early thirteenth century, this historic castle was one of the first great Irish country houses to open for guests, becoming a hotel in 1973. The castle keep is a venue for banquets, and larger groups of up to 150 people are entertained in the sixteenth-century banqueting hall. The Elizabethan part dates from the second half of the sixteenth century, and the Victorian house was built in the 1830s. It is said that a man is interred between the top of the stairs and the roof of the tower. His family did this to prevent their eviction as tenants, as the lease stated that if he was put underground, it would expire. The bedrooms are spacious and comfortable and each is individually decorated. All rooms have hairdryer, trouser press, telephone and TV.

Barberstown has a good reputation for its food, which is creative and beautifully served. It is an interesting and relaxing place to stay, within easy reach of Dublin and the airport. No pets. All major credit cards accepted.

OWNER Kenneth Healy OPEN All year ROOMS 20 double, 6 twin; all en suite TERMS B&B IR£66; reduction for children; single supplement IR£10 MEALS Dinner IR£29.50

THE CURRAGH

Martinstown House
The Curragh, Co. Kildare
Tel: 045 41269

This unusual house was built as a shooting lodge for the second Duke of Leinster, and was constructed in the "Strawberry Hill" Gothic style 200 years ago. It is set in 70 hectares of parklike grounds and farmland and has a wonderful walled garden full of flowers, fruit and vegetables, and a hard tennis court. At the back of the house is an unusual gothic stable yard. Mrs Long has had some interesting decoration done to the house recently. The entryway has a faux mural, giving one the feeling of the entrance to a church, and then opens out to countryside views. The house is very comfortably furnished with some lovely furniture in a simple, unfussy way. There is a smaller sitting room, and grander, more formal drawing room with a high, decorated ceiling. The bedrooms are spacious and the bathrooms newly tiled, one or two reached up a narrow winding staircase. Dinner, served in the attractive, intimate dining room and cooked by a French chef, is available if arranged in advance. No pets or small children and no smoking in the bedrooms. Martinstown House can be found from the N7 in Kildare by passing the Japanese Gardens, forking right and following the signs. All major cards accepted, except Diners Club.

OWNER Meryl Long OPEN Closed at Christmas & Easter ROOMS 2 double, 2 twin; 2 en suite TERMS B&B IR£50–60; single supplement by arrangement MEALS Dinner IR£28

COUNTY KILKENNY

Kilkenny, the county town, is one of the oldest and most interesting towns in Ireland. It comes alive at the end of August during the Kilkenny Festival, which is one of Ireland's foremost cultural festivals. Kilkenny Castle stands in the centre, dominating the town, and just opposite are the Kilkenny Design Centre workshops, which can be visited.

The cathedral stands on the site of a monastery built by St Canice in the sixth century and from which the city took its name. The Kilkenny Archaeological Society houses its collection in a most interesting Tudor merchant's house – Rothe House – and the City Hall, built in 1761, was formerly the Tolsel or Toll House. Some well-known writers, including Swift, Berkeley and Congreve, were educated at Kilkenny College, a fine Georgian building.

The Kilkenny countryside is pretty and compact, and places of interest to visit are the attractive town of Thomastown, near Dysart Castle, former home of George Berkeley, after whom the city and university in California, Berkeley, is named. Near to Callan on the King's River is Kells, a fortified, turreted and walled collection of early ecclesiastical buildings, and near Urlingford are the ruins of four castles.

CASTLECOMER

Wandesforde House
Castlecomer, Co. Kilkenny
Tel: 056 42441

Wandesforde House was built in 1824 by Lady Ann Ormonde as a school for the children of the Castlecomer estate. When the Flemings bought it in 1989 it was almost a ruin. They have cleverly united the whole building by enclosing the front porch behind glass and putting in a new front door. The two enormous school rooms with high ceilings to each side of the house have been converted into a sitting room/restaurant for guests, and into the family living quarters. The central area, where the teacher lived, has been altered to accommodate the bedrooms, which are comfortable and attractively decorated, each having tea making facilities. David is a trained chef, and interesting meals are available, if booked in advance. At the back of the house is a lovely conservatory, which leads onto a sunny patio. The Flemings have horses, and guests are welcome to bring their own. No pets and smoking in the conservatory only. Located 15 km from Kilkenny on the main Dublin road. Visa, Mastercard, Access accepted.

OWNER Phil & David Fleming   OPEN January 1 – December 21 ROOMS 3 double, 3 twin; all en suite   TERMS B&B IR£20; reduction for children; single supplement IR£5   MEALS Dinner IR£15, supper IR£10

FRESHFORD

Kilrush House
Freshford, Co. Kilkenny
Tel: 056 32236 Fax: 056 32588

Kilrush House stands in lawns, gardens and parklands, surrounded by its 100-hectare farm, which supports sheep and a few thoroughbred National Hunt mares. The St George family has lived at Kilrush for three centuries, and until the present house was built in 1810, they inhabited the old Tower House, which still stands. One of the features of the house is the graceful cupola that is set high above the hall, the circular landing on the first floor accentuating its lines. The dining and drawing rooms contain a collection of early nineteenth-century Irish furniture, and the enormous dining room has old, somewhat faded wallpaper dating from around 1820. Home-cooked dinners including vegetables, lamb and free-range pork from the farm are available if booked in advance. There is a hard tennis court, pleasant walks through the garden and parkland, and farm walks. Hunting holidays can be arranged during the winter. Pets are accepted outside only. Kilrush is on the Kilkenny road, 10 km from Urlingford. All major credit cards accepted.

OWNER Richard & Sally St George   OPEN April 1 – September 30 ROOMS 1 double, 1 twin, 1 double or twin; all en suite   TERMS B&B IR£45; reduction for children by arrangement; single supplement MEALS Dinner IR£25

Berryhill

Inistioge, Co. Kilkenny
Tel: 056 58434 / 087 461532 Fax: 056 58434

This most attractive country house was built by the Dyer family in 1780 and stands in 80 hectares of farmland with wonderful views to the Nore Valley and to the hills on the other side. It is a favourite retreat of actress Mia Farrow who has stayed here with her six children. Accommodation is in the three exceptional suites, one of which has an outside terrace where one can enjoy the view. Breakfast is a specialty and is served in the dining room, which has a fireplace and bay window. Guests can relax in the long drawing room, which has a baby grand piano, in front of the log fire with a drink from the honesty bar. Belinda Dyer is a charming and attentive hostess, and both she and George, who takes care of the 80-hectare farm, love meeting people. There is a pleasant garden, a cross-country croquet course, private fishing, lovely walks and two excellent restaurants within walking distance. No pets, and smoking in the drawing room only. Access, Mastercard accepted.

OWNER George & Belinda Dyer   OPEN mid-April – end October
ROOMS 2 double, 1 family; all en suite TERMS B&B IR£40; reduction for children by arrangement; single supplement IR£10

Cullintra House

The Rower, Inistioge, Co. Kilkenny
Tel: 051 423614 E-mail: cullbse@indigo.ie

This attractive, ivy-covered, 200-year-old house is approached by a long driveway through a park of grazing cattle, and has been in Patricia Cantlon's family since the turn-of-the-century. It is an animal and bird sanctuary, and there are a great many friendly cats and a local fox who comes to eat dinner in the garden every evening. The rooms, including a garden conservatory and a converted barn, reflect Patricia's artistic talents. She is also an accomplished cook and serves dinner by candlelight at 9 p.m. in an unhurried fashion. Breakfast can be taken as late as you wish. The studio/conservatory with a small kitchen for making drinks is available for guests and can also be used as a small conference room. There are 93 hectares of farmland, and a private path leads to beautiful Mount Brandon and the ancient Cairn. Pets by arrangement, and smoking in the drawing room or studio/conservatory only.

OWNER Patricia Cantlon OPEN All year ROOMS 6 double/twin/single/family; 3 en suite TERMS B&B IR£20–25; reduction for children; single supplement IR£10 MEALS Dinner IR£16

Garranavabby House

The Rower, Inistioge, Co. Kilkenny
Tel: 051 23613

This attractive country house, parts of which date back to the seventeenth century, is set in a pretty garden and is part of a large mixed farm, mostly sheep and cattle. There are ornamental pheasants, chickens to provide eggs for the house, and lovely views. Garranavabby is a nice, comfortable, well-lived-in family home, with some faded furnishings, but a welcoming atmosphere pervades. Guests have use of a comfortable sitting room, and breakfast is served in the pleasant dining room with a sideboard full of silver. This is an excellent spot for fishing, hill walking, riding and shooting. No smoking in the bedrooms.

OWNER Mrs Johanna Prendergast OPEN Easter – September 30 ROOMS 1 double, 1 twin, 1 family TERMS B&B IR£19; reduction for children; single supplement

JENKINSTOWN

Swift's Heath
Jenkinstown, Co. Kilkenny
Tel: 056 67653 Fax: 056 67653

This splendid house, built in 1650, was lived in by the Swift family until 30 years ago, when it was bought by the present owners, who have done a wonderful job restoring it. It is reached from the main road through an impressive stone archway and down a long driveway, and is surrounded by its own grounds. Brigitte Lennon is originally from Germany, and is a friendly and welcoming hostess. The very large rooms have good, old furniture, and one bathroom is the original bathroom dating from 1845, still with its old fixtures and a splendid loo with a painted porcelain basin and flush handle – which has to be treated with the utmost care as it is very difficult to repair. The single room is Jonathan Swift's old room. There is an incredible billiard room, a comfortable drawing room, and large dining room with one long table where both breakfast and dinner, by request, are served. Tea or coffee are offered to guests upon arrival, and can be ordered at other times. There is a grass tennis court, and nearby there is fishing on the River Nore, golf, riding, and hunting and shooting in season. No pets and smoking downstairs only. Visa, Access accepted.

OWNER Brigitte Lennon OPEN February 1 – December 20 ROOMS 1 double, 2 twin; all en suite TERMS B&B IR£30; reduction for children MEALS Dinner IR£18

KILKENNY

Burwood Bed & Breakfast
Waterford Road, Kilkenny, Co. Kilkenny
Tel: 056 62266

This modern bungalow with old-fashioned hospitality is set back off the main road, with a small, pretty front garden. Joan Flanagan is a most accommodating host, and she is proud of the personal attention she gives her guests, making them feel relaxed and welcome. A cup of tea or coffee is offered upon arrival and in the evening. The bedrooms are all on the ground floor and are immaculate and individually decorated. Three are now en suite, the fourth bedroom having a private bathroom, and they have tea and coffee making facilities. There's a comfortable TV lounge for guests and breakfast only is served in the dining room. The large rear parking area has 24-hour surveillance. Burwood can be found on the Waterford road, 1 km from the centre of medieval Kilkenny. Pets can be accommodated in an outhouse. No smoking.

OWNER Joan Flanagan OPEN April – September ROOMS 2 double, 2 twin; 3 en suite TERMS B&B IR£17; reduction for children; single supplement IR£8

Danville House
New Ross Road, Kilkenny, Co. Kilkenny
Tel: 056 21512

This 200-year-old Georgian house is set in open countryside, with a pretty garden and a long driveway up from the main road. The house has been split into two, with Kitty Stallard's son and his wife living in one half and taking care of the farm. Kitty is a friendly, cheerful hostess and the house has a relaxed atmosphere. One bedroom is on the ground floor, and the TV lounge is combined with the dining room, which has a large table where breakfast is served. In summer croquet is set up on the lawn, and there is a walled kitchen garden. Fishing, golf and riding are available nearby. Smoking only in the dining room. Danville House is 1 km from Kilkenny on the New Ross road.

OWNER Kitty Stallard OPEN April 1 – October 31 ROOMS 4 double, 1 twin; 4 en suite TERMS B&B IR£15–17.50; single supplement

Dunromin
Dublin Road, Kilkenny, Co. Kilkenny
Tel: 056 61387 Fax: 056 70736

The standard of maintenance is exceptionally high throughout the public rooms and bedrooms of this house. The bedrooms are spacious, have recently been completely refurbished and are immaculately clean. Guests enjoy the secluded, landscaped garden,

and there are views of the countryside at the back of the house; a golf course lies to the front. Dunromin is well known for its informality and great musical evenings, set off by Tom Rothwell playing the accordion. There is a wonderful, friendly atmosphere and tea or coffee is offered on arrival. Breakfasts include home-baked breads and homemade preserves. The house is on the edge of the town, reached off the N10. Pets outside only and no smoking. Visa, Mastercard accepted.

OWNER Valerie & Tom Rothwell OPEN Closed at Christmas ROOMS 4 double or twin; all en suite TERMS B&B IR£17; reduction for children; single supplement

Hillgrove
Bennettsbridge Road, Kilkenny, Co. Kilkenny
Tel: 056 51453 / 22890

This delightful family home is set back off the New Ross Road, 3 km from Kilkenny. Margaret Drennan used to work for the Irish Tourist Board and knows everything there is to know about Kilkenny. She is happy to suggest itineraries and help with planning your stay. The house is furnished in a mixture of old and reproduction furniture and the en suite bedrooms all have hairdryers. Tea and coffee making facilities are available in the TV lounge and there is a varied breakfast menu No pets and no smoking.

OWNER Margaret & Tony Drennan OPEN February 1 – November 30 ROOMS 2 double, 2 twin, 1 family; all en suite TERMS B&B IR£18; reduction for children; single supplement IR£5

Newlands Country House

Sevenhouses, Kilkenny, Co. Kilkenny
Tel: 056 29111 Fax: 056 29171 E-mail: newlands@indigo.ie

The Kennedys originally owned Shillogher House in Kilkenny, then decided to move out into the countryside and designed and built Newlands, moving in over Christmas 1995/96. It is set in 28 hectares of farmland, supporting cattle and sheep, and nearer to the house, peacocks and ducks can be seen. Although the house has every comfort, and wonderful food, it is the personalities and hospitality of Seamus and Aileen that make a stay here so memorable. The house is very well built and insulated, so one hears no noise from other guests. The bedrooms are very comfortable, with lavish décor; four have whirlpool baths, and they all have telephones, TVs and trouser presses. Outstanding breakfasts, orchestrated by Seamus, with a choice of duck or free-range hen eggs from the farm, are served in the conservatory-style dining room, which has bright, cheerful colours and an attractive tiled floor. There are special weekend packages available, which include a seven-course dinner on Saturday night. These are very popular with people wanting to get away for peace and quiet in comfortable surroundings. Kilkenny is but a short drive away, with all its historical attractions, and a variety of restaurants. No pets and no smoking in the bedrooms. Visa, Mastercard, American Express accepted.

OWNER Seamus & Aileen Kennedy OPEN Closed at Christmas ROOMS 3 double, 2 twin; 4 whirlpool baths, 1 shower en suite TERMS B&B IR£20–27.50; single supplement (at weekends) MEALS Dinner IR£20

Shillogher House

Callan Road, Kilkenny, Co. Kilkenny
Tel: 056 63249 / 64865 Fax: 056 64865

This large, modern brick house stands in its own grounds on the outskirts of Kilkenny, a 10-minute walk to the centre. Shillogher

House is professionally run and offers immaculately clean, well-equipped bedrooms, all with hairdryers, TVs and telephones. Tea and coffee are available in the conservatory and there is a lounge off the breakfast room. The menu gives guests an excellent choice for breakfast. No pets and no smoking. Mastercard, Visa accepted.

OWNER Margaret & Bill Morgan OPEN All year ROOMS 1 double, 1 family, 3 triple; all en suite TERMS B&B IR£19; reduction for children; single supplement

KNOCKTOPHER

Knocktopher Hall
Knocktopher, Co. Kilkenny
Tel: 056 68626 Fax: 056 68626

This lovely Georgian country house was bought and lovingly restored by John and Carmel Wilson. It was built in 1740 using the foundations and basements from a castle dating back to 1540, and has splendid views of Mount Leinster and the Blackstairs Mountains. It is surrounded by 4 hectares of its own land, including a pretty garden with peacocks. John and Carmel are passionate about their house and all the improvements they are making to it, and guests really get to share their lovely home. Dinner is available for parties of six or more, if arranged in advance, at weekends, with excellent locally produced food – and puddings are celebrated, especially the Grand Marnier mousse. The bedrooms are enormous, and most have French antique beds and wonderful views. The drawing room, where afternoon tea is served to arriving guests, has Edwardian oak panelling, a large open log fire and a grand piano. The famous Mount Juliet Golf course is 5 km away, and the medieval city of Kilkenny 18 km. No pets and no smoking.

OWNER John & Carmel Wilson OPEN All year ROOMS 4 double; all en suite TERMS B&B IR£35; single supplement IR£10 MEALS Dinner IR£25

MADDOXTOWN

Blanchville House
Dunbell, Maddoxtown, Co. Kilkenny
Tel: 056 27197   Fax: 056 27636

This elegant Georgian country house stands in its own grounds and is approached by a tree and shrub-lined private drive. It has a warm and friendly atmosphere and is beautifully furnished with antiques. The large, comfortable en suite bedrooms overlook the lovely green countryside and have hairdryers and tea and coffee making facilities, and some have TVs and trouser presses. The spacious drawing room, with the original wallpaper and service bells, has a TV, grand piano and open fireplace. Evening meals, if booked in advance, are served in the atmospheric dining room, and are tastefully prepared with homegrown produce. There is a tennis court for guests' use, and local amenities include golf, racing, fishing and flying at the Kilkenny Air Club. There are a wide range of archeological and historical attractions, and Blanchville is at the centre of a Craft Trail incorporating five prominent studio workshops in County Kilkenny. Kennels are available for pets, and smoking is permitted in the drawing room. To reach the house take the N10 Carlow/Dublin road from Kilkenny. First right 1 km after the Pike Pub, left at next crossroads, entrance 2 km on the left. All major credit cards accepted.

OWNER Monica Phelan   OPEN March 1 – November 1   ROOMS 3 double, 2 twin, 1 family; all en suite   TERMS B&B IR£30–35; reduction for children; single supplement IR£5   MEALS Dinner IR£22

THOMASTOWN

Abbey House

Jerpoint Abbey, Thomastown, Co. Kilkenny
Tel: 056 24166 Fax: 056 24192

Abbey House is an attractive building located opposite Jerpoint Abbey. The house may have been built as early as 1540, and a mill here dates from the twelfth century. Ruins of the old mill, which Helen Blanchfield would love to restore, lie behind the house. The house itself was in a very bad condition when the Blanchfields bought it in 1988, and only one original wall is left after doing the restoration work. Helen is an amusing, chatty lady with a lot of energy. The house is spacious, with a drawing room, and simply furnished bedrooms all equipped with hairdryers, telephones and TVs. The pleasant dining room has small tables. Helen is building on a new extension at the back of the house, with a room for disabled people and a lovely terrace, which will overlook the river and catch the evening sun. Dogs are allowed in their baskets in bedrooms, smoking only in the drawing room. Visa, Mastercard, Access accepted.

OWNER Helen Blanchfield OPEN All year ROOMS 2 twin, 2 single, 4 double or twin; 7 en suite TERMS B&B IR£20–25; single supplement IR£5

Ballyduff House

Ballyduff, Thomastown, Co. Kilkenny
Tel: 056 58488

This attractive eighteenth-century manor house is set in lovely, peaceful countryside, reached down a series of country lanes and entered through a gateway and up a long pot-holed driveway. It stands just above the River Nore and enjoys views of the river and hills. Mrs Thomas is a charming young widow with two children, and is a kind and thoughtful hostess. Ballyduff is a wonderful old family home, with an interesting collection of family portraits. The bedrooms are huge and comfortably furnished and have good-sized bathrooms. Breakfast is served in the dining room, and guests also have use of a wonderful library and drawing room with TV. Arrangements can be made for guests to fish on the estate's own stretch of the River Nore, and hunting is also available. No smoking in bedrooms. Visa, Mastercard accepted.

OWNER Mrs Breda Thomas OPEN All year ROOMS 2 double, 1 twin; all en suite TERMS B&B IR£20–25; reduction for children

COUNTY LEITRIM

Leitrim is a county of charming beauty, with distinctive hill formations and lovely lakes. This long, narrow county is divided in two by Lough Allen, one of the many lakes of the River Shannon. The county is a very popular place for anglers, and the main topic of conversation everywhere seems to be fishing.

Dromahair is a pretty village, located about 12 km from Manorhamilton. The road from here is superbly scenic, with views of Lough Gill and beautiful wooded countryside.

Fenagh, which is located in the hills, has the ruins of a Gothic church, all that remains of the monastery St Columba founded as a school of divinity. You can fish to your heart's content in this area, which is full of lakes, beautiful scenery and wildlife.

Carrick-on-Shannon is the centre of river cruising on the Shannon. There is a large marina, several cruising companies, and lots of restaurants and pubs, which during the season have traditional Irish music.

BALLINAMORE

Glenview
Aughoo, Ballinamore, Co. Leitrim
Tel: 078 44157 Fax: 078 44814

Glenview is a most attractive farmhouse on the new Shannon-Erne link, 500 m from lock 4, beside the Woodford River. This is a delightful rural setting; there are extensive gardens, a pony, and a donkey and cart for children's enjoyment. A games room and pool table are available for guests' use. The house is efficiently run and guests are always made to feel part of the family. The residence has undergone extensive renovations and there is now a fully licensed restaurant offering the meal of the house and a table d'hôte menu. The lounge has a marble fireplace where log fires burn on cool days, and an antique chaise longue. There are many lakes close by and guests are advised on the best places to fish. A tackle shed, cold room and bait service are provided. Teresa Kennedy has been very successful with her bed & breakfast business for the past 14 years, and is the proud recipient of the BHS Agri-Tourism Award. Three self-catering bungalows are available, two of which have full wheelchair facilities. There is plenty to keep the visitors busy, including barge cruises, walking, golfing, horseback riding, canoeing, a Genealogy Centre and in the local pubs traditional Irish music. Visa, Mastercard, Access accepted.

OWNER Teresa Kennedy   OPEN March 1 – October 31   ROOMS 5 twin, 1 family; 5 en suite   TERMS B&B IR£19–25; reduction for children; single supplement IR£6.50 MEALS Dinner

Riversdale Farm Guesthouse
Ballinamore, Co. Leitrim
Tel: 078 44122 Fax: 078 44813

This large, spacious country residence surrounded by an 32-hectare farm overlooks the new Shannon-Erne waterway, which borders the farm for 1 km and is adjacent to Aghoo lock. All of the rooms have views and are furnished to a high standard. There are two lounges, one with TV, and both have open fires. Breakfast and excellent dinners are served in the conservatory dining room, which is furnished with chestnut and beech furniture made by a local craftsman. This is a wonderful spot for an all-purpose holiday – in the courtyard of the farm there is a small leisure complex which consists of a heated pool, sauna, and squash court. The cut-stone hay barn has been converted to a large games room, which could also be used for small seminars. The Ballinamore-Ballyconnell canal, which is based at Riversdale Farmhouse, also offers barging holidays; the barges are a modification of the traditional narrowboat, but are wider and offer more living space and comfort. Full details are available from Riversdale Farm, which is run by a member of the Thomas family. Cooking is done by the Ballymaloe-trained family and there is a wine licence. There is a 9-hole golf course at Ballinamore and five minutes away is

Drumcoura City Western Riding Centre. Special breaks are available. Access, Mastercard, Visa accepted.

OWNER Raymond Thomas OPEN All year ROOMS 10 rooms double/ twin/ family; all en suite TERMS B&B IR£22; reduction for children 25%; single supplement IR£7 MEALS Dinner

CARRICK-ON-SHANNON

Ard na Greine
St Mary's Close, Carrick-on-Shannon, Co. Leitrim
Tel: 078 20311

Ard na Greine is an ideal property for people looking for an angling holiday – this well maintained house is situated in the centre of town, yet is within walking distance of the River Shannon and a choice of 41 fishing lakes. Helen Dee is a most welcoming lady who runs her B&B in a friendly but efficient manner and serves a hearty breakfast. Evening meals are not served, but there are several establishments within walking distance. The rooms are spotlessly clean in this comfortable modern house, and there is a video and TV in the guest lounge. Guests are welcome to return at any time during the day and Helen is happy to help with things to see and do in the area – there is a heated swimming pool, sports complex tennis courts, and a 9-hole golf course, and for folks interested in a little night life there are several local bars and hotels that provide music. Visa, Mastercard accepted.

OWNER Helen Dee OPEN All year ROOMS 4 double, 4 twin, 2 family; 2 en suite TERMS B&B IR£17; reduction for children 50%; single supplement IR£3

Caldra House
Carrick-on-Shannon, Co. Leitrim
Tel: 078 21606

This family-run, beautifully restored Georgian house offers the highest standards of hospitality and good home-cooked food. It stands in a secluded spot in 30 hectares of farmland overlooking the Shannon Waterways and is an ideal location for visiting local beauty spots. Guests are made to feel immediately welcome; tea or coffee is offered upon arrival. In addition to the lounges, there is a conservatory, which is a delightful spot in which to relax on pleasant days, and both the dining room and lounges have fires on chilly days. There are boats and a bait and tackle room for guests' use. There are 41 coarse fishing lakes within a 8-km radius. Evening meals must be pre-arranged. Traditional music can be enjoyed in local pubs. Visa accepted.

OWNER Maura O'Donnell   OPEN March – November   ROOMS 3 double, 1 twin, 1 family; 3 (2 with shower) en suite TERMS B&B IR£20; reduction for children: under 5s free, 10% for 6–10; single supplement IR£2 MEALS Full and light dinners

Corbally Lodge
Dublin Road, Carrick-on-Shannon, Co. Leitrim
Tel: 078 20228

Corbally Lodge is a country-style house furnished with antiques, set in an attractive garden in a peaceful spot. The bedrooms are well maintained and are spotlessly clean and comfortable; two are on the ground floor. The comfy lounge has turf fires and a TV. Mrs Rowley is a friendly, hospitable lady who takes excellent care of her guests. Tasty breakfasts and pre-arranged home-cooked dinners are served in the bright dining room, featuring fresh vegetables, home-baked bread and excellent desserts. The River Shannon is close by and there are numerous lakes in the area. Golf, swimming and local boat hire are also available. Visa, Mastercard accepted.

OWNER Valerie & P. J. Rowley OPEN All year ROOMS 2 double, 3 twin; 3 en suite TERMS B&B IR£15–17; reduction for children 25%; single supplement IR£3–6 MEALS Dinner

Lakeview Glebe House
Drumcong, Carrick-on-Shannon, Co. Leitrim
Tel: 078 42034

This old-style country house is adjacent to the Shannon Erne Canal and overlooks Carrickport Lough to the front and Lough Scur to the rear. It has a warm and welcoming atmosphere and the owners, Tom and Nancy McKeown, are hospitable and friendly.

The house was originally owned by the parish priest; the house and 2 hectares were purchased by Tom and Nancy in 1972, and they have been welcoming guests into their home since that time. The house has a lived-in feel, the bedrooms are large and modestly furnished and most have lough views. There are seven lakes close by and guests can fish for perch, pike, bream and rudd, while Loughs Carrickport and Scur are within a five-minute walk. Guests have use of a three-bedroom self-catering cottage.

OWNER Nancy & Tom McKeown   OPEN April 1 – November 30
ROOMS 2 double, 1 twin, 1 family; 2 en suite   TERMS B&B IR£18;
reduction for children 50%; single supplement IR£2   MEALS Dinner

COUNTY LONGFORD

The most central county in Ireland, Longford lies in the basin of the Shannon. The landscape is consequently low and flat, interspersed with small streams and lakes dotted with islands. Longford has strong associations with writers, particularly Oliver Goldsmith, Padraic Colum, Maria Edgeworth and Leo Casey, and is a popular place for coarse fishing.

The town of Longford is spaciously laid out with wide streets, a Renaissance-style court house and a nineteenth-century cathedral, which is built of grey limestone and has impressive towers.

Close to Newtonforbes is beautiful Castleforbes, a fine seventeenth-century castellated mansion. St Patrick is said to have founded a church at the old village of Ardagh in a pretty wooded setting, the ruins of which can still be seen.

LONGFORD

Sancian House
Dublin Road, Longford, Co. Longford
Tel: 043 46187

Sancian House has been welcoming guests for many years; they return often to enjoy the warm and informal atmosphere and high standards found here. A pot of tea and scones is offered upon arrival. The rooms are spotlessly clean and simply furnished. The house sits back off the main road, the front garden is full of roses and there are colourful window boxes. Martha O'Kane is a friendly, outgoing lady who is very knowledgeable regarding family heritage, and is willing to assist guests who are interested in tracing their family history. An 18-hole golf course is located across the street, and it is a five-minute drive to the lovely village of Ardagh.

OWNER Martha O'Kane OPEN All year ROOMS 2 double, 1 twin, 2 single; 3 en suite TERMS B&B IR£18; reduction for children; single supplement IR£5 (in double room)

COUNTY MONAGHAN

Monaghan is a sportsman's paradise, with many lakes and small roads winding round the hills and through Monaghan's pastoral landscape. It is an unspoilt area, rich in farming land, and ideal country for outdoor activities and exploring. Among the prettiest lakes are Lake Muckno, Glaslough Lake, Lough Emy and the Dartry Lakes. Monaghan is a market town, and is home to an award-winning museum which houses the Clogher Cross, a fine example of early Christian metalwork. In July, Monaghan hosts the Fiddler of Oriel Festival of Irish dance and music.

CARRICKMACROSS

Shanmullagh House
Killanny Road off Dundalk Road, Carrickmacross, Co. Monaghan
Tel: 042 966 3038 Fax: 042 966 1915

Shanmullagh House is an attractive, modern, red brick house in a rural setting with countryside views. With nothing in sight but green fields and mature trees, it is a peaceful and tranquil "away from it all" spot. The property is adjacent to the well-known Nurenmore Hotel and Country Club with its excellent golf course. The house is tastefully decorated throughout and has pine floors, immaculately kept bedrooms and power showers. Mr

Flanagan runs a gift shop in town and Margaret Flanagan takes care of the bed & breakfast – and her three delightful young daughters. Excellent breakfasts are served in the dining room which overlooks the view, allowing a peaceful start to the day. The owners are a congenial and friendly couple who obviously enjoy what they do, and guests are well taken care of here. Visa accepted.

OWNER Margaret Flanagan   OPEN All year, including Christmas ROOMS 2 double, 2 twin, 2 family; 5 en suite   TERMS B&B IR£16; reduction for children 50%; single supplement IR£4

NEW BLISS

Glynch House
New Bliss, Co. Monaghan
Tel: 047 54045

Glynch House is an impressive Georgian residence set in beautiful countryside, part of an 80-hectare farm where they raise calves and a beef suckling herd. The house has spacious rooms, furnished in keeping with its character, and there is an original marble fireplace in the lounge, where peat fires burn on chilly days. The original casement shutters are still in working order. Most of the bedrooms overlook peaceful countryside and a fairy fort. John O'Grady can easily be persuaded to tell guests stories about the fairies. An additional bonus of staying at Glynch Farm are the owners themselves – a down-to-earth, friendly and hospitable couple who have created a wonderful, informal atmosphere, and have a great sense of humour. John obviously enjoys chatting with guests and sharing his knowledge of the area. The house was originally built for a member of the Hugonuck family. New Bliss is an artist's colony; Richard Morris, a well-known architect, left his home for artists and musicians. More details on this interesting aspect can be obtained from John O'Grady. Excellent, freshly prepared break-fasts are served family-style and there are several eating establish-ments close by for evening meals. Visa, Mastercard accepted.

OWNER Martha O'Grady OPEN March 1 – September 30 ROOMS 1 double, 2 twin, 1 family, 1 single; 3 en suite TERMS B&B IR£20–25; reduction for children; no single supplement in single room

COUNTIES OFFALY AND LAOIS

Both counties lie in the central part of Ireland, with the River Shannon forming their western border.

Clonmacnois is an important name in Irish history. St Ciarán founded a monastery here in A.D. 548, which became one of Ireland's best-known religious centres. A pilgrimage is held here each September on the feast of St Ciarán.

There is an attractive castle at Clononey, and Anthony Trollope first started writing novels whilst living at Banager, a pretty little village on the canal. At Birr, the gardens of the castle are open to the public, and in Portarlington, built on the canal, the gardens of the old town houses run down to the river.

BIRR

Minnocks' Farmhouse
Roscrea Road, Birr, Co. Offaly
Tel: 0509 20591

This Georgian-style house with colonnades, Georgian doors, windows, ceiling rose and cornices was cleverly converted from a farmhouse in 1991. It is part of a 40-hectare working dairy farm. There are two ground floor bedrooms, which have firm beds and are individually decorated with matching fabrics and curtains. Breakfasts include freshly made scones, potato bread, eggs, bacon, cream and milk from the farm. Five-course dinners are available, if pre-arranged, and there are some good value restaurants close by, which Veronica will be happy to give you information on. Veronica Minnock is a gracious host and has been awarded the Golden Thoughts Tourist Award, an accolade for "service above and beyond the call of duty." A cup of tea is offered upon arrival – in fact, at Minnocks' farm, the kettle is rarely off the boil! Visa accepted.

OWNER Noel & Veronica Minnock OPEN All year ROOMS 1 double, 2 twin, 2 family, 1 single/double; all en suite TERMS B&B IR£17.50; reduction for children; single supplement IR£8 MEALS Dinner

RAHAN

Canal View Country House
Killina, Rahan, Co. Offaly
Tel: 0506 55868 Fax: 0506 55034

Canal View is an attractive, modern dormer bungalow in a peaceful position backing onto the Grand Canal. Guests can fish from the back garden for bream, rudd, tench and perch, or walk along the canal bank and watch the cruisers pass by. Angling maps are available. A 10-minute stroll brings you to the ancient Rahan Church. A patio, picnic and play area and rowing boats, as well as a sauna, steam room and jacuzzi, are all available at no extra charge. Breakfast and evening meals are served in the pretty dining room, which overlooks the canal. The bedrooms are tastefully decorated with matching fabrics and wallpapers. Canal View offers extremely high standards and guests are assured of a warm welcome and attention to detail in this pleasant house. Guests often have the opportunity of watching the local farmer's cows swimming from one yard to another across the canal, which occurs in the morning and the evening. Guided bog tours, horseback riding and a 9-hole golf course are all available close by. Visa, Access, Barclaycard accepted.

OWNER Bernadette Keyes OPEN All year ROOMS 1 double, 2 family, 1 single; 3 en suite TERMS B&B IR£24; reduction for children; single supplement IR£5 MEALS Dinner

TULLAMORE

Pine Lodge
Tullamore, Co. Offaly
Tel: 0506 51927 Fax: 0506 51927

This exceptionally well-maintained house with high standards is delightful in every way. It is set in almost one hectare of lawned gardens with outstanding views of the surrounding countryside, providing the ultimate in relaxation. All but one of the well-appointed bedrooms have pine furnishings. There is a sitting room with TV and a separate dining room, where excellent wholesome breakfasts are served at separate tables. Claudia Krygel, who is from Germany, prides herself on the wholesome food served. Breakfast consists of smoked salmon, eggs and pancakes as well as traditional fare. Little wonder that Claudia has been the recipient of the National Irish Breakfast Award. Imaginative evening meals are also served (advance notice is required). Vegetarian and special diets can also be catered for. There are some enjoyable countryside walks, and golf and fishing are close by. There is a log cabin, which houses a large, heated indoor pool, sauna and steam room and sun bed. Massage and reflexology are also available. There is a charge for the pool, sauna and steam room of £3.50 per session. Not suitable for children under 12.

OWNER Claudia Krygel OPEN February 15 – December 15 ROOMS 2 double, 2 twin; all en suite TERMS B&B IR£25–30; single supplement negotiable MEALS Dinner

DONAGHMORE

Castletown House
Donaghmore, Co. Laois
Tel: 505 46415 Fax: 505 46788 E-mail: castletown@tinet.ie

Castletown House has been awarded for the third time the prestigious Agri-Tourism Provincial Award. This warm and welcoming nineteenth-century farmhouse stands in scenic countryside surrounding an 80-hectare beef and sheep farm, on

which the ruins of a Norman castle remain. It is approached via a private drive through open fields full of grazing sheep. The house continues to improve, upgrading is ongoing, it is spotlessly clean and there is a comfortable and relaxed atmosphere. This must be one of the best value accommodations in Ireland; the bedrooms are all a good size, and there are several pieces of antique furniture. Fresh farmhouse breakfasts and pre-arranged light evening meals are served in the dining room, which has a marble fireplace; there is also a sitting room with TV and information on what to see and do in the area. Guests enjoy gathering in the family kitchen for a cup of tea and a chat with the friendly owners. A conservatory games room is available to guests and there is an open farm on the property with star billing going to the three donkeys Mollie, Donna and Wilkie. Access, Mastercard, Eurocard, J.C.B. accepted.

OWNER Moira Phelan OPEN March 1 – November ROOMS 2 double, 1 family, 1 triple/twin; all en suite TERMS B&B IR£17; reduction for children MEALS Light meals

KILMINCHY

Chez Nous
Kilminchy, Co. Laois
Tel: 0502 21251

Chez Nous is a classic Irish vernacular design residence, situated in a quiet spot in a peaceful cul-de-sac. Guests who book in here are treated as friends and enjoy first-class accommodation. The luxuriously appointed bedrooms are very tasteful, the sunshine suite has a half tester canopied bed, and all are tastefully decorated in soft pastels of pink sorbet, peach blossom, and lavender blue. The family suite has two double rooms and a separate single, ideal for families or friends travelling together. Just about everywhere you look is decorated with bows, ribbons and pretty curtains. Breakfasts are a banquet, and include sugar-rimmed orange juice, edible flowers, potato cakes, pan-fried trout, home-baked brown bread, homemade preserves and marmalade, or for those who prefer, a traditional Irish breakfast. There is a conservatory with a blue and yellow décor, where guests may help themselves to tea and coffee, and cosy log fires in the sitting room. Evening meals are served, if arranged in advance, but there are options for eating out at several venues close by. The house was featured in *Select*, a yearly magazine which features houses and furnishings of special interest. Not suitable for children under 10.

OWNER Audrey & Tony Canavan OPEN All year ROOMS 2 double, 2 twin, 2 family; all en suite TERMS B&B IR£18.50–20; reduction for children; single supplement IR£5 MEALS Dinner

BORRIS-IN-OSSORY

Ballaghmore House
Borris-in-Ossory, Co. Laois
Tel: 087 407588

This modern cream-and-green shuttered farmhouse sits way back off the road in a large landscaped garden with a pond and a small waterfall. It is part of a 30-hectare mixed farm and there is a lake on the property with free fishing; the land runs adjacent to an 18-hole golf course. Beautifully maintained with tasteful décor, the bedrooms are reached by a split mahogany staircase, and have cast-iron beds, lace canopies, and restful pastels of peach, cream, lemon and grey. Excellent breakfasts and pre-arranged high tea or evening meals are served in the inviting dining room and there is a turf fire in the lounge. The warm hospitality shown to guests and the extremely high standards found at Ballaghmore House make this an excellent choice for touring this unspoiled area. Visa, Mastercard accepted.

OWNER Carole England OPEN All year including Christmas ROOMS 1 double, 2 twin, 1 family; all en suite TERMS B&B IR£17; reduction for children; single supplement IR£3 MEALS Dinner, high tea

COUNTY ROSCOMMON

County Roscommon is an island county 60 km in length. Two-thirds of the county is surrounded by water. In the north are the largest lakes: Lough Key, Lough Gara and Lough Boderg. The great Lough Ree is in the east. The limestone foundation of the whole county and the numerous lakes make it a fisherman's paradise.

Large areas of arable land are to be found in the centre of the county, and the principal occupation of the people is raising cattle and sheep.

Roscommon is a county of abbeys and castles. You can visit Clonalis House, Castlerea, once the home of two of Ireland's high kings in the twelfth century; Strokestown Park House, with its records of Famine-ridden Ireland; prehistoric Rathcroghan; St John's Interpretative Centre; medieval Boyle and picturesque Lough Key with its forest park.

For those interested in contemporary art, the Glebe House Gallery is situated midway between Boyle and Carrick-on-Shannon at Crossna, Knockvicar.

CARRICK-ON-SHANNON

Avondale House
Roosky, Carrick-on-Shannon, Co. Roscommon
Tel: 078 38095

This attractive house stands in its own grounds 500 m from the River Shannon. This friendly, family-run establishment has a relaxing, cosy atmosphere. Carmel Davis was formerly in the hotel trade but missed the personal contact with people and decided to open her own bed & breakfast establishment. Carmel and her husband were successful from the beginning and soon added on additional bedrooms. The bedrooms are clean and comfortable and have orthopedic beds. The cosy TV lounge has a turf fire. Excellent home-cooked evening meals are available if ordered in advance, and there is a new hotel within walking distance which has an excellent restaurant and bar food. Avondale is a good base for anglers; there is a tackle room with fridges and drying facilities are also available. For people who enjoy walking there is a pleasant river walk close by. Guests are well taken care of at Avondale and are assured of personal attention from the pleasant owners. Visa, American Express accepted.

OWNER Carmel Davis OPEN All year ROOMS 2 double, 2 twin, 1 family; all en suite TERMS B&B IR£18; reduction for children; single supplement IR£5 MEALS Dinner

Glencarne House
Ardcarne, Carrick-on-Shannon, Co. Roscommon
Tel: 079 67013

This charming Georgian house, approached up a private drive, is located in scenic countryside with lovely views overlooking green fields and grazing sheep. A very warm welcome awaits you at Glencarne House. Agnes Harrington has won several awards, including the Galtee Breakfast Award and the Agri-Tourism National Award. The house is well maintained and freshly decorated. It is warm and relaxed, and the bedrooms have every comfort, including armchairs, hot water bottles and electric blankets, and some have antique brass beds. There is a peaceful, old-fashioned lounge with a marble fireplace which, along with the dining room, has a real fire on chilly days. Agnes Harrington is an excellent cook; evening meals are prepared fresh daily and desserts feature some of the best pastry in Ireland. There is a golf course within 1 km and lots of outdoor activities and wildlife walks in the nearby 325-hectare Lough Key Park. Many guests have been returning to this special place over the years and early reservations are recommended.

OWNER Patrick & Agnes Harrington OPEN March – November ROOMS 3 double, 1 twin, 1 family, 1 single; all en suite TERMS B&B IR£25; reduction for children; single supplement IR£5 MEALS Dinner

STROKESTOWN

Church View House
Strokestown, Co. Roscommon
Tel: 078 33047 Fax: 078 33047

This spacious, 200-year-old, rambling country house stands in a scenic location. It has been in the Cox family for four generations and is part of a 100-hectare working farm. The original structure of a Famine fever hospital is found on the grounds. The house continues to be well maintained, and the good-sized bedrooms are simply furnished. One of the lounges has the original marble fireplace. Evening meals are available, but must be ordered in advance, and include tasty homemade dishes and desserts. Church View House is not licensed, but guests may bring their own wine. Strokestown House and the Famine Museum and gardens are 6 km away.

OWNER Harriet Cox OPEN April 1 – September 30 ROOMS 2 double, 2 twin, 2 family; 3 en suite TERMS B&B IR£17–20; reduction for children; single supplement peak season only MEALS Dinner

COUNTY TIPPERARY

Located in the centre of the southern part of Ireland, Tipperary is a beautiful county of rich farmland. From the top of Slievenamon there is a splendid view. To the north you can see the Rock of Cashel, a steep outcrop of limestone topped by impressive ruins – a truly spectacular sight, particularly during the summer when it is floodlit at night. From early times the rock was a fortress and seat of chieftains, and later it became an important religious site.

Today you can see the vast ruins of the gothic cathedral, which dates from the thirteenth century; the tower of the Castle; the cross of St Patrick, the massive base of which is said to be the coronation stone of the Munster kings; and Cormac's Chapel, which dates back to 1130.

The Cashel Palace Hotel is a very fine Queen Anne-style house, formerly the residence of Church of Ireland archbishops, located in the busy town of Cashel.

A fine collection of sixteenth-century and seventeenth-century books can be found in the Diocesan Library in the precincts of St John the Baptist Cathedral. There's a good craft shop where you can buy Shanagarry tweed. Situated between Thurles and Cashel, Holy Cross Abbey was built in 1110, to house a part of the True Cross, and later became a popular place of pilgrimage.

Cahir, a most pleasant town on the River Suir, has a beautifully restored fifteenth-century castle on an island in the river, and now houses the tourist office. Tipperary, famous for the song "It's a

Long Way to Tipperary," is a great farming centre. The mountains between Nenagh and Toomvara were the home of Ned of the Hill, the local Robin Hood. Nearby is Nenagh Round, all that remains of a castle built in 1200.

Kilcooly Abbey, the Abbey of the Holy Cross and the attractive old church at Fethard are all worth seeing. At Ahenny are two elaborately carved eighth-century stone crosses, and at Carrick-on-Suir, there is a fine example of a Tudor mansion, which can be visited by request.

BANSHA

Bansha House
Bansha, Co. Tipperary
Tel: 062 54215

This impressive Georgian residence is approached by an avenue of beech trees, set in 40 hectares of land. The house is furnished in keeping with its character and there are several pieces of antique furniture about. The bedrooms are large, and two are on the ground floor. The charming lounge has a log fire and leads out onto the gardens. A relaxed and comfortable atmosphere pervades, and guests can often be found in the kitchen with Mary, chatting about what to see and do in the area. John and Mary breed racehorses, and their stables-registered Equestrian Centre offers horseback riding. There is an all-weather 1-km track on the farm.

Cooking is of a very high standard, with homemade breads, tarts and pies. Glorious scenic tours can be taken from here. This is superb place for guests wanting some peace and tranquillity. A self-catering cottage is also available. Visa, Mastercard accepted.

OWNER John & Mary Marnane   OPEN January 1 – December 20
ROOMS 4 double, 3 twin, 1 single; 5 en suite   TERMS B&B IR£25;
reduction for children; single supplement IR£5   MEALS Dinner

Lismacue House
Bansha, Co. Tipperary
Tel: 062 54106 Fax: 062 54126 E-mail: lismac@indigo.ie

Lismacue House has been in Kate Nicholson's family since it was built in 1813. It is a classic, beautifully proportioned Irish country house, set in its own extensive grounds at the foot of the magnificent Galtee Mountains. The approach to the house is via one of the most impressive lime-tree avenues in Ireland. The spacious drawing room and library have their original wallpaper. Breakfasts and dinners are served in the imposing dining room. Traditional log fires burn in the warm and welcoming reception rooms. Special interest holidays are available, such as pony trekking for adults and children and, from November to February, hosted hunting holidays. There is also trout fishing on the estate's own river (tuition available). There are three golf courses and tennis courts close by and the Rock of Cashel and Cahir Castle are just a short drive away. Visa, Mastercard, American Express accepted.

OWNER Kate Nicholson   OPEN All year   ROOMS 2 double, 1 twin, 2
family; 3 en suite   TERMS B&B IR£38–45; reduction for children; single
supplement IR£7   MEALS Dinner

CAHIR

Ashling
Old Cashel Road, Cahir, Co. Tipperary
Tel: 052 41601

This pink-washed low building is situated 2 km outside Cahir, and has lovely views from the front of the house. Breda Fitzgerald is a very friendly, chatty lady who keeps an immaculately clean and tidy house. The rooms are on the small side, but are comfortably furnished, and there is a large sitting room off the dining room.

OWNER Breda Fitzgerald OPEN All year ROOMS 2 double, 2 twin; 3 en suite TERMS B&B IR£16.50–18; reduction for children; single supplement IR£7

CASHEL

Ardmayle House
Cashel, Co. Tipperary
Tel: 0504 42399 Fax: 0504 42420 E-mail: ardmayle@iol.ie

Ardmayle House is a spacious, creeper-covered, unpretentious farmhouse surrounded by an 80-hectare working farm. The bedrooms, furnished with solid old-fashioned and antique furniture, are large and comfortable. The open log fire in the sitting room is the ideal place for making friends and enjoying a hot drink and some delicious homemade scones. Guests are welcome to explore the dairy farm; sheep and horses are also kept. Annette is a warm, kindly host who likes guests to enjoy the best of rural living. They are welcome to fish both banks on the 2.5-km-long private stretch of the River Suir that runs through the property. A ghillie is also available by arrangement. Golf, forest walks and horseback riding can be arranged locally. Evening meals by advance arrangement only. There are also two four-star self-catering cottages on the farm.

OWNER Annette Hunt OPEN April 1 – October 1 ROOMS 1 double, 1 twin, 3 family, 1 single; 4 en suite TERMS B&B IR£20; reduction for children; single supplement IR£6.50

Ballyowen House
Cashel, Co. Tipperary
Tel: 062 61265

This impressive, listed Georgian country house is approached up a long private drive and stands in 120 hectares of farmland and woodland with specimen trees and lakeshore walks. It is still operated as a working farm, and the house has been in the McCann family for six generations. The house is full of family portraits and other treasures. Many interesting features include the Venetian ground floor windows; the staircase hall rising through three floors capped with a large dome skylight; decorative plasterwork in the drawing room; and the false door in the Adams style in the front hall. The house is elegantly furnished with antiques and the original service lift is still operable. The bedrooms are enormous and a stay here is a genuine opportunity to experience Irish country life. The McCann family are gracious hosts who enjoy sharing their family home. A two-night minimum stay is recommended, which allows guests to explore the grounds, the Oak Wood and Mount O'Meara and share in the everyday life of Ballyowen. Imaginative breakfasts are served in the elegant dining room, and the McCanns will be happy to make recommendations for evening meals.

OWNER The McCann Family   OPEN May – September   ROOMS 1 double, 2 twin; 2 en suite   TERMS B&B IR£22.50; reduction for children; single supplement IR£5

Knock-Saint-Lour House
Cashel, Co. Tipperary
Tel: 062 61172

A circular driveway leads to this large, square, modern whitewashed house with its stone pillared porch, surrounded by 13 hectares of beef and tillage farming. There is a formal drawing room, but the TV lounge has comfortable chairs, a piano and a fireplace. The rooms are large and comfortable, and the house has good views of the Rock of Cashel. There is a good supply of information on the area, and Eileen O'Brien is happy to advise guests on what to see and do in the area.

OWNER Eileen O'Brien   OPEN April 1 – November 1   ROOMS 2 double, 3 twin, 2 family, single; all en suite   TERMS B&B IR£18; reduction for children; single supplement IR£6.50   MEALS Dinner

Rahard Lodge
Cashel, Co. Tipperary
Tel: 062 61052

Rahard Lodge is approached up a tree-lined driveway and set amidst glorious landscaped gardens with superb views of the Rock of Cashel, which is floodlit at night. Built by the owners 30 years ago, this long, low, whitewashed house is surrounded by a 52-hectare beef and sheep farm. The bedrooms, all on the ground floor, are large and comfortable. An additional bonus are the delightful owners, Mr and Mrs Foley, who are interested in antiques; there are some excellent pieces about. Guests are greeted with a hot drink on arrival and very often a slice of delicious home-baked cake or some scones. The house is impeccably maintained; there are rich carpets and the spacious lounge has an open fireplace. Freshly prepared breakfasts only are served, but there is no shortage of venues for evening meals in the Heritage town of Cashel. Guests are welcome to sit in the lovely gardens, which were awarded first prize in County Tipperary and third place in the All-Ireland competition. Visa, Mastercard accepted.

OWNER Moira Foley OPEN March 31 – November 30 ROOMS 2 twin, 4 family; all en suite TERMS B&B IR£18.50; reduction for children; single supplement IR£3 MEALS Light meals on request

Ros Guill House

Dualla Road, Cashel, Co. Tipperary
Tel: 062 61507

This small, neat-looking house was built by the owners 28 years ago, and Mrs Mahoney has been running a bed & breakfast here for 26 years. Ros Guill House is well shielded from the road by evergreen trees and a small front garden, which has been a winner in the Bord Fáilte National Garden Competition. Evelyn Mahoney is also a proud recipient of the Galtee Breakfast Award. The house has been freshly decorated and new carpets have been fitted. The rooms are a little on the small side, but immaculately clean, and the dining room has views of the castle and the Galtee Mountains. Evelyn is a very friendly lady who takes excellent care of her guests. Visa, Mastercard, Access, Eurocard accepted.

OWNER Evelyn Mahoney OPEN May – October ROOMS 2 double, 2 twin, 2 family; 3 en suite TERMS B&B IR£20; reduction for children; single supplement IR£7

CLONMEL

Woodruffe House

Cahir Road, Clonmel, Co. Tipperary
Tel: 052 35243

This spacious and elegant house, set on 110 hectares of mixed farming, is surrounded by a lovely garden full of mature trees and flowers. This is a warm and inviting house, and even though it was only built in 1977, it has the ambience of a bygone era. The four spacious bedrooms are beautifully decorated with matching Sanderson wallpapers and fabrics. Guests enjoy the log fires on chilly evenings. Owner Anne O'Donnell is a gracious host who offers complimentary refreshments on arrival. Evening meals are available, if pre-arranged. Anne is an excellent cook; a favourite dish with guests is her baked fish with its delicious sauce, and her mouth-watering desserts, such as pavlova with fresh fruit, are equally popular. There are walks through the farm, and Cahir, Cashel and Clonmel are within driving distance.

OWNER Anne O'Donnell OPEN April 4 – September 30 ROOMS 3 double, 1 twin; 2 en suite   TERMS B&B IR£15–17; reduction for children; single supplement IR£5 MEALS Dinner

MULLINAHONE

Killaghy Castle

Mullinahone, Co. Tipperary
Tel: 052 53112

This Norman castle, whose original owners were Cromwellian planters, has been added on to and extended over the years. Originally it was just a Motte and Bailey, still visible to the left of the castle. During Tudor times a long house was added to the rear of the property, and in 1800 two other buildings were added, making Killaghy the castle we see today. It is part of a 96-hectare dairy and tillage farm. The present owners, the Collins family, moved here in 1995 from Cork. Moira Collins is a down-to-earth and friendly lady, who has created an informal, welcoming atmosphere, adding her personal touch by redecorating and installing new curtains and orthopedic beds. The house is full of antiques purchased specifically for the house to enhance the old-world ambience. The bedrooms are enormous and some have original fireplaces, as do the dining room and the drawing room; the latter is a wonderful spot to relax in and help yourself to tea or coffee. The drawing room has interesting coving and a terra-cotta border. The house has glorious views all round. There is a nature trail and walled garden, as well as games and two tennis courts for guests' use. Visa, Mastercard accepted.

OWNER Moira Collins OPEN All year ROOMS 2 double, 1 twin, 1 double/single; 3 en suite TERMS B&B IR£22.50; reduction for children; single supplement IR£5

NENAGH

Otway Lodge Guest House
Dromineer, Nenagh, Co. Tipperary
Tel: 067 24133 / 24273

Otway Lodge is in a lovely position overlooking Lough Derg. Parts of the house, which was formerly part of a barracks, are over 100 years old. It has been extended and tastefully modernised since that time. The modestly furnished bedrooms are a good size, as are the bathrooms. There is a spacious guest lounge with a peat fire, TV, harp and piano. Frank and Ann work as a team and enjoy their business, and always have a pot of tea on the hob. There is a small shop on the premises offering sweets, lemonade and other snacks. This is an ideal spot for families and water sports enthusiasts as there is windsurfing, sailing, water-skiing and trout and coarse fishing available. There are also boats for hire.

OWNER Ann & Frank Flannery OPEN All year ROOMS 2 double, 4 twin; all en suite TERMS B&B IR£18; reduction for children; single supplement IR£6

Gurtalougha House
Ballinderry, nr. Nenagh, Co. Tipperary
Tel: 067 22080 Fax: 067 22154

Bessie and Michael Wilkinson have retired and this beautiful home has been taken over by the Pettits, who have been busy refurbishing and improving on the high standards already established. Gurtalougha is approached via a peaceful avenue that winds for 1.5 km through 60 hectares of mature forest. Built in the nineteenth century, the house is in an ideal location on the banks of the River Shannon; in the distance can be seen the mountains of Clare and Galway. This is an informal and relaxed house – the emphasis here is on relaxation, and there are log fires and antique furnishings. The spacious and elegant bedrooms have wooden floors and comfortable beds. One has a balcony overlooking the lake. Breakfasts are served in the dining room, which has a view, as do the drawing room and library. The Pettits have introduced an imaginative and extensive menu, featuring the finest ingredients, fresh produce and splendid tasty sauces. There are lovely woodland walks available with a great variety of wildlife such as red squirrels, badgers, otters and kingfishers. Boats and windsurfing boards are available at no extra charge, and there is swimming from the jetty and croquet on the lawn. There are four golf courses, pony trekking, two hard tennis courts and a sailing school close by.

OWNER Ann Pettit OPEN All year ROOMS 8 double, 2 twin; 8 en suite
TERMS B&B IR£50; reduction for children MEALS Dinner

TERRYGLASS

Riverrun House
Terryglass, Co. Tipperary
Tel: 067 22125 Fax: 067 22187

Riverrun House stands in its own beautifully landscaped grounds of 0.5 hectares in the centre of Terryglass, the recipient of the famous Tidy Village Award. Tom and Lucy Sanders have been running their bed & breakfast very successfully since 1991 and are as enthusiastic as ever. Three of the well-appointed bedrooms are located on the ground floor, tastefully decorated in pretty pastel floral colours with matching fabrics and pine furniture. Two have lake views. This house of character is very comfortable and full of interesting antiques. A pleasant five-minute stroll away is the busy harbour set on the northeast shore of Lough Derg – the largest of the lakes on the Shannon system. Riverrun House has a hard tennis court, bicycles for guests' use, and fishing boats for hire. There is an 18-hole golf course close by. Excellent breakfasts are served, including freshly squeezed orange juice, home-baked soda bread and yoghurts, as well as traditional fare. Vegetarian breakfasts are available on request. Evening meals are not available, but Tom and Lucy Sanders would be happy to make recommendations on where to eat. Visa, Mastercard, American Express accepted.

OWNER Lucy Sanders OPEN All year ROOMS 2 double, 2 twin, 2 family; all en suite TERMS B&B IR£25; reduction for children; single supplement IR£5

TIPPERARY

Clonmore House
Galbally Road, Tipperary, Co. Tipperary
Tel: 062 61637

Guests continue to enjoy this immaculate, detached house set back from the main road on the edge of town. The bedrooms are tastefully decorated and colour-coordinated with modern fitted wardrobes. Breakfasts only are served in the attractive dining room with its pretty lace tablecloths. The spacious lounge overlooks the garden – both are available to guests. A fire is lit in the lounge on chilly days, and guests may enjoy a hot drink in the evening; it is a pleasant spot to unwind after a busy day of sightseeing. On fine days the sun lounge is a popular place to sit. Mary Quinn is a delightful hostess who prides herself on personal service. She is pleased to advise on good local restaurants. The town centre is just a five-minute walk away.

OWNER Mrs Mary Quinn OPEN March 1 – November 1 ROOMS 2 double, 3 twin, 1 family; all en suite TERMS B&B IR£18; reduction for children; single supplement IR£5

Woodlawn
Galbally/ Cork Road, Tipperary, Co. Tipperary
Tel: 062 51272

This traditional-style house, with an English russet brick exterior, stands a good distance off the road in a quiet spot behind a large, landscaped garden. It was built as a family home 12 years ago, and when the two sons left home, the owners used the excess space for a bed & breakfast. It is beautifully maintained, has a tranquil ambience and the rooms to the rear of the house overlook horses grazing in the fields. The bedrooms are individually decorated with restful pastel colours and have plenty of wardrobe space. Nuala O'Sullivan is extremely hospitable, and goes out of her way to ensure her guests are well taken care of. Excellent breakfasts are served and include a wide cereal choice and fresh fruit, followed by a traditional Irish breakfast.

OWNER Nuala O'Sullivan OPEN April 1 – November 30 ROOMS 2 double, 1 twin, 1 double/single; all en suite TERMS B&B IR£17; single supplement IR£6.50

COUNTY WESTMEATH

Centrally located, this county offers a peaceful and beautiful landscape, excellent fishing and lots of history.

The main attractions are its lakes. The four largest are Loughs Owel, Ennell, Derravaragh and Lene. Beautiful Lough Sheelin is farther north and there a number of small lakes too, as well as Lough Ree, an expansion of the Shannon, which is now popular for sailing, cruising and coarse fishing. On many of the islands that dot the lakes are remains of early Christian churches.

Mullingar, the county town, is a thriving commercial centre and attractive market town. It is in one of the best cattle-raising districts of Ireland, and is also a great centre for hunting, shooting and fishing.

Athlone is the largest town in the country. Originally a fording point of the Shannon, Athlone is now a busy market town, major road and rail terminus, and harbour on the inland waterways system. Athlone Castle, now housing a museum dealing with local history, is a strongly fortified building with many interesting features. It has been a famous military post since its original construction in the thirteenth century.

Lough Derravaragh, one of the most beautiful in County Westmeath, is associated with the most tragic of Irish legends, when the Children of Lir were changed into swans by their jealous stepmother and spent 300 years on dark waters.

Tullynally Castle is near Castlepollard. Seat of the Earls of Longford, the castle has a spectacular façade of turrets and towers. Fore is the most historic Christian site in Westmeath. There are several ruins to see, dating from the tenth century, among them St Fechin's Church, an unusual feature of which is the massive cross-inscribed lintel stone.

ATHLONE

Cluain-Innis
Summerhill, Galway Road, Athlone, Co. Westmeath
Tel: 0902 994202

Cluain-Innis is a friendly, cosy bungalow situated 4 km from Athlone. The bedrooms are fresh and bright, prettily decorated and are all on the ground floor. Improvements are ongoing and TVs and hairdryers have been added to the rooms. The lounge is tastefully decorated with matching pink and red fabrics, attractive lights and wall lamps, and tea and coffee makers. Breakfast only is served but there is a good choice of restaurants and pubs in Athlone for evening meals. This is an ideal location for touring Clonmacnois and Deer Park. Fishing and golf are close by.

OWNER Kathleen Shaw OPEN April – October ROOMS 1 double, 1 twin, 1 family; 1 en suite TERMS B&B IR£15–17; reduction for children; single supplement IR£4–6

Shelmalier
Cartrontroy, Athlone, Co. Westmeath
Tel: 0902 73190

Shelmalier House is a spacious, modern house standing in its own grounds with an attractive front garden. The bedrooms, two of which are on the ground floor, are beautifully appointed and have firm, comfortable beds. This is very much a family-run establishment, with considerate hosts who extend a very personal service to ensure their guests' comfort. The TV lounge is spacious, and there is a sun porch where guests may help themselves to complimentary tea or coffee at any time. Jim and Nancy specialise in coarse fishing holidays, but a warm welcome is extended to all visitors. Evening meals are served with the emphasis on fresh food and home-baking, but they must be ordered in advance. There is an 18-hole golf course on the shores of Lough Ree, trail walks and a heated swimming pool within 10 minutes' walk. This is a delightful house with hospitable hosts. Visa, Mastercard.

OWNER Jim & Nancy Denby OPEN All year ROOMS 3 double, 2 twin, 2 family; all en suite TERMS B&B IR£17; reduction for children; single supplement IR£3.50

CASTLEPOLLARD

Whitehall Farm House
Castlepollard, Co. Westmeath
Tel: 044 61140

This creeper–covered, nineteenth-century farmhouse is approached up a private drive. It is set among mature trees and a garden, part of a working cattle, sheep and tillage farm. The house is furnished in keeping with its character and retains the original casement shutters. The bedrooms are warm and cosy with attractive bed linens and comfortable beds. There is a good-size TV lounge and a separate dining room where freshly prepared breakfasts and home-cooked, four-course evening meals are served. Abigail, a friendly, outgoing lady, has been running her bed & breakfast establishment for over eight years. Guests enjoy the special warmth and hospitality here and many folks are happy repeat visitors. Guests are welcome to wander around the farm and watch the animals. The ancient monastic village of Fore nearby contains an interesting seventh-century church. Traditional Irish music can be heard at local pubs and perhaps, too, some of the folklore tales of the area.

OWNER Donagh & Abigail Smyth   OPEN April 1 – November 1
ROOMS 1 double, 2 twin; all en suite   TERMS B&B IR£15–17.50;
reduction for children 33%; single supplement IR£5 MEALS Dinner

HORSELEAP

Woodlands Farm
Streamstown, nr. Horseleap, Co. Westmeath
Tel: 044 26414

This charming 200-year-old farmhouse, surrounded by ornamental trees, is part of a 50-hectare cattle farm, and is a marvellous
spot for families. Mary Maxwell has created a wonderful, informal,
welcoming atmosphere. Guests are encouraged to explore the farm
and there are free pony rides for children. The bedrooms are
spacious and there are lots of antique furnishings, including a
chaise-longue and a lovely dresser. Guests enjoy sitting around in
the spacious lounge, which has a grand piano, and musical
evenings are encouraged. Four of the bedrooms are on the ground
floor. Breakfast and pre-arranged dinners are served in the very
large dining room; when possible, meals feature fresh, home-
grown produce. Vegetarians can be catered for with advance
notice.

OWNER Mary Maxwell OPEN March 1 – October 1 ROOMS 2 double,
2 twin, 1 family, 1 single; 4 en suite TERMS B&B IR£18; reduction for
children; single supplement IR£6 MEALS Dinner

Cooleen

Ballymore Road, Moate, Co. Westmeath
Tel: 0902 81044

This well maintained, attractive bungalow with hanging baskets
and flower tubs is situated in a country setting of 0.5 hectares.
Ethna Kelly is a considerate host and guests are greeted with a hot
drink upon arrival. The good-sized rooms are tastefully furnished
and decorated, and have comfortable beds. Breakfasts are excellent
and include fresh, home-baked scones, and are served in the lush
conservatory on warm days. There is a lounge where turf fires burn
in the evening. Bicycles are available and there are some lovely
walks winding past the bog. This is perfect for folks who are
looking for an informal, home-away-from-home atmosphere.

OWNER Ethna Kelly OPEN All year ROOMS 1 double, 1 family; both
en suite TERMS B&B IR£17; reduction for children; single supplement
IR£3

Temple

Horseleap, Moate, Co. Westmeath
Tel: 0506 35118 Fax: 0506 35118

This lovely, 200-year-old country house sits in a secluded position
amidst mature trees and gardens on a 57-hectare cattle farm. It was
built on the site of a sixth-century monastery – hence the name.
The house has been in the same family for three generations and
is full of old-world charm; there are marble washstands and
fireplaces, and brass beds. Bernadette is an excellent cook; dinners
are served in the large dining room and feature tasty, healthy
foods, fresh vegetables, local meats and delicious homemade
desserts. After dinner, guests gather round the open fire in the
lounge, often joined by Bernadette and Declan. A games room and
a library were added three years ago. Special breaks are offered for
individual or small groups in the recently created "Temple Spa" in
the new, stone-finished courtyard. Guests can partake of yoga,
steam baths, massage, beauty therapy and total relaxation
packages, as well as walking and cycling. Fishing and golfing
holidays at championship courses can also be arranged.

Reservations should be made as far ahead as possible. Temple House is a haven of peace and tranquillity, the food is excellent and Bernadette and Declan are the perfect hosts. Vegetarian and special diets can be catered for with advance notice. Visa, Mastercard accepted.

OWNER Declan & Bernadette Fagan OPEN February 1 – December 1 ROOMS 2 double, 4 twin, 1 family, 1 single; all en suite TERMS B&B IR£30–40; reduction for children; single supplement IR£10 MEALS Dinner

MULLINGAR

Hilltop Country House
Delvin Road, Rathconnel, Mullingar, Co. Westmeath
Tel: 044 48958 Fax: 044 48013

This exceptionally well maintained, spacious, split-level house is approached by a private gravel drive. The house sits in an elevated position with views of Sheever Lough in the distance and the city at night. The house was specifically designed for bed & breakfast; the bedrooms are all large, with a high standard of décor, and have comfortable firm beds. One of the bedrooms is on the ground floor and has its own entrance. Freshly prepared breakfasts are served in the bright dining room overlooking pretty countryside. Dympna and Sean are extremely hospital and helpful, and are happy to assist with itinerary planning. Hilltop has facilities for the angler, including a tackler with drying facilities. Boat hire can be arranged. There are several options in the area for evening meals.

OWNER Sean & Dympna Casey OPEN All year ROOMS 2 double, 3 twin; all en suite TERMS B&B IR£20; reduction for children; single supplement IR£6.50

Keadeen
Innishtown, Mullingar, Co. Westmeath
Tel: 044 48440

There is a comfortable, easygoing atmosphere at this well maintained, freshly decorated bungalow, situated in a peaceful location on the edge of town. To quote Madge Nolan, "I have never met a guest I didn't like," which could have something to do with her friendly and welcoming personality. The bedrooms are spotlessly clean and are individually decorated in bright colours, with warm duvets and rich carpets. Breakfasts are served from 7 a.m. to 10:30 a.m. and consist of homemade marmalades, preserves and freshly baked bread. Dinners are no longer available, but Madge Nolan will be happy to recommend local establishments for evening meals. Local amenities include golf, swimming, fishing and boating.

OWNER Madge Nolan OPEN All year ROOMS 1 double, 1 twin, 1 family; 2 en suite TERMS B&B IR£18; reduction for children; single supplement IR£3

Lough Owel Lodge
Cullion, nr. Mullingar, Co. Westmeath
Tel: 044 48714

Lough Owel Lodge is a delightful country house approached by a long private drive. It has panoramic views of Lough Owel and the surrounding countryside. There are 20 hectares of fertile farmland, and the property extends down to the lake, where there are ghillies and boats available. The house is well maintained and appointed, and the spacious lounge overlooks the gardens and hard tennis court. There are several interesting pieces of antique furniture about. The bedrooms are individually furnished; two have four-poster beds, and all rooms have had TV installed. Guests looking

for the perfect place to unwind will be well satisfied with this charming house situated in this secluded, tranquil setting. Wind-surfing and golf are available close by. Visa, Mastercard accepted.

OWNER Martin & Aideen Ginnell OPEN March 1 – December 1
ROOMS 3 double, 1 twin, 1 family; all en suite TERMS B&B IR£18–20;
reduction for children; single supplement IR£5 MEALS Dinner

MULTYFARNHAM

Mornington House
Multyfarnham, Co. Westmeath
Tel: 044 72191 Fax: 044 72338

Mornington House, a gracious family home, was built in 1854 and extended in 1896. It is surrounded by beautiful trees – the Mornington Oak is over 200 years old. It is within easy walking distance of Lough Derravarragh – the Lake of the Oaks – one of the three lakes where the children of Lir spent 300 years of their 900-year exile. The grounds are inhabited by foxes, badgers, storks and a variety of birds and there is a wealth of flora and fauna. The house is furnished with much of the original furniture and many family portraits, and retains the ambience of a bygone era, lovingly combined with all-modern comforts. Mornington is an oasis of peace and tranquillity and is an ideal location in which to explore the Midlands and the surrounding scenic area; Dublin is within a

90-minute drive. The reception rooms have open log and turf fires. Anne and Warwick are charming hosts; Anne is an excellent cook, and wonderful dinners are served by candlelight in the Victorian dining room, featuring fresh fruit, vegetables and herbs from the walled garden. Vegetarians can be catered for with advance notice. The bedrooms are large. Two have brass beds. Children are welcome by arrangement. Canoes, boats and bicycles are available for hire. American Express, Visa, Mastercard accepted.

OWNER Warwick & Anne O'Hara OPEN April 1 – October 31 ROOMS 3 double, 1 twin, 1 single; 2 en suite TERMS B&B IR£35; reduction for children; single supplement IR£5 MEALS Dinner

Northern Ireland

COUNTY ANTRIM

County Antrim's attractions are many. The county town of Belfast lies on the shores of Belfast Lough, in a most attractive setting, surrounded by hills that can be seen from most parts of the town.

It became a thriving commercial centre and port in the nineteenth century, and now has a population of 300,000, nearly a third of the population of Northern Ireland. Among the many sights to see in Belfast is the Ulster Museum, which contains the treasures from the wreck of the Spanish Armada vessel, the *Girona*.

The town of Antrim is set back from Lough Neagh, the largest expanse of inland water in the British Isles, and famous for its eels. The main fishery is in Toomebridge. One of the best ways to see the lough is from the Shane's Castle Railway at Randalstown, Ireland's only working narrow-gauge railway.

The Country Antrim stretch of coastline is among the most spectacular and scenic in Europe. Carrickfergus to the south, the oldest town in Ireland, is dominated by its castle. Farther north lies Larne, an important port, only a two-and-a-half hour ferry ride from Scotland. Beyond Larne, the coast road built in the 1830s affords breathtaking views of the coast and cliffs. Along this road, it is possible to see the formation of the earth's outer crust.

The coast road connects each of the nine famous Glens of Antrim: green valleys running down to the sea, with rivers, waterfalls, wildflowers and birds. From south to north they are: Glenarm, Glencloy, Glenariff, Glenballyeamon, Glenaan, Glencorp, Glendun, Glenshesk and Glentaisie, which are said to mean: glen of the army, glen of the hedges, ploughman's glen, Edwardstown glen, glen of the rush lights, glen of the slaughter, brown glen, sedgy glen, and Taisie's Glen (referring to the legendary princess of Rathlin Island).

The resort town of Ballycastle is famous for its "Oul Lammas Fair," which once lasted a week and now takes place over two hectic days at the end of August. Ballinatoy, a picturesque, Mediterranean-looking fishing village, is one of the prettiest towns on the coast. Beyond the town is one of the word's most amazing natural wonders, the Giant's Causeway. This is made up of a mass of basalt columns, altogether some 40,000, which are all tightly packed together, reaching heights of 12 m, and which disappear into the sea. They appear at Staffa Island on the Scottish coast, and there are many legends attached to this natural phenomenon.

BALLYCASTLE

Colliers Hall
50 Cushendall Road, Ballycastle, Co. Antrim
Tel: 012657 62531

This eighteenth-century, pebble-dashed farmhouse lies just off the main road 3 km from Ballycastle. The bedrooms are spacious, with the washbasins cleverly incorporated into marble washstands, and all have tea and coffee making facilities and hairdryers. The house is furnished with a mixture of traditional and antique furniture, and one room has a four-poster bed. The large TV lounge has an original marble fireplace, and dinner, if booked in advance, is served in the dining room. Colliers Hall offers comfort, excellent value and a warm atmosphere. There are lovely walks through the woods, with views of the Knocklayde Mountains and Glenshesk Valley. An 18-hole golf course is close by, and it is 3 km to the ferry terminal serving Ballycastle to Campbelltown in Scotland. No pets. Smoking only in the lounge. Visa accepted.

OWNER Gerard & Maureen McCarry   OPEN April – September
ROOMS 3 double; all en suite   TERMS B&B £18; single supplement
£10   MEALS Dinner from £12

BELFAST

Ash-Rowan Town House
12 Windsor Avenue, Belfast, Co. Antrim   BT9 6EE
Tel: 01232 661758   Fax: 01232 663227

This late Victorian house stands in its own garden in a quiet, tree-lined avenue in south Belfast. Ash-Rowan is a most attractive house of character, with interesting colours and furnishings, antiques and all kinds of knick-knacks. It is a cosy place with a friendly atmosphere, and Sam and Evelyn have thought of just about everything for their guests, combining all the facilities of a hotel with personal service at a reasonable price. There are flowers and newspapers, and a laundry service is available. The en suite bedrooms all have TVs, hairdryers, trouser presses, information packs, bathrobes, linen sheets and tea and coffee making facilities. Ash-Rowan is known for its breakfast – a great selection from the menu, including freshly squeezed orange juice and home-baked bread. No pets. Smoking only in the lounge and two designated bedrooms. The house is 10 minutes from the city centre and five minutes from the M1 and M2, and is found between the Malone and Lisburn Roads. Visa, Mastercard accepted.

OWNER Evelyn & Sam Hazlett   OPEN Closed at Christmas & New Year's   ROOMS 5 double/twin/single; all en suite   TERMS B&B £33–39.50; single supplement £8.50–15

Avenue House
23 Eglantine Avenue, Belfast, Co. Antrim
Tel: 01232 665904 Fax: 01232 291810

Stephen and Alice Kelly have totally renovated this late Victorian terraced brick-built house, which stands on a fairly busy residential tree-lined street. The rooms are spacious and light and furnished with elegant simplicity. The en suite bedrooms vary in size and all have TVs, telephones and tea and coffee making facilities. Both the breakfast room and drawing room have their attractive, original marble fireplaces, and the rooms are separated from each other by an interesting pull-up wall. Stephen and Alice, who started in business at the start of 1998, are an enthusiastic couple who do everything possible to make their guests comfortable. Avenue House is located between the Malone and Lisburn roads. It is conveniently placed for the University and centre of town, which can easily be reached by bus. No pets.

OWNER Stephen & Alice Kelly   OPEN All year   ROOMS 2 double, 3 family; all en suite   TERMS B&B £22.50; reduction for children; single supplement £4.50

Hermitage Lodge
62 North Road, Belfast, Co. Antrim BT5 5NJ
Tel: 01232 203322

Hermitage Lodge is an attractive Victorian detached house standing in its own gardens off a fairly busy residential street, within a few kilometres of the city centre. It was a virtual ruin when the Frews bought it, and it has been almost completely rebuilt, some of its older features unfortunately lost in the process. The rear garden is quite private and a peaceful spot to sit, away from the bustle of the city. There is plenty of parking space in the front driveway. The entrance door is flanked by two large, stone, sitting lions. The rooms are bright and cheerfully decorated and simply furnished in pine. Every convenience is available for the visitor including TV, trouser press, hairdryer, tea and coffee making facilities and telephone. There is a bright sitting room, off which is the small breakfast room with individual pine tables. Hermitage Lodge is popular with business people, and the Frews prefer guests on shorter stays. No pets, no smoking and not suitable for children. It is located off the Newtownards Road. Visa, Access, American Express accepted.

OWNER Jean & Terry Frew   OPEN Closed at Christmas   ROOMS 2 twin, 2 single; 4 showers en suite   TERMS B&B £27.50; single supplement £7.50

Laburnum Lodge Guest House
16 Deramore Park, Belfast, Co. Antrim BT9 5JU
Tel: 01232 665183 Fax: 01232 681460

Laburnum Lodge is a comfortable house in a very pleasant residential street only 3 km from the city centre. For ten years it was a nursing home. It became a bed & breakfast during 1997 and still has a lift. Anna Johnston is a friendly, welcoming host who runs the house in a professional manner. It is clean, comfortable and furnished with simple elegance. The large dining room has separate tables, with a small sun lounge separating it from the sitting room. The en suite bedrooms have hairdryers, trouser presses, TVs, telephones and tea and coffee making facilities. No pets. Visa, Mastercard accepted.

OWNER Anna Johnston   OPEN Closed at Christmas   ROOMS 2 double, 3 family, 1 single; all en suite   TERMS B&B £27.50; reduction for children; single supplement £7.50

Maranatha Guest House

254 Ravenhill Road, Belfast, Co. Antrim BT6 9GL
Tel: 01232 460200 Fax: 01232 460200

This attractive Victorian terraced house is set back a little from the main road and lies just opposite the Ormeau Leisure Centre. It is 2.5 km from the city centre, easily reached by bus, and has some car parking space in front of the house. The McCreas moved here from a guest house farther up the road in 1996, and totally renovated Maranatha. Although not many of the original features of the house remain, it is warm, comfortable and well equipped. The entrance to the house is through a small sun porch with a tiled floor, and guests have use of a TV lounge. Breakfast is served at separate tables in the dining room. The good-sized bedrooms have TVs, telephones and tea and coffee making facilities, and some of the upper rooms have views of the hills beyond the city. No pets and no smoking.

OWNER Stuart & Edna McCrea OPEN Closed at Christmas ROOMS 2 double, 5 twin, 2 single; 8 en suite TERMS B&B £19.50; reduction for children; single supplement

Roseleigh House

19 Rosetta Park, Belfast, Co. Antrim BT6 0DL
Tel: 01232 644414 Fax: 01232 644414

This restored Victorian-style, brick-built house is surrounded by a small garden. It is in a residential area of south Belfast, conveniently located for bus routes leading into the city centre. Roseleigh House was completely renovated by the McKays, and most recently they have opened up a couple of new bedrooms and a lounge. The rooms are decorated in pastel colours and are clean and comfortable. The en suite bedrooms all have TV and tea and coffee making facilities. Packed lunches are available if arranged in advance. Smoking is only permitted in the lounge. No pets. There is a car park to the rear of the house. Visa, Mastercard, American Express accepted.

OWNER Peter & Dorothy McKay OPEN All year ROOMS 3 double, 2 twin, 1 family, 2 single; all en suite TERMS B&B £23.75; reduction for children; single supplement £12 MEALS Packed lunch £5–7

Tara Lodge

36 Cromwell Road, Botanic Avenue, Belfast, Co. Antrim BT7 1JW
Tel: 01232 590900 Fax: 01232 590901 E-mail: info@taralodge.com

A purpose-built, small hotel/guest house, Tara Lodge was opened in the spring of 1998. It is situated on a quiet residential street, close to the University and within easy access of the city centre. It offers well-planned, functional, bright bedrooms, simply and attractively furnished with all amenities including hairdryers, trouser presses, telephones, TVs and tea and coffee making facilities. One bedroom is suitable for disabled guests. There is a small TV lounge on the first floor and a quite extensive dining room, where currently breakfast only is served, although there are plans to offer other meals in the future. There is also a large off-street parking area. Tara Lodge is particularly suited to business people. No pets. All major credit cards accepted.

OWNER Conor O'Donnell OPEN All year ROOMS 4 double, 2 twin, 12 family; all en suite TERMS B&B £27–32.50; reduction for children by arrangement; single supplement £8–17.50

The Old Rectory

148 Malone Road, Belfast, Co. Antrim BT9 4LH
Tel: 01232 667882 Fax: 01232 683759

When the Old Rectory was built in 1896, it was out in the countryside. Now it is within a comfortable distance of the city centre – 3 km – and still has views of the Belfast mountains. It was designed by the architect Henry Seaver, who was also responsible for the neighbouring Church of St John's (he was the brother of the then minister, Rev. Richard Seaver). Later in life it became a nursing home, before becoming the family home of the Callans. It is furnished and decorated with individual taste and has some interesting pieces whilst retaining the feel of a family home. Books and newspapers can be found in the sitting room, and a complimentary "hot Irish whiskey" is served each evening. The bedrooms each have TV, hairdryer, trouser press and tea and coffee making facilities. Malone Road is one of the principal streets leading into the centre of town and is right on the bus route. No pets. Some rooms are designated non-smoking.

OWNER Mary Callan OPEN Closed at Christmas & 2 weeks in summer
ROOMS 4 double, 1 single; 4 en suite TERMS B&B £30; reduction for
children; single supplement £10 MEALS Dinner £14

BROUGHSHANE

Dunaird House
15 Buckna Road, Broughshane, Co. Antrim BT42 4NJ
Tel: 01266 862117

Built in 1920, this substantial house stands just outside
Broughshane. The Grahams bought the house, partly to do B&B,
and partly because 20 hectares went with the house, which
extended John Graham's existing farm. The house provides luxury
accommodation, with carpets and wallpapers of all types and
varieties adorning every square inch. Some of the rooms have their
original fireplaces, and two of the bedrooms are front-facing with
lots of windows and lovely views. All rooms are en suite with
telephones, TVs and tea and coffee making facilities. John and
Sylvia are a friendly young couple who do everything they can to
make their guests' stay comfortable.

OWNER Sylvia Graham OPEN All year ROOMS 2 double, 1 twin; all
en suite TERMS B&B £22.50; reduction for children; single
supplement £2.50

BUSHMILLS

Billy Old Rectory
5 Cabragh Road, Castlecat, Bushmills, Co. Antrim BT57 8YH
Tel: 012657 31208

The little hamlet of Billy surrounds its old parish church. The Old
Rectory, suitably, stands next to the church. Billy is the oldest –
and oddest – of names, an anglicised form of "Bile" (or Bille) a
Gaelic word meaning "ancient or sacred tree, venerated by the
Druids." The late Georgian house is most attractive and was
bought by the Pages at the end of its rectory days in a dilapidated
state – a gradual deterioration over the previous 150 years! The

central, front part of the house is rounded, with a circular staircase leading from the cellar to the first floor. Handsome door trims surround the doorways to the comfortable drawing room and dining room, both of which overlook the lovely and extensive garden. The smaller double bedroom has a large private bathroom which was once a bedroom with corner tub and bidet. The larger bedroom has a well designed, en suite shower room constructed so as not to spoil the proportions of the room. Mrs Page is a delightful, welcoming host and Mr Page is the local pharmacist. Billy Old Rectory has been their family home for some 20 years. The original lodge to the house has been converted to self-catering accommodation. No smoking and no pets. Billy is located 2.5 km southeast of Bushmills.

OWNER Meta Page OPEN Easter – October 31 ROOMS 1 double, 1 twin; 1 shower (en suite) TERMS B&B £20–25; reduction for children; single supplement £5

Craig Park
Bushmills, Co. Antrim BT57 8YF
Tel: 012657 32496 Fax: 012657 32479

Craig Park, situated in open countryside, has views of the Donegal and Antrim hills, and is 3 km inland from Bushmills. The original house has had a new piece added to it, built in the Georgian style, giving it an imposing look. This new part of the house accommodates the guests with three good-sized bedrooms, a large sitting room and a dining room, where breakfast only is served. There are great walks, cycling and golf, and the Giant's Causeway is nearby. Visa, Mastercard accepted.

OWNER Jan Cheal OPEN Closed at Christmas ROOMS 2 twin, 1 family; 3 showers en suite TERMS B&B £25; single supplement £5

Killen's Restaurant
28 Ballyclough Road, Bushmills, Co. Antrim BT57 8UZ
Tel: 012657 41536 Fax: 012657 41070

Formerly the Auberge de Seneirl, this establishment was taken over by the Laffertys in 1997 and its name changed to Killen's Restaurant. Once an old schoolhouse, the building was extended and recently refurbished, and it has pleasant views. The bedrooms are light and attractively decorated in bright colours, with refitted en suite bathrooms. All the rooms have TVs, hairdryers and tea and coffee making facilities, and one is a suite with a four-poster bed and jacuzzi bath. Families are very welcome and there is a children's play area. There's also an indoor swimming pool, sauna, sun bed and sun lounge. Peter Lafferty, who's from Scotland and is an award-winning chef, runs the restaurant, featuring local, international and vegetarian cuisine. Killen's is close to the scenic Antrim coast and the Bushmills Distillery. No smoking in the restaurant. All major credit cards accepted.

OWNER Peter Lafferty OPEN All year ROOMS 5 double, 1 suite; all en suite TERMS B&B £25; reduction for children; single supplement £10 MEALS Dinner £19.50

Valley View

6a Ballyclough Road, Bushmills, Co. Antrim BT57 8TU
Tel: 012657 41608 / 41319

This whitewashed, modern house was built by the McFalls and extended recently to provide more guest accommodation. It is surrounded by its own 24 hectares of farmland, supporting beef and sheep, and is 6 km inland from Bushmills. Mrs McFall is a cheerful, friendly host with young children, and is welcoming to families. The accommodation is simple and bright. Guests have use of a comfortable sitting room and breakfast only is served at separate tables in the dining room. One room is suitable for the disabled. No pets and no smoking. The attractions of the north Antrim coast are within easy reach, including the Giant's Causeway, Carrick-A-Rede Rope Bridge, Bushmills Distillery, Dunluce Castle and Rathlin Island. Valley View is signposted off the B67 and B17.

OWNER Mrs Valerie McFall OPEN All year ROOMS 2 double, 2 twin, 2 family; all en suite TERMS B&B £15–16.50; reduction for children; single supplement £5

Caldhame Lodge

102 Moira Road, Nutts Corner, Crumlin, Co. Antrim BT29 4HG
Tel: 01849 423099 Fax: 01849 423099

Caldhame Lodge is just off the main Moira Road, in its own grounds and just five minutes from the airport. It was built in the early 1990s as the McKavanaghs' family home. It has recently been upgraded to have six en suite rooms, all with TVs, hairdryers, telephones and trouser presses. There are also jacuzzi baths. It is comfortable and pleasantly furnished with brand-new furniture. Breakfast only is served in the dining room/sun lounge, and guests have use of two further lounges, one with TV. Certain bedrooms are reserved for smokers. Pets are permitted outside. Caldhame Lodge can be found on the A26 17 km from Junction 9 on the M1. Access, Visa, American Express, Mastercard accepted.

OWNER Anne McKavanagh OPEN All year ROOMS 6 double/single/ twin/family; all en suite TERMS B&B £20; reduction for children; single supplement £8

Keef Halla

20 Tully Road, Nutts Corner, Crumlin, Co. Antrim BT29 4SW
Tel: 01232 825491 Fax: 01232 825491

Keef Halla, meaning "welcome" in Arabic, acquired its name because Charles Kelly used to work in Saudi Arabia and bought the house with the money he earned there. It is an old country house that has been renovated and recently extended. Charles Kelly, who runs the guest house (Siobhan is a teacher in Belfast), is fast earning a reputation for the level of comfort and service he provides – borne out by being awarded the accolade of Northern Ireland Guesthouse of the Year. All the en suite bedrooms have telephones, hairdryers, trouser presses, TVs, information packs and mineral water. The comfortable sitting room has an open fire, leather sofa and chairs, and leads into the dining room, where meals are available all day long if arranged in advance. Packed lunches can also be provided. One guest arriving by helicopter landed in the garden, and Keef Halla claims to be the nearest guest house to the airport. Pets can be accommodated in outbuildings.

Smoking is permitted only in the designated bedrooms. The house stands just off the main A26 road, five minutes from Belfast International Airport. Visa, Mastercard, Delta, American Express accepted.

OWNER Charles & Siobhan Kelly OPEN All year ROOMS 1 double, 1 twin, 5 family; all en suite TERMS B&B £20–22.50; reduction for children; single supplement £7.50–10 MEALS Lunch £5; packed lunch £3; high tea £10; dinner £15

CUSHENDALL

Glendale
46 Coast Road, Cushendall, Co. Antrim BT44 0RX
Tel: 012667 71495

This attractive, white, pebble-dashed house is down a private driveway off the main A2 road in the village of Cushendall. It enjoys lovely views of the Antrim plateau and sea. The O'Neills are friendly and welcoming hosts, attracting a lot of repeat visitors. Mr O'Neill works on the Larne-Cairnryan ferry, and enjoys outlining sightseeing itineraries for guests. The house has been extended to provide for two more bedrooms and a new dining room, where breakfast only is served. The house is well maintained and comfortably furnished and the bedrooms have TVs and tea and coffee making facilities.

OWNER Mrs Mary O'Neill OPEN All year ROOMS 5 family; all en suite TERMS B&B £17; reduction for children; single supplement £4

DUNDONALD

The Cottage
377 Comber Road, Dundonald, Co. Antrim BT16 0XB
Tel: 01247 878189

This charming, low, whitewashed, 250-year-old cottage is a relaxing, comfortable house, with a delightful and friendly owner. It lies just off the main Belfast to Comber road in open countryside, has a most attractive small garden and enjoys lovely views. It has been very prettily decorated and furnished throughout, completely in keeping with its cottage atmosphere. The bedrooms are small and both have antique double beds, pretty wallpaper and fabrics, telephones and hairdryers. The large breakfast room/lounge with open fireplace is full of character. The Cottage is a popular place to stay, combining proximity to Belfast and rural tranquillity. All bedrooms are on the ground floor. Pets outside only. No smoking.

OWNER Elizabeth Muldoon OPEN All year ROOMS 2 double TERMS B&B £20; reduction for children; single supplement £5

LARNE

Cairnview
13 Croft Heights, Ballygally, Larne, Co. Antrim
Tel: 01574 583269 Fax: 01574 583269

Cairnview is a modern house in an area of newer buildings standing above the coast road, with views of the sea and the Glens of Antrim. The bedrooms have TVs and tea and coffee making facilities, and there is a ground floor room suitable for the disabled. Breakfast is served in the large conservatory, which enjoys a lovely view. Guests may also use the exercise equipment. No smoking and no pets. Cairnview is 500 m from the beach and is well located for touring the Glens of Antrim, the north coast or getting the ferry to Scotland. It can be found by turning left (coming from the Larne direction) in Ballygally by the restaurant, and left again after 200 m in Croft Park, then turning right.

OWNER Mrs Jennifer Lough OPEN All year ROOMS 1 double, 1 twin, 1 family; 3 showers en suite TERMS B&B £18; reduction for children; single supplement £7

The Beeches Country House

10 Dunadry Road, Muckamore, Co. Antrim BT41 4RR
Tel: 01849 433161 Fax: 01849 432227

This Edwardian country house stands in a large, pleasant garden just off the A6 between Templepatrick and Antrim and only 8 km from Belfast airport. The Allens, a very friendly couple, offer comfortable accommodation and hold a Taste of Ulster award. The bedrooms have every possible amenity, including hairdryers, trouser presses, telephones, irons and ironing boards and TVs. There is a snack menu and evening meals are available if booked in advance. No smoking and no pets. Visa, Mastercard, Access, American Express accepted.

OWNER Mrs Marigold Allen OPEN Closed at Christmas & New Year's ROOMS 3 double, 2 single; all en suite TERMS B&B £32.50; single supplement £7.50 MEALS Snack menu £2–5; dinner £5

Glenkeen Guest House

59 Coleraine Road, Portrush, Co. Antrim BT56 8HR
Tel: 01265 822279

Glenkeen is a well maintained, clean guest house located on the edge of Portrush. It is set back a little, by its car park, from the busy main A29 road. Mrs Little is a friendly and efficient lady who has been in the bed & breakfast business for a number of years, and is most particular about keeping the house in good decorative order. The large, comfortable en suite rooms have TV, telephone and tea and coffee making facilities. Breakfast, and evening meals by arrangement, are served in the dining room, and the pleasant sitting room has comfortable chairs and sofas. There is now a chair lift on the stairs for infirm or disabled guests. Some bedrooms are non-smoking. Pets outside only. Visa, Mastercard, American Express accepted.

OWNER Mrs Roberta Little OPEN All year ROOMS 4 double, 3 twin, 3 family; all en suite TERMS B&B £20; reduction for children; single supplement £5–7 MEALS Dinner £8–10

Maddybenny Farm

Loguestown Road, Portrush, Co. Antrim
Tel: 01265 823394 Fax: 01265 823394

Maddybenny Farm, meaning "sanctified or holy post," dates from the 1600s. It was built as a plantation house on lands belonging to the Earl of Antrim. The first Presbyterian minister, Rev. Gabriel Cornwall, lived here. Added on to over the years, the house floor plan is unusual in allowing one to walk completely around the house from the inside. It is approached up a long track and stands in a wonderful, rural location. It is part of a big complex of buildings consisting of the farm, stables and six self-catering cottages. The riding school is run by Rosemary White's son, and offers tuition to guests by an international rider. Maddybenny farm is a comfortable, relaxed place. It is a bright and spacious house with a comfortable drawing room and dining room where breakfast only is served. The bedrooms are all en suite and very large, and have hairdryers and telephones. There is a fridge for

guests' use and laundry facilities. Rosemary White is a marvellous host with a wonderful sense of humour. Her breakfasts are copious and include home baking and fresh trout. Maddybenny is very near the Royal Portrush Golf Club, the Giant's Causeway, the University and beaches. Pets can be accommodated in the stables. Smoking is not allowed in the dining room. The self-catering cottages are equipped to a high standard and sleep six to eight people. The farm is signposted on the A29 both at Portrush and Coleraine. Visa, Mastercard accepted.

OWNER Mrs Rosemary White OPEN Closed at Christmas & New Year's ROOMS 1 double, 2 twin/family; all en suite TERMS B&B £25; reduction for children; single supplement £2

COUNTY ARMAGH

County Armagh is the smallest and most varied county in Northern Ireland, ranging from magnificent mountain scenery in the south to rich fruit-growing land in the north, interspersed with small lakes and dairy farms.

Armagh, the ancient capital of Ulster and former great centre of learning, has been the spiritual capital of Ireland for 1,500 years and is the seat of both Catholic and Protestant archbishops.

The two cathedral churches are prominent features in the city. The Church of Ireland cathedral stands on the hill where St Patrick built his stone church, and the twin spires of the Catholic cathedral, which was finished in 1873, rise from the opposite hill.

In the south of Armagh the mountains of Slieve Gullion contain an unspoilt area of small villages and beautiful scenery. Crossmaglen has the largest market square in Europe and has become the centre of the recently revived lace-making industry. There is an enormous open-air market every Sunday at Jonesborough.

Whilst driving down a country lane, you might come across the great Armagh game; roads bowls, which is shared with County Cork. The object is to hurl a metal bowl weighing 1 kg as far as possible, covering several miles in the shortest number of shots. Children are sent ahead to warn motorists.

The orchard of Ireland, rich, fruit-growing country in the northeast, is at its best in May. Apple Blossom Sunday takes place in late May.

ARMAGH

Ballinahinch House
Richill, Armagh, Co. Armagh
Tel: 01762 870081 Fax: 01762 870081

This early Victorian house is part of a working arable and beef farm of 50 hectares. It has an informal, welcoming atmosphere and John and Elizabeth Kee are delightful hosts. The rooms are spacious and traditionally furnished, the bedrooms comfortable, and the dining room has its original black slate fireplace. There is half a hectare of newly landscaped gardens in front of the house, and the setting is peaceful with lovely walks close by. No smoking. Pets outside only. To locate Ballinahinch House, turn off the A3 onto the B131, take the second road on the left and continue over the crossroads – the house is approximately 1.5 km down on the left.

OWNER John & Elizabeth Kee OPEN April 1 – September 1 ROOMS 2 double, 1 twin, 1 single TERMS B&B from £16; reduction for children; single supplement £2

Dean's Hill

34 College Hill, Armagh, Co. Armagh BT61 9DF
Tel: 01861 524923

This substantial Georgian country house was built by a dean of the cathedral in 1760, and it has been in Mr Armstrong's family since 1870. The house has been restored and offers a large four-poster room, an enormous twin-bedded room and a single room with a newly created large bathroom. Guests have use of a cosy library/study/TV room with comfortable chairs and an open fire. Thirty-two hectares of farmland, ideal for walks, surround the house. Dean's Hill is located close to the centre of Armagh and is in a superb position for visiting all the local places of interest. Smoking in TV lounge only.

OWNER Jill & Edward Armstrong OPEN Closed at Christmas & New Year's ROOMS 3 double/twin/family; 2 en suite TERMS B&B £25; reduction for children

Hillview Lodge

33 Newtownhamilton Road, Armagh, Co. Armagh
Tel: 01861 522000 Fax: 01861 528276

Hillview is a modern building about 2 km outside Armagh, set just back from the road beside a golf driving range, which is under the same ownership. The accommodation is functional and well designed, and the entire house has plain wood-type floors, unalleviated by any rugs. The bedrooms all have hairdryers, telephones, TVs and tea and coffee making facilities. One ground floor room is suitable for the disabled. The dining room, where breakfast only is served, has a sitting area, and there is a further place to sit in the entrance/reception room. Hillview is well suited to business people, or those who want to practise their golf swing. No pets and no smoking. It is located on the B31 Newtownhamilton road. All major credit cards accepted.

OWNER Mr & Mrs McBridge OPEN All year ROOMS 1 double, 5 family; all en suite TERMS B&B £20; reduction for children; single supplement £5

Padua House

63 Cathedral Road, Armagh, Co. Armagh
Tel: 01861 522039 Fax: 01861 523584

Guests are made to feel like part of the family at Padua House. Mr and Mrs O'Hagan are a friendly, welcoming couple who thoroughly enjoy their visitors. The family lounge is shared with guests, who are encouraged to join the owners after a busy day's touring. A hot drink is almost always available, and the O'Hagans are always happy to assist guests with itineraries and recommendations on places to eat. The house has a lived-in, family feel to it and a collection of dolls line the staircase. The accommodation is clean and basic and all bedrooms have a TV. A hearty breakfast is served in the dining room. No pets. Smoking in the TV lounge only. Padua House is located within 100 m of St Patrick's Cathedral.

OWNER Mrs Kathleen O'Hagan   OPEN All year   ROOMS 2 twin
TERMS B&B £14; reduction for children

COUNTY DERRY

Derry is probably best known for the tune "Derry Air," also known as "Danny Boy." The city of Derry is situated on a hill on the banks of the Foyle. The city acquired the name Londonderry in the seventeenth century when the City of London financed building and resettlement in the city. The seventeenth-century walls, about 1.5-km-round and 5.5-m-thick, have withstood several sieges and are still intact, giving magnificent views of the surrounding countryside. Derry still preserves its medieval layout, and amongst the historic buildings is the 1633 Gothic Cathedral of St Columb.

From the quay behind the Guildhall, hundreds of Irish emigrants left Derry for America during the eighteenth and nineteenth centuries, amongst them the families and ancestors of Davy Crockett and US President James Polk.

The Mussenden Temple, built by the eccentric Earl Bishop of Derry as testimony of his affection for Lady Mussenden, stands on a windswept headland on the coast at Downhill; adjacent, the castle is now in ruins but exudes an aura of romance and grandeur, and is worth visiting.

One of Ulster's finest fortified farmhouses can be seen at Bellaghy, and whiskey is produced at Bushmills near Coleraine, the town which St Patrick is supposed to have founded.

AGHADOWEY

Greenhill House
24 Greenhill Road, Aghadowey, Coleraine, Co. Derry BT51 4EU
Tel: 01265 868241 Fax: 01265 868365

A nice old Georgian house standing in its own grounds of trees, lawns and shrubs, with lovely views over farmland to distant hills. This is a 60-hectare arable and beef farm and the Hegartys have owned the property for about 15 years. Upgrading is ongoing; two of the bathrooms now have baths and showers, and are well-appointed with every convenience. Mrs Hegarty, formerly a teacher, now devotes her time to running her successful bed & breakfast; she is a most friendly and cheerful lady. There is a spacious lounge which overlooks the fields, and a marble fireplace where fires burn brightly on chilly evenings. Breakfasts and pre-arranged dinners are served at separate tables, and guests may

bring their own wine to dinner. Greenhill House is the recipient of several awards, including the Taste of Ulster and British Airways Awards. Visa, Access, Mastercard accepted.

OWNER Mrs James Hegarty OPEN March 1 – October 31 ROOMS 2 double, 2 twin, 2 family; all en suite TERMS B&B £25; reduction for children; single supplement £5 MEALS Dinner

CASTLEROE

Camus House
27 Curragh Road, Castleroe, nr. Coleraine, Co. Derry
Tel: 01265 42982

Camus House is reputed to be built on the site of an old monastery, and is a listed building, dating from 1685, the oldest house in the area. The house is in a delightful setting, close to the River Bann, and Mrs King owns 2 km of river frontage. This lovely old ivy-covered house is approached by a private driveway through parklike grounds, and has a pretty front garden. Mrs King is a most friendly and accommodating lady who runs a warm and comfortable bed & breakfast, and is also a member of the "Healthy Eating Circle Galtee Breakfast Awards." Her passion is fishing, and this is a great fishing family; her daughter has represented Ireland. The house has lots of character and is comfortably furnished as a family home. In winter, guests use Mrs King's cosy sitting room, which has an open fire. There is another sitting room, and a dining room where breakfasts only are served. Not suitable for children.

OWNER Josephine King OPEN All year ROOMS 1 double, 1 family, 1 single; 1 en suite TERMS B&B £20; single supplement £5 MEALS Packed lunches

COLERAINE

Killegue Lodge
157 Drumcoone Road, Coleraine, Co. Derry BT49 9EF
Tel: 01265 868229

Margaret Moore previously ran her bed & breakfast from the farm, which is now lived in by her son. Guests are still welcome to wander around the farm, but the accommodations are now in a beautiful new property built on the land. Two of the bedrooms are on the ground floor and they are all very tastefully decorated: one has a semicircular wall, old pine furniture and a pastel lemon décor; another has mahogany furniture and pine décor; the third large upstairs room is blue, with rich mahogany furnishings. There is a sun lounge and two other lounges for guests' use. Breakfast, and excellent home-cooked four-course dinners are served upon request, and packed lunches can also be provided.

OWNER Margaret Moore OPEN All year ROOMS 1 double, 1 twin, 1 family; all en suite TERMS B&B £20; reduction for children; single supplement £3 MEALS Dinner, packed lunches

DERRY

Number 10
10 Crawford Square, Derry, Co. Derry
Tel: 01504 265000/ 360304

This family-run modernised Victorian house is in an unspoiled Victorian square, five minutes' walk from the city centre. Improvements have been ongoing; all the bedrooms have en suite bathrooms. Grace McGoldrick is a very personable and helpful lady who keeps a spotlessly clean house. A freshly prepared tasty breakfast is served in the attractive dining room. A popular venue with tourist and business people.

OWNER Grace McGoldrick OPEN All year ROOMS 2 double, 1 family; all en suite TERMS B&B £17.50; reduction for children; single supplement £3

EGLINTON

Longfield Farm
132 Clooney Road, Eglinton, Co. Derry BT47 3DX
Tel: 0154 810210

This spacious old house stands in a pleasant garden with lawn and shrubs. Improvements have been ongoing, and en suite facilities added to one of the bedrooms. The farmyard, which serves the 80-

hectare farm of potatoes, beef and cereals, is to the back of the house. It is a comfortable family home with a lived-in feeling. A cosy smaller lounge with open fire is used in winter; in summer, the large lounge is preferred. The bedrooms are of a good size, and breakfasts only are served in the dining room.

OWNER Mrs Elma Hunter OPEN May 31 – October 30 ROOMS 1 twin, 2 family; 1 en suite TERMS B&B £16; reduction for children; single supplement £3

LIMAVADY

Ballyhenry House
172 Seacoast Road, Limavady, Co. Derry BT49 9EF
Tel: 015047 22657

This large, bright and airy farmhouse is close to the sea between Limavady and Castlerock. It was built around the turn of the century by Mr Kane's grandfather, and the flat and fertile land extends to 140 hectares. The farm is managed by Rosemary Kane's two sons and their uncle; it is a very successful operation, and they have won a variety of awards. Rosemary Kane is a very friendly lady, who prepares excellent evening meals, if arranged in advance. The rooms are nicely proportioned and pleasantly decorated and furnished with some interesting antique furniture. A large en suite room has been added with a double and a single bed and its own balcony, and a loft has been converted to provide a self-catering unit that sleeps six.

OWNER Rosemary Kane OPEN All year ROOMS 1 double, 1 twin, 1 family, 1 single; 1 en suite TERMS B&B £17; reduction for children; single supplement £3

PORTSTEWART

Lis-Na-Rhin
6 Victoria Terrace, Portstewart, Co. Derry
Tel: 01265 833522

This fresh and bright house is located in a pleasant spot a few metres away from the sea, overlooking the golf course. The town centre and the promenade are just a few minutes' walk away. All the rooms have recently been refurbished and high standards pervade the house. The beds are comfortable and all rooms have sea views. There is a good supply of information on the area provided and the pleasant owner, Lynne Gardiner, is happy to offer advice. The spacious lounge is well furnished and is a good spot in which to relax after a busy day. Modestly priced evening meals are available, if pre-arranged, and vegetarians can be catered for with advance notice. Visa, Mastercard, Access accepted.

OWNER Miss Lynne Gardiner OPEN All year ROOMS 1 double, 1 twin, 5 family, 1 single; 6 en suite TERMS B&B £15–21; reduction for children; single supplement £5–7 MEALS Dinner

Oregon Guest House

168 Station Road, Portstewart, Co. Derry BT55 7PU
Tel: 01265 832826

About 1 km from the sea, and within walking distance of the city centre, this well maintained and well-kept guest house lies on the outskirts of Portstewart, just off a fairly busy main road. The house has a high standard of furnishings and fresh, bright rooms, prettily decorated with floral curtains and bed covers. One of the double bedrooms has a corner bath, and some are on the ground floor. The small, cosy, panelled dining room, with fine china and flowers on the table, overlooks the sunny patio with a pond and a small fountain. The lounge is comfortable and breakfast and pre-arranged evening meals are served in the dining room, which is very bright and has windows all round. There is plenty of information for the visitor. Access, Visa, Mastercard, American Express accepted.

OWNER Mrs Vi Anderson OPEN February 1 – October 31 ROOMS 4 double, 2 twin, 1 family, 1 single; all en suite TERMS B&B £22.50; reduction for children; single supplement £8.50 MEALS Dinner

COUNTY DOWN

A county rich in monuments of antiquity, County Down has been subject to many invasions throughout its history, the fiercest of all from the Vikings in the ninth century.

Legend has it that St Patrick landed here in A.D. 432 at the place where the Slaney River flows into Strangford Lough. During the 30 years between his arrival and death in A.D. 461, St Patrick converted the pagan Irish to Christianity.

The Ards Peninsula, bordered by Strangford Lough to the west and the Irish Sea to the east, is a narrow strip of land with a bracing climate, reputedly the sunniest and driest part of the North. It has some charming villages and towns that were first settled by the Scots and English.

Bangor was a famous centre of learning from the sixth century, until it was devastated by the Vikings in the ninth century. It was from here that the missionaries St Columbanus, St Gall and many others set off to bring Christianity to the rest of Europe.

The breezy coast road runs from Bangor past Ballycopeland – the only working windmill in Ireland – past the pretty village of Kearney to the attractive town of Portaferry, where the 8 km-long ferry ride to Strangford affords lovely views of Strangford Lough. The Lough is a famous bird sanctuary and wildlife reserve, and the small rounded hills, called "drumlins," that cover North Down are to be found in Strangford Lough, appearing as small islands. Amongst the historic places to visit are Castle Ward, built by the first Lord Bangor in 1765, and Mount Stewart, the childhood home of Lord Castlereagh, a former British Foreign Secretary. Out of the Cistercian Abbeys in medieval County Down, three were built around the Lough: Inch Abbey, Grey Abbey and Comber.

Downpatrick, at the southern tip of Strangford Lough, is an attractive Georgian town and contains the burial site of St Patrick, which is in the graveyard of the Church of Ireland cathedral.

The Mourne Mountains cover a small area, 22.5 km long and 12 km wide, with 12 rounded peaks. The barren peak of Slieve Donard, climbing steeply to 860 m, dominates this peaceful landscape, which is a paradise for walkers. From the summit you can see the Isle of Man, the Belfast hills and Lough Neagh. There are also two artificial lakes or reservoirs that supply Belfast with water.

These are surrounded by a huge dry stone wall over 2 m high and 33 km long. The Mourne Wall Walk attracts thousands of walkers from all over the world each June.

The coast south from Newcastle, a lively seaside resort, was notorious for smuggling in the eighteenth century. Newry was once a prosperous mercantile town with large town houses and public buildings, as well as the earliest Protestant church in Ireland, St Patrick's.

BANGOR

Cairn Bay Lodge

278 Seacliffe Road, Bangor, Co. Down BT20 5HS
Tel: 01247 467636 Fax: 01247 467636

Cairn Bay Lodge is a most interesting and substantial house, built in 1880, in a large and beautifully maintained garden. It is set back from the shore with uninterrupted views of the sea. Its rather heavy woodwork and panelling in some rooms can make it a little oppressive, and there are all kinds of unusual pieces of furniture and décor. The drawing and sitting rooms occupy the front of the house, affording lovely views over Belfast Lough. The three well-equipped, spacious, comfortable bedrooms, each with hairdryer, trouser press, telephone, TV, tea and coffee making facilities and desks, have a yesteryear feel to them. No pets and no smoking. Cairn Bay is a quiet, peaceful place, and is just a five-minute walk from the centre of Bangor at the southern end of town. Access, Visa accepted.

OWNER The Mullen Family OPEN All year ROOMS 2 double, 1 twin; all en suite TERMS B&B £30–35

Carrig-Gorm

27 Bridge Road, Helen's Bay, Bangor, Co. Down BT19 1TS
Tel: 01247 853680

Carrig-Gorm is a rambling, old, white house standing in its own grounds on the edge of Helen's Bay village. It is thought that the oldest wing of the house dates back around 300 years, and the newest, which includes the elegant drawing room, from 1870.

Some of the older furnishings have a rather worn appearance, but the house exudes a warm, friendly atmosphere. There are sea views from all bedrooms, which have TVs, hairdryers, trouser presses and tea and coffee making facilities. Breakfast only is served in the dining room. Guests tend to sit around the open fire in the well-lived-in panelled hall, and also in the conservatory during fine weather. Smoking in the hall only. No pets. To reach Carrig-Gorm take the A2 from Belfast, turn to Helen's Bay, after 2 km, turn right into Bridge Road and it is the fourth house on the left.

OWNER Elizabeth Eves OPEN Closed at Christmas & New Year's ROOMS 1 twin, 1 family, 1 single; 1 en suite TERMS B&B £22–27; reduction for children; single supplement £5

Chablis

9 – 11 Gray's Hill, Bangor, Co. Down BT20 3BB
Tel: 01247 467747 Fax: 01247 469098

Many years of work and experience led to the creation of Chablis, opened in 1997. Jean-Pierre Carre lovingly restored part of a derelict seafront terrace into a charming restaurant with accommodation. It is located right in the middle of Bangor and has lovely views of the harbour and sea. Jean-Pierre was first trained in baking and butchery and was then a pastry chef. He worked for many years in restaurants and hotels and comes from a great culinary background. His grandfather was a shepherd and cheese maker, his grandmother a Cordon Bleu cook and his father was a baker. The restaurant offers very reasonably priced, wonderful French food both at lunchtime and in the evening, and an excellent choice of wines – there is a full-time wine waiter. The bedrooms, named after the different French wine regions, are bright, comfortable and attractively decorated and furnished, and all have en suite facilities, TVs, telephones, trouser presses, hairdryers and tea, coffee and mineral water, as well as delivery of morning newspapers. Either continental or Irish breakfast is served in the restaurant, and guests are at all times attended by enthusiastic staff members. No pets. All major credit cards accepted.

OWNER Jean-Pierre Carre OPEN All year ROOMS 4 double, 1 twin; all en suite TERMS B&B £39–46; reduction for children; single supplement MEALS Dinner; lunch

Hebron House

59 Queens Parade, Bangor, Co. Down BT20 3BH
Tel: 01247 463126 Fax: 01247 274178

Hebron House is part of an attractive Victorian terrace of houses, set back from and above the sea front and harbour. The Maddocks took over the house in 1996 and are gradually working on bringing it up to a high standard. It is comfortable and attractively decorated and provides excellent service. The bedrooms have hairdryers, telephones, TVs and tea and coffee making facilities. Evening meals are available, as are packed lunches, a laundry service and baby-sitting. There is a combined TV lounge and dining room. No pets and no smoking. All major credit cards accepted.

OWNER Mrs I. Maddock OPEN All year ROOMS 3 double; 2 en suite
TERMS B&B £20–22; reduction for children; single supplement £3–5
MEALS Dinner £10

DOWNPATRICK

Havine Farm

51 Ballydonnell Road, Downpatrick, Co. Down BT30 8EP
Tel: 01396 851242

This comfortable, eighteenth-century, pebble-dashed farmhouse, part of a farm of 50 hectares, is highly acclaimed and has received an award for hospitality. Mrs Macauley is a most welcoming, friendly lady and tries to think of everything for her guests' comfort, including such items as sewing kits, dressing gowns and slippers. The bedrooms are small and cosy, with sloping wooden ceilings and hairdryers, trouser presses and tea and coffee making facilities. There are two lounges, one with a TV, and one for relaxing or reading in which also has all kinds of musical instruments for guests to use – which they do! Havine Farm is a place you will look forward to returning to. No pets and no smoking. Located on the Downpatrick road 3 km from Clough, turn right at Tyrella – the house is 3 km on the left.

OWNER Myrtle Macauley OPEN Closed at Christmas ROOMS 1 double, 1 family, 1 single TERMS B&B £16–17; reduction for children

Tyrella House

Downpatrick, Co. Down BT30 8SU
Tel: 01396 851422 Fax: 01396 851422

This large, elegant country house, with a porticoed, classical façade, stands in 120 hectares of parkland and farmland that stretches down to the sea and its private beach. Most of the house dates from around the eighteenth century, with the Georgian front added in the early nineteenth century. The grounds include a private event course, and a point-to-point course which is used a couple of times a year. Horses are available for beach, forest or mountain rides, or guests are welcome to bring their own horses. Hunting can be arranged and tuition is available in cross-country riding and polo. Guests can also enjoy a game of croquet or tennis on the grass court. The house has a welcoming feeling, with a large hallway and stairs leading up to the three large bedrooms, two with en suite bathrooms featuring pre-war fittings. Dinner (if pre-booked) is served by candlelight in the elegant dining room, and a cheerful fire is lit in the drawing room where coffee is served after dinner. No smoking in the bedrooms or dining room. Pets can be accommodated in the kennels or owner's car. Tyrella House is on the A2 Ardglass road, 6 km out of Clough – it has blue gates with a gate lodge on the right. Visa, American Express accepted.

OWNER David & Sally Corbett OPEN February 1 – November 20
ROOMS 1 double, 1 twin, 1 family; 2 en suite TERMS B&B £40; reduction for children; single supplement £5 MEALS Dinner £20

DROMORE

Sylvan Hill House

76 Kilntown Road, Dromore, Co. Down BT25 1HS
Tel: 01846 692321 Fax: 01846 692321

This listed Georgian house was built in 1781 and stands in beautiful gardens with mature trees and panoramic views of the Mourne and Dromara mountains. Mr and Mrs Coburn are solicitous hosts, entertaining their guests either in their well-lived-in sitting room, or in the more formal drawing room. They join their guests for dinner, which in summer is sometimes served in the conservatory. Mrs Coburn is a gourmet cook, all breads and desserts are home-made, and a special treat at breakfast is her elder flower marmalade. The three very large bedrooms, all with hairdryers and tea and coffee making facilities, overlook the garden, and furnishings are a mixture of antique and traditional. Pets are accepted by arrangement. Smoking is discouraged. To find the house, turn off the A1 onto the Lurgan road, take the first right (Kilntown Road) signposted to Moira, go 2.5 km to the top of the hill and the house is on the right.

OWNER Jimmy & Elise Coburn OPEN All year ROOMS 1 double, 1 twin, 1 family; 2 en suite TERMS B&B £25; reduction for children by arrangement MEALS Dinner £14

HOLYWOOD

Ardshane Country House
5 Bangor Road, Holywood, Co. Down BT18 0NU
Tel: 01232 422044 Fax: 01232 427506

Ardshane means "hill of John" and is built on the 800-year-old campsite of King John's army. It is a large, Edwardian, brick family home standing in most attractive mature gardens, approached up a long driveway. It is a restful, spacious and elegant house, beautifully appointed, with every comfort. There is a TV lounge and an elegant dining room with a marble fireplace. The bedrooms are large, with modern bathrooms, telephones, TVs, hairdryers, trouser presses and tea and coffee making facilities. There is a croquet lawn for the enjoyment of guests, and the house is well suited for the disabled. Pets are accepted by arrangement. Non-smoking bedrooms are available. Ardshane is located at the Bangor end of Holywood off the main road.

OWNER Judith Caughey OPEN All year ROOMS 3 double, 3 twin, 1 family, 1 single; 7 en suite TERMS B&B £35–45; reduction for children MEALS Dinner

Rayanne House

60 Demesne Road, Holywood, Co. Down BT18 9EX
Tel: 01232 425859 Fax: 01232 423364

Rayanne House, a substantial brick building dating from the nineteenth-century, stands in its own grounds and enjoys lovely views across Belfast Lough to Carrickfergus and the Antrim Hills. It offers a warm welcome, good food and a high standard of comfort and service. Raymond and Anne, who made their names at the Schooner Restaurant in Holywood, continue to attract a wide clientele of food lovers here. The house has been refurbished, and offers six comfortable en suite bedrooms, all with TVs, hairdryers, fresh fruit, hospitality trays, toiletries and reading material. The two sitting rooms and the dining room are comfortable, informal and filled with all sorts of china and knick-knacks. Breakfasts are memorable with a wide selection from the menu, and guests are offered every imaginable extra, such as a laundry service, video library, baby-sitting and minicom telephone for the deaf. No pets. Smoking in the lounge only. Visa, Access accepted.

OWNER Raymond & Anne McClelland OPEN Closed at Christmas & New Year's ROOMS 2 double, 1 twin, 1 family, 2 single; all en suite TERMS B&B £45; reduction for children; single supplement £10 MEALS Dinner à la carte

KILKEEL

Heath Hall

160 Moyadd Road, Kilkeel, Co. Down
Tel: 016937 62612

Heath Hall is a turn-of-the-century, stone-built farmhouse set in 6.5 hectares of farmland with sheep and cattle. It has views of the sea and the Mourne Mountains. The house was completely renovated a few years ago and has been attractively decorated, and some rooms have harbour views. All three bedrooms have hairdryers and tea making facilities. The TV lounge has the original marble fireplace, and there is also a snooker room. The house was formerly run as a bed & breakfast by Mrs McGlue's mother-in-law, and has a reputation for offering good value meals and accommodation. Dinner and high tea must be arranged in advance. Pets outside only. No smoking. Heath Hall is located on the B27, 2.5 km north of Kilkeel.

OWNER Mary McGlue OPEN Closed at Christmas ROOMS 1 double, 1 twin, 1 family; 1 en suite TERMS B&B £16; reduction for children MEALS Dinner £8; high tea £6

NEWCASTLE

The Briers
Middle Tollymore Road, Newcastle, Co. Down
Tel: 013967 24347 Fax: 013967 26633

This 200-year-old former farmhouse, once part of Lord Roden's estate, is set in 0.75 hectares of grounds, which include a newly planted arboretum and large ornamental pond. The original house is a low, whitewashed building. It has a modern two-storey addition, which is where most of the guests' accommodation is located. Here there are two ground floor bedrooms suitable for the disabled. The upstairs twin bedroom is very spacious and has a beamed pitched roof. The old part of the house was totally derelict when the Bowaters bought it; it has thick stone walls, beamed ceilings and the original fireplace, made from local stone. The entrance, a small lounge and a couple of bedrooms are in this old part. The bedrooms are all en suite and have hairdryers, TVs and telephones. Both lunch and dinner are available if arranged in advance. Smoking is allowed in the lounge. Pets are allowed outside only. Horseback riding and fishing are available close by. The Briers is signposted opposite Tollymore Forest Park. All major credit cards accepted.

OWNER Mary Bowater OPEN All year ROOMS 9 twin/double/family; all en suite TERMS B&B £25; reduction for children; single supplement £10 MEALS Lunch from £5; dinner from £8

NEWTOWNARDS

Ballycastle House
20 Mountstewart Road, Newtownards, Co. Down BT22 2AL
Tel: 012477 88357 Fax: 012477 88357
Web Site: www.mni.co.uk/formhol

A warm welcome always awaits you at Ballycastle House, the comfortable home of the Deerings. The house was built over 150 years ago and is set in 16 hectares of lovely grounds that were once part of the Mount Stewart estate. The bedrooms have some interesting furniture, the guest lounge features the original fireplace, and a conservatory has recently been added. Mr Deering collects and restores old farm machinery and tractors. The house is minutes from the sea, with lovely walks close by. It can be found 1 km off the A20, turning left at the Ballywalter signpost, 6 km south of Newtownards. Pets can be accommodated in the garage or owner's car. No smoking.

OWNER Margaret Deering OPEN All year ROOMS 2 double, 1 family; all en suite TERMS B&B £20; reduction for children; single supplement £2

Beech Hill
23 Ballymoney Road, Craigantlet, Newtownards, Co. Down
Tel: 01232 425892 Fax: 01232 425892

This long, low, whitewashed house was built 40 years ago by Victoria Brann's grandmother in the Georgian style. It stands on a slight rise surrounded by its own farmland (which is let out) with lovely views over the north Down countryside. Beech Hill has a very pleasant country house atmosphere with the public rooms leading from one to another. The elegant dining room and comfortable drawing room are tastefully furnished with antiques, and beyond is the conservatory, which is used for breakfast. The bedrooms are on the ground floor. The beds are made up with Irish linen and all the rooms have en suite facilities, TVs, hairdryers, trouser presses and tea and coffee making facilities. Dinner is available if booked in advance. Smoking is not allowed in the bedrooms. Pets are accepted in the kennels and by arrangement. Nearby are Mount Stewart House and Gardens,

Rowallane Gardens, Dundonald Motte and Greyabbey, with its herb garden and antiques centre. To find Beech Hill, take the A2 from Belfast, 2.5 km from the bridge at the Ulster Folk Museum, turn right up Ballymoney Road, signposted Craigantlet. The house is 3 km on the left. Visa, Access accepted.

OWNER Victoria Brann OPEN All year ROOMS 3 double; all en suite
TERMS B&B IR£30; single supplement £5

Edenvale House

130 Portaferry Road, Newtownards, Co. Down BT22 2AH
Tel: 01247 814881 Fax: 01247 826192

Approached up a long driveway, Edenvale House is a small Georgian country house located above Strangford Lough. It stands in its own grounds surrounded by fields, and is immaculately kept, both inside and out. Diane Whyte is a welcoming host, and the atmosphere is informal and relaxed. The house has been beautifully furnished and decorated with great taste, and there are lovely views from the first floor rooms. Guests generally prefer to have breakfast, which includes fried potato bread and hot homemade bread, in the large kitchen at the big kitchen table. Diane's daughter looks after the livery business, and guests are welcome to bring their horses. The beautifully kept stables and barn lie to the side of the house, and within the half a hectare of gardens is a croquet lawn. Pets can be accommodated in the

kennels or stables. Smoking is only allowed in the sun room. Edenvale House can be found 3 km from Newtownards on the Portaferry road. Access, Visa, Mastercard accepted.

OWNER Diane Whyte OPEN Closed at Christmas ROOMS 2 double, 1 twin; all en suite TERMS B&B £25; reduction for children; single supplement £5

PORTAFERRY

The Narrows
8 Shore Road, Portaferry, Co. Down BT22 1JY
Tel: 012477 28148 Fax: 012477 28105
E-mail: the.narrows@dial.pipex.com

The Narrows stands at the very end of the Ards Peninsula, and right on the shorefront overlooking the "narrows" and village of Strangford on the opposite side of Strangford Lough. It is owned by Will and James Brown, two brothers who returned to their father's family home in 1992 and skilfully and sympathetically transformed a series of derelict buildings into a place of charm and rustic simplicity. The original house contains most of the bedrooms, which are simply decorated and furnished and have telephones, TVs and tea and coffee making facilities, and every room except the single has a sea view. Behind is the old renovated stone byre, which has a sauna (free for guests). The restaurant building is new and very cleverly designed, still retaining its big arched entranceway, allowing cars to be driven into the small courtyard. Upstairs is a conference/function room with big windows on each side overlooking the sea or charming walled garden. Here weekend workshops are sometimes held on such subjects as painting, basket making and stonewalling (some of the garden walls were rebuilt by students – nothing like being paid to have the work done!). The restaurant, offering deliciously cooked local food, with a strong emphasis on seafood, is very popular. The floors and furniture are pine, there is a small bar in the corner, the day's menu is posted on a blackboard, and every table enjoys views of the water. Will's wife, Sarah, is the pastry chef, and she is also responsible for the décor in the house. Some of the paintings around the house are hers; paintings and weavings by local artists also hang on the walls. Equally welcoming to families and functions, The Narrows is a great place for a break in this beautiful and interesting area of Ireland. Pets by arrangement. No smoking in the restaurant or bedrooms. All major credit cards accepted.

OWNER Will & James Brown   OPEN All year   ROOMS 6 double, 6 twin, 1 single; all en suite (3 with bath)   TERMS B&B £33; reduction for children; single supplement £6   MEALS Dinner; lunch

COUNTY FERMANAGH

County Fermanagh is lake or land – one third of the county is under water – and is traversed by the Erne River, which meanders its way across the forested county into a huge lake dotted with drumlins. A paradise for fishing, boating and other water-related activities, Lough Erne is a magnificent 75-km-long waterway offering uncongested cruising opportunities with 154 islands and many coves and inlets to explore. It has an interesting mix of pagan and Christian relics and traditions that have withstood the centuries.

The medieval town of Enniskillen is built on a bridge of land between Upper and Lower Lough Erne. The town's origins go back to prehistory, when it was on the main highway between Ulster and Connaught. The County Museum, housed in the Castle keep, displays the brilliant uniforms, colours and Napoleonic battle trophies of the famous Inniskillings Regiment, which fought at Waterloo.

Amongst the many islands to visit, Devenish is particularly interesting, with its perfect twelfth-century round tower, tiny church and remains of a fifteenth-century Augustinian abbey. In the cemetery of Boa, the largest island, are two ancient stone Janus idols, thought to date from the first century. Belleek is famous both for its fishing and its china, which comes mostly in the form of objets d'art. Two of Northern Ireland's most attractive Georgian houses are to be found in Fermanagh – Castle Coole, a neo-classical mansion with Paladian features, built in 1795 for the Earl of Belmore, and Florencecourt House, seat of the Earls of Enniskillen, which has wonderful rococo plasterwork.

BELCOO

Corralea Forest Lodge
Belcoo, Co. Fermanagh
Tel: 01365 386325

The Lodge stands in a superb location on 14 hectares of a forested nature reserve on the shores of Lough Macnean, with glorious views over the lough and to the hills beyond. When the Catteralls came here 22 years ago, the farmhouse was derelict, and they built a new house amidst this breathtaking scenery. The bedrooms, all on the ground floor, have patio doors, enabling guests to step outside and enjoy the view. The property has its own private landing stage and boats are available for hire. Sika deer roam the estate and in 1970, 37,000 trees were planted. The lounge is large and the separate dining room is where breakfast and evening meals can be served, if booked in advance. Guests may bring their own wine to dinner. This is the perfect place for bird-watching, painting and walking. Upper Lough Macnean has the reputation of being the most pollution-free lake in Northern Ireland and the best place for pike in western Europe.

OWNER Mr & Mrs Peter Catterall   OPEN March 1 – October 31 ROOMS 2 double, 2 twin; all en suite   TERMS B&B £20; reduction for children; single supplement £5   MEALS Dinner

KESH

Ardess House
Kesh, Co. Fermanagh
Tel: 013656 31267 Fax: 0135656 31267

Ardess House is a Georgian stucco building situated at the top of a hill in secluded grounds and gardens where peacocks stroll and Jacob sheep graze in the paddocks. It was built in 1780 as the rectory for the church opposite and has lovely views. The Pendrys bought it in 1984 and have done a great deal of work on restoring the house, and are continuing to upgrade the property. Dorothy Pendry was a teacher in a girls' school in Belfast and did weaving and spinning as a hobby. The basement has been converted into small workshops, where courses on different crafts are taught. The students who attend the courses get full board in the house, though even those not attending courses can partake of evening meals if they wish. Guests are also welcome to join in the activities in the craft centre. The kitchen is the preferred place for breakfast, but there is a dining room as well, and a drawing room. The bedrooms have been freshly decorated and good-sized bathrooms have been added. The former are large, airy rooms, with high ceilings and wonderful views and they are furnished with antiques. The house has been awarded a British Airways Tourism Endeavour Award. Smoking is not encouraged. Pets by arrangement. Follow the signs to Kesh; turn off onto the B72 before you reach the village. Access, Mastercard, American Express accepted.

OWNER Dorothy Pendry OPEN January 15 – December 15 ROOMS 3 double, 1 twin; all en suite TERMS B&B £22.50; reduction for children; single supplement £5.50 MEALS Dinner

COUNTY TYRONE

The least populated of the six counties in Northern Ireland, Tyrone is in the heart of Ulster and is bordered to the north by the Sperrin Mountains, bare hills with fertile green valleys. The main towns are Omagh, the county town, Cookstown and Dungannon, which has a textile industry and crystal factory.

The meaning of the Beaghmore stone circles, consisting of seven Bronze Age stone circles and cairns, is still unknown. The Ulster-American Folk Park at Camphill, Omagh, which recreates the America of pioneering days and the Ireland those pioneers left, grew up around the cottage where Thomas Mellon was born in 1813.

Also in County Tyrone is the ancestral home of Woodrow Wilson. The farm is still occupied by Wilsons, who will show callers around the house.

BALLYGAWLEY

The Grange
15 Grange Road, Ballygawley, Co. Tyrone BT70 2HD
Tel: 016625 68053

Dating from 1720, the Grange Guest House had a thatched roof
until recently. It now has the appearance of a more modern house,
with white stucco and new windows. It stands in a lovely, walled
garden of lawns surrounded by flower beds. Mrs Lyttle is very
friendly, and the house has a pleasant, lived-in feeling. The
attractive lounge has a piano and TV. The dining room, from
which stairs lead to the next floor, has lots of character and is full
of knick-knacks. There are sideboards decorated with silver and
china. There is one ground floor bedroom. No smoking. Pets
outside only. The Grange Guest House is on the edge of
Ballygawley a few metres from the roundabout.

OWNER Mrs Ella Lyttle OPEN All year ROOMS 2 double, 1 twin; all
en suite TERMS B&B £18; reduction for children; single supplement

DUNGANNON

Grange Lodge
7 Grange Road, Dungannon, Co. Tyrone BT71 7EJ
Tel: 01868 784212 Fax: 01868 723891

This attractive Georgian country house is set in 1.25 hectares of
pleasant gardens. It is a spacious house with well proportioned
reception rooms which include a large drawing room, a cosier,

smaller study with a TV and a panelled snooker room with a piano. The Browns, who also own a retail concern in Dungannon, are superb hosts – friendly, welcoming and perfectionists in maintaining their very high standard of accommodation and food. The bedrooms are pretty and comfortable and all have en suite facilities, TVs, hairdryers, telephones and tea and coffee making facilities. A stay here would not be complete without sampling Norah Brown's cooking, which is superb both in the extremely high standard of the food itself and the way in which it is presented. Dinner for house guests is served in the elegant dining room, on separate tables covered in white tablecloths and decorated with pretty flowers and candles. Non-residents are accommodated in a newly added dining room, which is completely self-contained with its own entrance. Dinner must be booked in advance. No pets. Smoking in the TV lounge only. Visa, Mastercard accepted.

OWNER Ralph & Norah Brown OPEN Closed at Christmas ROOMS 3 double, 1 twin, 1 single; all en suite TERMS B&B £35.50; single supplement £14.50–20.50 MEALS Dinner

Stangmore Country
65 Moy Road, Dungannon, Co. Tyrone BT71 7DT
Tel: 01868 725600 Fax: 01868 726644

Approached through an impressive entrance and down a winding driveway flanked by mature, landscaped grounds, Stangmore is a substantial country house built in the Georgian style. It was built 10 years ago as a private home, then became a guest house. The present owners took it over in the summer of 1997 and opened the restaurant, which has proved to be a popular venue for the local population. The rooms are large and furnished in luxurious opulence. Drinks before dinner and coffee after dinner are served in the comfortable drawing room. Excellent dinners, beautifully presented, are served by candlelight in the elegant drawing room. All 10 bedrooms are en suite and have hairdryers, trouser presses, telephones, TVs and tea and coffee making facilities. Four of them are in a mews building to one side of the house. Pets by arrangement. No smoking in the dining room. All major credit cards accepted.

OWNER Norman & Hilary Bell OPEN All year ROOMS 7 double or twin, 2 family, 1 single; all en suite TERMS B&B from £35; reduction for children; single supplement from £10 MEALS Dinner from £16.95

Tullydowey House
51 Tullydowey Road, Dungannon, Co. Tyrone BT71 7HS
Tel: 01861 548230 Fax: 01861 548881

Built in 1740 as a manor house, Tullydowey House belonged to one family until it was recently bought by the present owners. Nothing had been done to the house for years, and there were branches of trees growing through the windows. Pauline Brown previously owned Ballycanal Manor Guest House in Moira, Co. Down. As well as running the accommodation and restaurant, she also owns and trains point-to-point horses. Tullydowey is an attractive house in a parklike setting, surrounded by its own land, and it has nicely proportioned rooms. There is a comfortable drawing room and a small sitting room, and elegant dinners are served in the dining room. The well-equipped bedrooms have hairdryers, trouser presses, telephones, TVs and tea and coffee making facilities. Other amenities on offer are a laundry service, packed lunches and baby-sitting, and newspapers are delivered every morning. Disabled people are catered for. The estate has a river boundary of approximately 2 km running along the River Blackwater, with exclusive fishing rights. Arrangements can be made for golfers with a local golf club. Tullydowey can be found halfway between Armagh and Dungannon on the B128. All major credit cards accepted.

OWNER Mrs Pauline Brown OPEN All year ROOMS 12 double or twin; all en suite TERMS B&B £30; reduction for children; single supplement £5 MEALS Dinner £15; packed lunches

Charlemont House

4 The Square, Moy, Co. Tyrone BT71 7SG
Tel: 01868 784755 Fax: 01868 784895

Charlemont House, a lovely Georgian townhouse, occupies a corner site in the central square of the small town of Moy, which lies halfway between Armagh and Dungannon. The McNeice family has been associated with innkeeping in Moy for many generations, and also runs Tomney's Bar and Lounge and Moy Reproductions, located just a few doors down the square. The bar is completely authentic, with small, dark rooms and a great atmosphere. The house has elegant proportions and is an amazing place, full of Victorian furnishings and furniture. The lounge has old floral wallpaper, pinkish chintzes, black and pink patterned carpeting, black furniture (including a piano), romantic pictures and all kinds of glass and china. The breakfast room, in the basement, is less flamboyant with an Aga cooker and pottery adorning the high shelf around the room. The property stretches right down to the River Blackwater at the back, reached through a courtyard. Guests can sit here on fine days, surrounded by old coach houses, then go through an archway to a pretty, partly walled, compact garden with more tables and chairs. No pets. Smoking in the TV lounge only. Visa accepted.

OWNER Laurence & Margaret McNeice OPEN All year ROOMS 9 double/twin/family/single; 1 en suite TERMS B&B £17; reduction for children; single supplement £3

Muleany House

86 Gorestown Road, Moy, Co. Tyrone BT71 7EX
Tel: 01868 784183

Muleany House was purpose-built some 12 years ago and is a substantial, porticoed whitewashed building. Mrs Mullen is a most friendly, chatty lady, who does her own baking and enjoys meeting her guests. The good-sized bedrooms have tiny shower rooms and additionally there are two public bathrooms with bathtubs. Two bedrooms are on the ground floor. Well suited for families, Muleany House offers a baby-sitting service, laundry facilities and a large games room with pool table, small organ and open fire. There is also a smaller lounge with TV, and a dining room where evening meals are served, if ordered in advance. No pets. No smoking in the bedrooms or dining room. There are two self-catering units in the grounds. The house can be found about 1.6 km from Moy by taking the B106 to Benburb, then the right fork towards Ballygawley. Visa, Mastercard, Delta accepted.

OWNER Mrs Mullen OPEN Closed at Christmas ROOMS 9 double/ twin/family/single; all en suite TERMS B&B £17; reduction for children; single supplement £5 MEALS Dinner £10–15

OMAGH

Bankhead
9 Lissan Road, Omagh, Co. Tyrone BT78 1TX
Tel: 01662 245592

This small farmhouse is at the end of a long private road and has pleasant views over farmland with the Drumragh River just below. It was built by the Clements in 1970 and is part of an 11-hectare beef and sheep farm. The bedrooms are furnished simply, and are fresh and bright. They are all on the ground floor. There is a small, neatly kept TV lounge with an open fire, and the dining room has a TV and sitting area. The terrace is pleasant for sitting outside on fine days, and guests have use of the garden. Smoking is not allowed in the bedrooms. Pets are permitted outside only. Bankhead can be found off the A5 towards Omagh by crossing the Drumragh River and turning left immediately into Lissan Road.

OWNER Sadie Christina Clements OPEN All year ROOMS 2 double, 1 twin TERMS B&B £15; reduction for children; single supplement £2

STRABANE

Mrs Jean Ballantine's
38 Leckpatrick Road, Artigarvan, Strabane, Co. Tyrone BT82 0HB
Tel: 01504 882714

This family home has a friendly atmosphere and stands in its own garden with lovely distant views of farmland and hills. It is a modern house with three small bedrooms equipped with hair-dryers, sharing two bathrooms. There is a TV lounge with an open fire, a conservatory and the dining room has one table, where evening meals are served if arranged in advance. The Ulster American Folk Park is 24 km away. No smoking. Pets outside only. The house is located by turning off the B40 opposite Leckpatrick Dairy and it is the first on the right.

OWNER Jean Ballantine OPEN January – November ROOMS 1 double, 1 twin, 1 single TERMS B&B £13.50–15; reduction for children MEALS Dinner £10

Area Maps

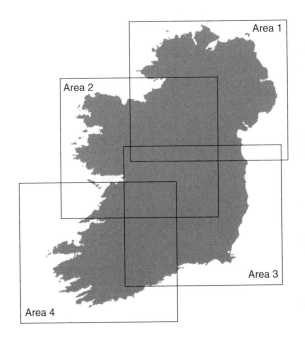

Area 1

Area 2

Area 3

Area 4

Area 1

Broad Haven

Belmullet
(Béal an Mhuirhead)

Ballycastle

Killala Bay

Bunnahowen

Killala

Enniscrone

Bangor Erris

Crossmolina

Ballina

Bunnyco

Blacksod Bay

MAYO

Foxford

Sv

Keel

Mulrany

Newport

Castlebar

Turlough

Kiltimagh

Kilt

Clew Bay

Westport

N5

Ballyhean

Balla

Claremorris

Ba

Louisburgh

Ballindine

Leenane

Letterfrack

Ballinrobe

Kilmaine

Clifden

GALWAY

Clonbur
(An Fhairche)
Cornamona

Neale

Shrule

Mannin Bay

Ballyconneely

Oughterard

Headford

Roundstone

Glinsk
(Glinsce)

Kilkieran
(Cill Chiaráin)

Spiddal
(An Spidéal)

Galway

Oranmore

Clarinb

Kilcolga

G A L W A

Ballyvaughan

Kinvarra

Gort

Lisdoonvarna

Kilfenora

Kilconnell

Ennistymon

Corofin

Crusheen

Lahinch

N18

Milltown
Malbay

CLARE

Ennis

Tull

Clarecastle

Broa

Doonbeg

Cooraclare

Newmarket-
on-Fergus

Sixmile

SHANNON

Kilkee

Killadysert

Kilrush

Killimer

Askeaton

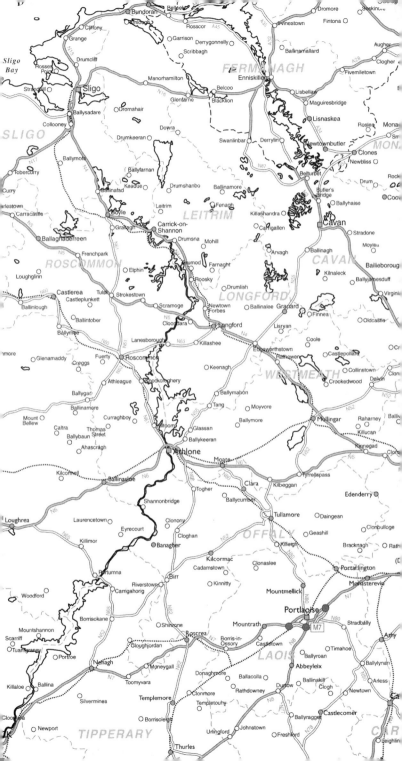

Area 3

Area 4

Index